"You Crown the Year with Your Goodness"

HANS URS VON BALTHASAR

"You Crown the Year with Your Goodness"

Radio Sermons

Translated by Graham Harrison

IGNATIUS PRESS   SAN FRANCISCO

Title of the German original:
"Du kronst das Jahr
mit deiner Huld": Radiopredigten

Cover by Victoria Hoke Lane

With ecclesiastical approval

ISBN 0-89870-058-2
Library of Congress catalogue number 89-83743
Printed in the United States of America

Contents

Preface

These radio homilies, broadcast over a period of several decades, were collected and arranged solely according to their place in the Church's calendar. This selection concerns the feasts of God, of Christ and of his Mother; the feasts of the saints could fill another volume: this one is already large enough. Naturally there is nothing systematic about the order in which the homilies appear, unless, that is, they are viewed from a higher perspective: then, indeed, constant themes do emerge—perhaps only a single theme—of which the individual items are only variations. For in the Christian Faith, after all, there is only one dogma, splitting like light into a rainbow of colors, or, like a living body, expressing itself in manifold members, each dependent on the others. Just as we cannot understand anything of Christ apart from the mystery of the Trinity, anything of the Church without faith in Christ's divinity and humanity, anything of the sacraments apart from the bridal mystery between Christ and the Church, so too we cannot understand anything of the Christian life (or morality) without the Christian Faith (or dogma): orthopraxy and orthodoxy are two sides of the same coin.

So it is that these homilies keep circling around the same center: the inexhaustible mystery of our one, indivisible Faith. Each piece was written for a particular occasion and, relatively speaking, stands on its own; consequently, it would be tiresome to read through the whole book as one would read a novel or a textbook. It is best to open it at random or to pick a topic and then read at most a couple of homilies. In that way the inevitable overlappings will not cause irritation. In all cases what we have written should be tested by the plumb line of the Word of God. Many readers, quite probably, would have preferred something more "practical", but human praxis "practically" arises of itself, once we have adequately appreciated God's own "praxis". No sermon or homily can or should have any other subject matter but the One Word, uniquely manifested every Sunday, every feast day.

New Year

To and Fro in the Immensity of God's Realm

We ended the old year with thanksgiving to God, and we begin the new with the worship of him. Worship means acknowledging God's divine nature, his absolute power and goodness. Whatever may be in store for us in the new year, we live in *him*, within the sphere of his kindly power and mighty kindness, from which nothing can fall away. We can put it in the words of a psalm that has been inserted at the beginning of the First Book of Samuel; it starts like this: "My heart exults in the Lord; my strength is exalted. . . . There is none holy like the Lord, there is none besides thee." There is no such thing as a plurality of gods (for every man, including every religious man, whether he knows it or not, is subject to the One, All-Holy God), nor is there any power in the world that can make itself independent of his power and act as if it were almighty. True, the world contains people who are lofty and lowly, the powerful and the powerless, the fruitful and the sterile, the energetic and those lacking in strength; and we are acquainted with the terrifying contrasts of victory and defeat, of life and death. Full of fear, we sail back and forth on life's swing without being able to stop it, and the only thing we are certain of is that one day the swing on which our life is sailing to and fro must arc over, out of the light into the darkness, and this time there will be no swinging back.

But now the psalmist is emboldened to comprehend all these contraries between which we hover (as individuals, but also as nations and continents and power blocs, threatening each other with atom bombs); he has the courage to grasp all this as something that takes place within the One, almighty, all-knowing and kind God, who is eternal and all-powerful life and thus can embrace and relativize all our contraries. Let us listen to what he says:

> For the Lord is a God of knowledge,
> and by him actions are weighed.
> The bows of the mighty are broken,
> but the feeble gird on strength.
> Those who were full have hired themselves out for bread,
> but those who were hungry have ceased to hunger.
> The barren has borne seven,
> but she who has many children is forlorn.
> The Lord kills and brings to life;
> he brings down to Sheol and raises up.
> The Lord makes poor and makes rich;
> he brings low, he also exalts.
> He raises up the poor from the dust;
> he lifts the needy from the ash heap,
> to make them sit with princes and inherit a seat of honor.
> For the pillars of the earth are the Lord's,
> and on them he has set the world.

These are staggering words. They go further than our reflections so far. They say that all the ups and downs of individual and national fortunes are acted out within an all-embracing divine sphere. Furthermore, and most importantly, they affirm that this sphere is the living God, who intervenes to reverse the apparently irreversible human value judgments and make them conform to his own, absolute evaluations. At this point the biblical view of God diverges from most religious and philosophical world views: it is not simply that the earthly contradictions are relativized in the face of the absolute, but the living God vindicates his absolute values and evaluations in history itself. Not arbitrarily either, but in accord with his own nature, which, by an inner necessity, demands unconditional recognition. Therefore:

> Talk no more so very proudly,
> let not arrogance come from your mouth. . . .
> The adversaries of the Lord shall be broken to pieces. . . .
> He will guard the feet of his faithful ones;
> but the wicked shall be cut off in darkness.

We can ask ourselves whether man, even the man who has faith, can observe this law operating in his own history and in the history of the world. Perhaps he cannot see it in the same way that many Old Testament people, and Job's friends, thought they could. So the psalmist's strength of faith that enables him to dare to say these things is all the more amazing. In faith he knows that God lifts the poor from the dust and the mire because by his very nature he shows solidarity with the lowly and humble. Conversely, he knows that if those who have been lifted up become proud and imagine that they have raised themselves up by their own strength, they are bound to fall down again, since such arrogant behavior is in opposition to God's sublime nature. The psalmist is even aware of something that few under the Old Covenant knew, namely, that God not only causes man to journey to the grave but also brings him up out of it. For God is not a God of the dead but of the living; he himself is eternal life.

But can this faith knowledge on the part of the psalmist stand firm in the face of the harsh realities of human experience? Can it stand up to the cries of Job, who says that God has banished him, guiltless, in the darkest of nights, and that nothing of his kindness, omnipotence and justice is visible anymore?

To provide an answer at this point, we need to step over the threshold into the New Covenant. The psalm we have quoted, which is put into the mouth of the unfruitful Hannah when, through divine intervention, she conceived and bore the child Samuel, is taken up by the Virgin Mary, who will know no man and, overshadowed by the Holy Spirit, will bring the Son of the Most High into the world. Her heart, too, exults in the Lord and rejoices in God, her Savior; in the first place because, like Hannah, she has personally experienced that God makes the unfruitful fruitful by the power of his Spirit, that he puts down the mighty from their thrones and raises the lowly, fills the hungry with good things and sends the rich away empty, and that, in all these acts within history, he fulfills his promises, remembering his mercy and the word he spoke to our fathers, to Abraham and his posterity forever.

It is exactly the same faith, with exactly the same inner certainty, that expresses itself in Mary's song and in the song of Hannah. But the new singer's certainty is drawn deeper into the mysteries of divine omnipotence; the one who exults is also the Mother of him who is appointed for the fall and rising of many in Israel; she is also the one whose heart will be pierced by a sword. Is it possible to rejoice at the same time as being the Mother of Seven Sorrows? Can her Child know that nothing can separate him from his God—and at the same time cry out, like Job, on the Cross: "My God, my God, why hast thou forsaken me?"

It is only here that the ultimate depths of the old psalm are uncovered. It is not simply that the terrifying oppositions of our life affect God's all-embracing sphere, nor are they simply balanced out by an omnipotent God in a way that accords with his nature: what is new is that this God takes human form and undergoes them himself. He himself experiences the pitiless depths of poverty, humiliation and dying abandoned by God. But what we see when the horror comes to its ultimate end is that it was Light and Life and Love itself that allowed itself to become poor and humiliated and to die in forsakenness, in order to plumb all the depths of the human lot, including the fate of the sinner, and to rescue it and keep it safe in the divine life.

This can only become a reality if the word of Jesus is true: "No one takes my life from me, but I lay it down of my own accord. I have power to lay it down, and I have power to take it again; this charge I have received from my Father" (Jn 10:18). In other words, the one who dies abandoned by God performs an act and a demonstration of the eternal love of God: God is so absolutely alive in Jesus Christ that he can even afford to be dead. Not merely apparently dead, but dead in the most brutal sense, as the Cross—Grünewald's crucifixion—shows. It is only the man who has divine authority to lay down his life in divine freedom who can really die the death of a sinner under the judgment of God—and take it up again! As Hannah sang: "God brings down to Sheol and raises up." Here, at last, this finally comes true. Here, as Paul says, death becomes swallowed up in life, and its sting is drawn. The other paradoxes, too, are solved: the poor, those who mourn and who hunger for righteousness, are called blessed because God has now entered into solidarity with them in the most intimate manner, because his almighty power is not a tyrannical and haughty omnipotence: it is gentle and even poor in a certain sense, because it has no other weapons than love and that justice that is inwardly one with it.

The first thing we should reflect on at the beginning of this new year is the tremendous act of God in the death and Resurrection of Jesus Christ. Let all that this year will bring be surrounded, evaluated and governed, from the very outset, by this act.

Let us not forget, however, that today, New Year's Day, the Church celebrates the feast of "Mary, the Mother of God", in which, for the sake of the indivisible unity of her Son, who is God and man, the Mother is given this astounding title, explicitly since the Council of Ephesus in 431. The significance for us—and it is both consoling and inspiring—is that a mere human being like ourselves can share in the destiny of one who is the Son of God and the Savior of a doomed mankind. As we have already said, she rejoices in God her Savior—and her heart is pierced by a sword. This happens time and again during her Son's life and ultimately under his Cross. The plumbing of these heights and depths requires more than a heroic or tragic human fate: it requires a life that is simply devoted to the discipleship of Christ. All of us, in very varying degrees, can have a share in such a destiny, whether it is present in us as a mere hint or totally overwhelms us.

We have urgent tasks to be performed in the world. We have to fight for earthly justice, against hunger and disease, tyranny and terrorism. We approach these tasks with courage, but all the time we know that we shall never be able to eliminate evil and negativity and death: light and darkness alternate in our life like the day and night that God has created. We must fight manfully, but we must also admit honestly that we can never change the world's laws, we shall never be liberated from the destiny that seesaws between high and low, life and death. Yet we find consolation in the fact that God in Jesus Christ is with us and that he is far more acquainted than we are with all the dimensions of existence. He has experienced them, and he allows us to participate in *his* experience. "When I am weak," says the Apostle, "then I am strong." If I am poor with Christ, in his Spirit, then I am rich. If my heart lets itself be pierced, together with Mary's heart, it will be open and maternal, able to give succor to those who are overburdened.

So let us not be afraid of the future that is opening up before us. It will continually swing us back and forth between the light and the dark, but we shall never swing beyond God's reach.

Living in the Interstices

We men are bound to the cycle of the seasons, to this strange circle of nature's growth and decay, its blossoming, maturating, fruiting and then the deathlike period of rest. In this cycle, which continually shows us life in its universal aspect and its transience, we see more clearly than anywhere else that our little life also shares in this circuit, at least if we are permitted to live out the succeeding periods between childhood and old age. From time immemorial all peoples have marked with some celebration the turning point that nature puts at the end of one year and the beginning of the next. Often it has been an occasion for inebriation and uninhibited revelry, as if to drown out the warning that speaks of that very different death that lies in store for us when we pass the final frontier: "Let us eat and drink, for tomorrow we die." Animals know nothing, or hardly anything, of this warning issued by nature. They have no "history", no more than circling nature itself. History is something that man alone has: he is subject to destiny, and at the same time he plans and triggers that same destiny, for himself, for his fellowmen and for mankind as a whole. Individuals, just like groups, parties, nations and power blocs, have different designs for the future destiny, designs that mostly conflict with one another. All speak of changing the world, of creating things and conditions, but in their innermost hearts they all know that, in spite of this, they are all subject to destiny and, with their preparations and rearming, they are sorcerers' apprentices who have forgotten the word of restraint and recall and can easily become the victims of their own magic.

Somewhere or other all of us have a hand on the great wheel that is rolling forward along with us. Many hands want to push it on faster, while others are trying to apply the brake so that the existing state of affairs may last longer and what is already past may fade away less quickly. So the wheel hesitates, unsure of which future to move toward. There are not only millions, there are billions of hands on the wheel; can such a huge collective as that which inhabits this earth ever plan anything together? Will it ever be able to do this unless the overwhelming majority of men are transformed into anonymous worker-animals operating mechanically under the draconian eye of a few supervisors? But will even *they* agree on the direction the wheel is to take? Strange: the more refined technology becomes, the more menacing grow the means of wielding power, the power to force one's opponent to his knees. And the person with greater power is always less inclined to share it with his partner or counterpart. Power isolates, polarizes and encourages particularism. And those who keep sight of the total picture, who are striving to unite all men on this planet for the benefit of the great interests they have in common, find themselves living in the narrow and narrowing interstices between the power blocs. We can see an illustration of this in the Israel of old, which lived in the narrow space between the major power of Egypt and the great powers of Mesopotamia, Assyria and then Babylon. It was courted, threatened and overrun first by one power and then by the other. From a political and cultural point of view, this tight situation had something utopian about it, but it was regarded by the great prophets as the appropriate situation for God's chosen people. Naturally, the political pundits in Israel were always enamored of pacts and collaboration with the great power to the left or the right, and for a short time, too, it did seem to be a favorable way out. But in the long run these ways out always turned out to be culs-de-sac and brought about new crises. The prophets presented this little nation, this buffer state that was so miserable to earthly eyes, with a different program: they were to stay on the side of the God who had chosen Israel as his particular people and who stood above all the broad and influential parties. At most, this God would use these parties to punish Israel whenever it was unfaithful and faithless. However, when the time had come, he would permit the great nations, for the sake of the little nation of Israel, to share in his complete, world-embracing salvation. The prophet Isaiah says, in a well-known verse: "Behold, I am laying in Zion for a foundation a stone, a tested stone, a precious cornerstone, of a sure foundation: 'He who believes will not be in haste' " (Is 28:16). That is, the believer will not feel he has to seek for premature guarantees vis-à-vis God, but he will wait, bide his time, have patience, rely on God; he will depend on God's guidance and providence and dispense with earthly security. That is the watchword for those who are appointed to live in the interstices between the world's great powers. It still applied for the period when Israel was an occupied territory, that is, under the Ptolemys and the Romans; and if Israel had not risen up again and again in armed rebellion against the latter, Jerusalem would not have been besieged and so bloodily taken and destroyed. (We may well ask today's Israel whether it has not been overhasty in returning to an occupied land; for thereby, in a new way, it has fanned the flames of a worldwide hatred and ultimately of war.)

Christians, too, live in the interstices, and these in-between spaces can sometimes be in occupied zones too. They are not guaranteed to be politics-free areas; they can be almost entirely invisible areas and regions, such as in the Gulag Archipelago, in the Cancer Ward, in the First Circle of hell. But these points are not vulnerable to attack because they are characterized by a freedom that is beyond the world's grasp. Furthermore, these points spread out and radiate, and in this way they protect and extend that freedom that is increasingly restricted on earth. They are invisible drops, wearing away the stone; they cause the clay feet of the iron colossus to disintegrate and make apparently impregnable fortresses collapse. Often the most beautiful flowers bloom from cracks in masonry, to delight the weary passerby as he walks along the concrete wall. What a lovely parable, after all, is the laughable procession of the Israelites around the walls of Jericho, which crumble as they go round for the seventh time. This ancient legend gives us a symbol of Israel's faith in the God of history who stands by his people and guides their fortunes, over and above the resistance of the great powers of the world. From the latter's point of view, the victory of this contemptible minority must always be a ridiculous fluke, a pure misunderstanding, to be cleared up once and for all by the next major onslaught. The most ridiculous of these episodes recorded in the Bible is the detailed description of the way in which Gideon falls at night upon the camp of the Midianites with a handful of men—a story we would do well to take to heart. Initially God had reduced Gideon's army from thirty thousand to ten thousand men; then he cut it down to three hundred and sent the rest home. Only those who really believed were to fight, and Israel was not to be able to say, "My own hand has delivered me." Then Gideon gives his men clay pots concealing torches, positions them around the enemy camp, and blows his horn, whereupon they all smash their pots and, unarmed as they are, utter the war cry: "A sword for the Lord and for Gideon!" The Midianites flee, howling, slaughtering one another in the process.

Naïve legends, you may say. Maybe. But they are highly significant. "Behold," says the Man from Nazareth, "I send you out as sheep among wolves." This is the same situation again; it is still a picture, but now it is not an ancient story but the sober reality of Church history. And while it may not have been true of the Church in the last thousand years, it will very probably be her situation for the next thousand years, creating a direct link with the first Christian centuries before Constantine. The original Christian territories emptied and de-Christianized, the missions (insofar as they still exist) under threat and decimated, the power blocs moving closer against each other and rolling into the geographical interstices. The spiritual interstices we have mentioned will remain, but here too the pressure can increase greatly. It will very likely be impossible to bring along a lot of baggage, a lot of chests full of Christian tradition, nostalgic former liturgies, works of art, theological summas and other jewels of a Christian culture that has ceased to exist as such. Many people think it absolutely essential to carry all this baggage since it will provide nourishment for the coming lean years; not only will it keep us alive, but in the long run it will be possible to reconstruct new

Christian forms of culture out of the elements of this cultural tradition. Over against a civilization that wants systematically to forget everything that has come down to us, with its specific validity, through tradition, and that, in its "flight into the future", aims to build up a barbarian, technological, one-dimensional, inhuman world, Christians should be the guardians of the great and truly human culture, keeping alive the memory of what has been achieved and, on the wings of this memory, being able to produce things of equal sublimity. It is indeed a beautiful thought. But will the sheep among wolves be allowed time to create such beautiful things? I think that, as Christians, if we are really to think ahead, we must apply rather different categories.

Do you actually know what today's feast is? Not the familiar secular new year celebrations but the feast celebrated by the Catholic Church? In fact it only exists since the liturgical reforms initiated by the last Council. Formerly it was the Feast of the Circumcision of the Lord, for the simple reason that the Child Jesus was circumcised eight days after his birth at Christmas. This was not a particularly inspiring feast-day idea, at least for Christians, because it pointed very much into the Jewish past, whereas this Child was to bring the past to something new and to fulfill it. Today, however, to introduce the new year, we celebrate the Solemnity of the Mother of God, "Mary, the God-bearer". It is logical, too, to prepare a celebration after the birth of this Child of this Mother; and, by a happy chance, it also initiates the new year.

In this way, therefore, as the new year begins, we are also brought back to the very beginnings of our Christianity. We are brought back, behind all later tradition, to the simple, almost unremarkable, event that gave rise to all that followed, that is, the consent of the Virgin Mary to God's saving decree: "Behold, I am the handmaid of the Lord." We are brought back to this simple, silent consent to all that God might have in mind for her, now, later, at any time: "Let it be to me according to your word." Prior to all the organization and formation of the human body, and ultimately of the human spirit and its cultural achievements, there is the act of generation and conception: two of the tiniest things join together. Even prior to that beginning in which Christ's disciples are sent out into all the world, to all nations and times, there is the scarcely audible "Yes" of man's perfect faith in response to the conclusive and fulfilling "Yes" of God to all his promises. Everything grows out of this first, original consent, out of this faith that produced and fulfilled the full measure of the faith required of Israel. This is precisely the act to which Isaiah referred when he said, "He who believes will not be in haste." Such a person will not want to go quicker or more slowly than God, but will walk in step with him. He will not hesitate or wonder whether God is right or whether it would not be better to plan his own future himself; he will not overtake God, mistakenly imagining that he has already guessed what God's plans contain. Not only has Mary elevated this simple "Yes", which exactly keeps God's tempo, to the most lonely dignity ever attained by a human being: she has also made it the norm of a perfection that everyone can grasp and imitate. Saying "Yes" is basically something man does most gladly and most easily; he only hesitates when he has reason for mistrust. But who would ever have a reason to distrust God instead of entrusting himself, right from the outset, to God's present and future guidance? And in concrete terms this implies accepting responsibility for the seed that God sows in us, for the word he entrusts to us, for the mission he imparts to us.

Now we can see what, fundamentally, tradition is. It does not consist primarily of the beautiful forms of the past, of theological systems, of Romanesque and Baroque churches or of Masses as celebrated in the days of Pius X. It is that we accept what God has handed over to us [Lat. *traditio* = "handing over"—TRANS.], that we receive, carry, cherish and bring it to birth, nourishing it with our own substance and bringing it up. Everything else, human and historical tradition, comes later. It has significance in its own place, but only if it is an expression of the prior sense of faithfulness to tradition, that is, to the task that we have received from God. I say "we" because the task is one we share with others; it is an ecclesial task and one performed by us personally within the Church. It is only in and because of the Church that we possess our personal, Christian responsibility, for we are her members. No Christian has the right to say, "The Church ought to . . ." unless he himself is prepared to do what he thinks she should do. And no one has the right to say, "I must . . ." unless he is certain that this "must" will be beneficial to the Church as a whole. Nowadays we need to proclaim more clearly than ever that the ecclesial and personal dimensions are inseparable. Only if the two are integrated into each other—and not in the rattling bones of a mere organization on the one hand or in the chaotic bustle of charismatic cliques on the other—can Christendom confidently step over the threshold of the new year at the Solemnity of the Mother of God. For in Mary Church and personality are one. Her "Yes" is the proto-cell of the Church and of every individual Christian life. She is both the Mother and the epitome of the Church and the Church's most outstanding member. Furthermore, she best illustrates how tradition is combined with what is new: she grew up entirely within the religion of her fathers, and more particularly within the tradition of the faithful and poor in Israel who, removed from all political action, waited in quiet and in prayer for the nation's salvation, in the faith of Abraham. Thus she was made perfect by Abraham's all-embracing obedience to God. But precisely because she has this obedient faith, God can lead her beyond all that has been, all that is codified in the law and the prophets, into the New and eternal Covenant that he now wishes to conclude with the whole of mankind by becoming a man in her womb. On this model, tradition only remains alive as long as it is ready actively to transcend itself. It should not lose itself or be neglected and despised: it should fulfill itself in something that, like all grace, comes to it out of the blue.

All we need to do, to recognize this as a general law, is to look at the way truly great artists appear in the history of mankind. They are always preceded by a long, cultivated chain of tradition. They need this long approach, they presuppose all that has been achieved, but then they crown it with something new and beyond the reach of the tradition, which comes down from above like the final central stone in a dome. Think of Mozart, Donatello, Dante or Goethe. Whole centuries, subsequently, live and draw sustenance from them, creating and delighting in their shadow, but no one can attain to their level again. Now the last part of the comparison cannot properly be applied to the Church and to ourselves. Naturally, no one in Christendom can attain to the level of Mary, for her immaculate quality and her virginal motherhood are essentially unique. But her sublime person spreads, not shadow, but only light. Those who stand and try to live within this light are not pale imitators: they are people who have been encouraged to progress, who have been liberated. The fruitfulness of the Christian tradition is something quite different from the continuing influence of a genius. Mary opens up countless possibilities of saying "Yes" for all who come after her. All of them are personal, all of them are original; according to God's commission, all of them are new and have never existed before; yet they are all related to one another in their positive aspects. For the Christian, above all else, is a man who says "Yes". His love is never sparked into flame by mere criticism of the status quo, of inherited patterns and conditions, of structures. First of all he becomes aware of God's "Yes" to the world and to every individual; then he too utters this "Yes" and tries to find people who will listen to it (for it receives so little attention and is allowed so little room in which to operate). God's "Yes", which has been spoken once for all in his Incarnation, does not gradually fade away in the course of history. In itself it is always equally new, equally audible and equally effective; it only seeks for men who will join in uttering this "Yes" and who will strive to find others in the world who are prepared to listen.

The origin is open to all, and there can be hope for mankind as long as it recognizes that the origin is open, as long as it strives and journeys toward the light radiating from it. The light that has shone forth in the origin is the ultimate light, for it is God's love for the world, and this light of love illuminates our goal, which is to respond to this love. But it also illuminates the path to the goal: again, it is a walking in the power of love. The problems of mankind are so difficult to solve—industrialization, the conservation of resources, the distribution of goods, world food provision—but unless we are grounded in love, unless we start from love, they will only become more and more intractable. Love must penetrate even into the hardest realism of economics and politics if we are not to perish at one another's hand. In John we read, "he who hates his brother is a murderer", and Jesus spoke in very similar terms in the Sermon on the Mount. There are entire nations, and great nations, who bring up their children to hate the others, the "enemies", and it is only a question of time before these latent murderous energies come out into the public arena. The fuse is already burning at the powder keg.

Yet, as we began by saying, there are still the mysterious interstices, the in-between spaces: there, by God's appointment, dwell those who desire to live in and for his love. They keep the world going. They cannot be ascertained statistically, for, according to Jesus' word, the kingdom of God is not coming with "signs to be observed" (Lk 17:20). Such people can live on either side of the totalitarian frontier, on either side of the barbed wire. Nor can their influence be completely assessed; often the best of it remains hidden. They are like subterranean springs and streams that moisten the roots from below. They carry the water of the origin, of the primal tradition, and thus make it possible for the future to sprout forth. Tradition means handing on, keeping nothing back for oneself. We ourselves, as persons, are handed on by the forward march of time; the passing moment hands us on to our neighbor. That is why it is pointless to cling to what is transitory. We are a journeying people. In this way, ultimately, we can hold to the Apostle's motto for life: "Forgetting what lies behind and straining forward to what lies ahead, I press on toward the goal" "to make it my own, because Christ Jesus has made me his own" (Phil 3:13–14, 12).

Joy in the Midst of Anxiety

Dear Listeners, we wish each other a happy new year. What good things may it bring, to us and to the world? We do not know. As always, the human caravan is journeying into an unknown region. There can be no doubt that the countryside around us has become wilder and more threatening; the thin layer of culture that had covered the soil is getting thinner and thinner, and everywhere the naked rock comes to light, jagged and sheer. In the wake of the moon flights, man is lonelier than ever on his narrow little planet; the air he breathes, the bread and water he needs to live are literally running out. He experiences *angst*, a deep-seated anxiety, and this existential anxiety produces more and more panic reactions. Everywhere we hear of bombs exploding, hostages being taken; everywhere people are using violence and terror with the aim of changing situations for the better or actually creating them. Man is afraid that the whole business is ultimately meaningless, particularly the way it seems to be advancing (and the direction it is taking is clear enough), and he expresses this meaninglessness by acting meaninglessly himself. By doing so he shows that he is on the way to losing all joy in existence. Joy, in a profound, all-embracing and buoyant sense, has become perhaps the rarest article and raw material in today's world. Its stocks are dwindling, and in many places it has been completely used up. But how can man go on living without joy in his existence? And this joy must be a fully human joy, not a mere biological sense of pleasure in one's own strength as an individual or part of a group but a joy that finds life, with all its difficulties, reversals, threats and disappointments, to be ultimately good and worth living. "Be it as it may, it *was* beautiful!"

We cannot blame the majority of people for not being able to echo these words of Goethe. So many people have become cogs in a machine, people whose future, like their past and present, is totally planned, people in social systems that they hate, people—and how many there are—who simply lack the minimum for survival.

There is a religion, however, that can say without bitterness or cynicism, "Blessed are the poor, the hungry, those who weep, and who are hated and persecuted" (Lk 6:20ff.). This religion believes it can proclaim the message of joy to the whole world; it has taken over the word *gospel* (*eu-angelion*, "joyful tidings") and made it its own. Its message is not incidentally a message of joy as well as being many other things: it is quite simply *joy*. And it proclaims this message in and for a world that, in all its representatives, Christians, Jews and pagans, hanged the Herald of this Good News on a gallows. Thus it proclaims the message in a world it sees in very realistic terms and in all its cruelty.

There are not many basic attitudes that are regarded as ultimate and comprehensive by the various world views. Apart from the Christian, there are perhaps only two others that are worth considering (because they alone are worthy of the human person).

The first is expressed in the introverted, quiet and smiling face of the Buddha, who has found peace and invites those who look at him to seek and find by following in his footsteps. This is the peace of calm resignation, which has cut through the rank tendrils of passion and so has escaped the circling whirlwind of fate. In the Western world the Stoics endeavored to take the same path: they call their ideal *apatheia*, resignation, a spiritual superiority to all that happens to us from outside. By not being affected by external things, we have a chance of getting in touch with the inner, absolute, divine realm. Nowadays, once again, many people are knocking at the door of this Eastern path.

The second basic attitude is the courageous determination to change the intolerable aspects of earthly conditions, cost what it may. Since so many people are unhappy today, I will dedicate my life to the task of ensuring that more people are happy tomorrow, or at some future time.

Resignation and courage are the two fundamental attitudes that man himself produces as a response to today's world, which seems to offer no joy as such. Both arise from a negation of the here and now: the Oriental negates it in order to take flight into a religious dimension above and beyond this world; the Communist negates it in order to place the center of gravity into a future, and chasing this future lends meaning to the horrors of the present day. Only Christianity dares to affirm "today", this New Year's Day, seeing it as the introduction to a *happy* new year; only Christianity dares to take the new year wishes quite literally. Why is this?

It is quickly said, but reflection on it takes a long time. Let us try to clarify Christian joy by seeing it from three sides.

1. In creating the world and reconciling it to himself after it has turned from him in its guilt, the God of Jesus Christ does not simply give *something*: he gives himself. The attitude of *giving* is not one attitude among others on this God's part but the revelation of his nature. In all that he gives, whether it is sweet or bitter, he gives himself. He does this freely, for no other reason, simply for the sake of giving. According to Christian Faith, self-giving constitutes the eternal blessedness of this God. Insofar as he is the primal source of everything, "Father", he gives his all, from all eternity, to his Son, and the absolute bliss of both of them is to give themselves to each other in return in the Holy Spirit, who is God as pure gift.

Giving is only free if it liberates, if it allows the recipient to move into freedom. It is only free if it refrains from fettering the recipient to the gift and consigning him to a tyranny in which he is eternally having to say thank you to the giver. The Father gives the Son his entire divine freedom and subsequently entire human freedom too. He also gives it to the Prodigal Son. He gives freely so that the recipient, for his part, can use the gift on the basis of his own freedom. In Christian terms the two forms of joy, the joy of receiving and the joy of giving, are one, and the second rests essentially on the first.

How often does it occur to us that we are a gift from God to ourselves? I have been given as a gift to myself. I can and should give joyful thanks for my existence, because God wanted thereby to make me a present—in fact, the greatest possible present. It may be that my life would seem less worthless if I were continually to remember that, in giving me life, God has made me so precious a present; his intention is to give me a share in his eternal, blessed existence. And as for our ability to give, to make a personal contribution, to create something, to give and bequeath things to others, how often does it occur to us that we owe all this to the same primal joy of God? We have been endowed with a freedom that enables us to beget, to give birth, to fashion and invent things and to be a blessing to others!

Our life is a gift and a giving to others; therefore, it is joy at a profound level. Anyone who seriously makes this idea his own and begins to practice it will find it to be true; he will discover that the will to live it out, that is, to accept everything as a gift from God, can transform our life right down to its roots. But can we do this while oppressed by anxiety in the face of the world's suffering?

2. Christianity is the only world view able to attribute a positive meaning to *suffering*, all suffering. All the others are either techniques of escaping from suffering or techniques of reducing it as far as possible in the future. Christianity by no means loves suffering for its own sake, and it is completely

behind all who try to mitigate it. But Christianity does not stop at the frontier where man can do no more. Teilhard de Chardin emphasized this most strongly, along with all the great Christian thinkers and saints: suffering that is unavoidable, that, humanly speaking, is hopeless, and even death itself have a positive meaning. Even suffering, *particularly* suffering, is a precious gift that the one suffering can hand on to others; it helps, it purifies, it atones, it communicates divine graces. The sufferings of a mother can bring a wayward son back to the right path; the sufferings of someone with cancer or leprosy, if offered to God, can be a capital for God to use, bearing fruit in the most unexpected places. Suffering, accepted with thanksgiving and handed on, participates in the great fruitfulness of everything that streams from God's joy and returns to him by circuitous paths.

Of course there is a great mystery at the heart of this idea, namely, the vicarious suffering of Jesus on the Cross. There we see that it was possible for someone to take on himself our guilt, and hence the fundamental cause of our sadness and hopelessness, and by so doing open up for us the path to unreserved joy once more. The Old Testament tells of Samson, how one night he lifted the gates of the city of Gaza from their hinges and carried them off. So, in the night when he was forsaken by God, Jesus unhinged the far more heavily bolted gates of our perdition and, on Easter morning, set us free to walk down the path into God's broad landscape. But at the same time he also enabled us to walk along with him, to a certain extent, on the path of his suffering. Paul immediately drew the consequences, in several passages in his letters. "In my flesh I complete what is lacking in Christ's afflictions for the sake of his body, that is, the Church" (Col 1:24). Christian suffering is fruitful, especially when—without our having occasioned it—it leads to spiritual darkness. This does not mean that we should wish to be abandoned by God in order to intensify our solidarity with our fellowmen who are far from him. Nothing of the kind was in Paul's mind. But where tangible joy is withdrawn from us, we are right to hope that other hearts may light up because of our darkness.

3. So the joy that Christians have is both a gift and a responsibility. As Paul says, they are to "shine as lights in the [dark] world" (Phil 2:15). All that they have is intended for those who have not. They must be affirmative, *positive people*, so that the negaters, the fault-finders, those who smell ideology everywhere, may meet with a resistance against which their criticism will smash itself to pieces.

Amid all the fear that characterizes our time, we Christians are summoned to live in joy and to communicate joy—joy in spite of fear, joy in the midst of fear. Easter joy in the midst of the passion of humanity. Nor is this an artificially produced joy but one that is simply a gift from God. It alone can change hearts and hence conditions. No one has transformed the world more profoundly than Jesus Christ, but his life among men consisted primarily in quite small, everyday and very natural attentions to those nearest to him: he loved children, the sick, the despised and outlawed and those excluded from society; he loved those who hated him and planned his death. And he required the same attitude in those who wanted to follow him. Through this joy of his he raised the level of joy in the world. His love and joy come from afar, from the deepest wellsprings of eternal Being; he communicates them to those who are his, not hesitantly and sparingly, but in all fullness: "As the Father has loved me, so have I loved you; abide in my love"—in a down-to-earth love both of those who are close to us and of those who are our enemies—"just as I abide in my Father's love. These things I have spoken to you, that my joy may be in you, and that your joy may be full" (Jn 15:9–11).

Epiphany

Falling Down and Worshipping

It is said that the three wise men who came to see the Child and his Mother "fell down and worshipped". What they worship is the epiphany, the manifestation, the shining forth of God in this poor Child. The Old Covenant worshipped God in his majesty, his judicial righteousness, his goodness as Lord of the Covenant. Now he is to be worshipped in a human Child, and this is so astonishing that it compels us to reflect about the act of worship itself—something largely alien to us in our secularized age.

If we still have a personal relationship with God, for the most part we address prayers of petition to him, and we are right to do so. More seldom, we give thanks to him—and we remember that, of the ten lepers healed by Jesus, only one returned to give thanks—or, if some suffering comes our way, we make an act of surrender to the eternal design that is beyond our grasp. Again, we are right to do so. But surrender, acceptance, is not the same as worship.

What is it? God is unique and infinitely mysterious. Consequently, the act in which, with all our being, we acknowledge him as God, our God, is also unique and difficult to talk about. Let us try, all the same. We acknowledge that God alone exists of himself, whereas all created things only exist because of his almighty will and power and have their roots in something beyond all conditions. So, too, we acknowledge that God is truth pure and simple, the epitome of all truth, and that as a result he is always right, whatever he does or allows to happen. We acknowledge that God is goodness pure and simple, the epitome of all that is good, and that, consequently, whatever he sends us, we can always love him unreservedly with wholehearted homage and surrender. We acknowledge that God is the epitome of all beauty, and as a result we are enraptured as we submit to his truth and are caught up in rejoicing as we serve him, as the Psalms show us, and as Paul urges the Christians: "Singing and making melody to the Lord with all your heart, always and for everything giving thanks." The Old Covenant is already aware of this; there too God's faithful ones commit their hearts to him in surrender, thanksgiving and trust and in a profound reverence that is yet devoid of anxiety.

What now, however, when God sends his eternal Word to the earth in the form of a Child? First we must understand what God is saying to us through this epiphany. As always in his word, he is telling us something about himself; in all that this Child is and is to become, the youth, the man, the teacher and worker of miracles, keeping silence before the judge, scourged, mocked, rejected, crying out in his abandonment by God on the Cross, buried, and living forever after having risen from the dead—all this is epiphany, God revealing himself.

By being a tiny Child, God is saying this: with all my almighty power, genuinely mine as it is, I am still as poor and humble and trusting as this Child; indeed, not just *as* this Child, for I really *am* this Child. Later, in his teaching, Jesus will speak about taking the lowest place, about serving, about giving one's life for the brethren, and this will not be a mere moral instruction addressed to men but something he himself does and is. Thus it will be a manifestation of the heart of God, his Father. Do this, because this is what God is like! And then comes the terrible side to it: when Jesus suffers for sinners and, carrying their sins, loses his awareness of his Father and cries out, forsaken and dying of his thirst for God: again we have to say, this is what God is like! And when Jesus shares himself out in the form of food and drink: this is what God is like! For it is the Father who offers us this word and flesh of God, bloodied, rent and torn asunder by men, so that we may share in his eternal life. And when Jesus' heart is pierced and becomes a hollow wound where a man can place his fingers and his whole self—"hide me in thy wounds"—this is what God is like! For this wound goes right to his heart, and in it we can find healing. All this is the epiphany of God.

In falling down and worshipping, therefore, we are not worshipping flesh, that is, ourselves, but God; we are worshipping the One who is completely Other, self-existent, all-powerful, and yet who has been pleased to show us that he is sufficiently all-powerful to be powerless, sufficiently blessed to be able to suffer, sufficiently glorious to be able to take the lowest place in his creation. And God does not act "as if": he really *is* humble and childlike and poor. How could the God who created children not know in his heart how a child feels?

At this point we can ask if there can be a more mysterious and incomprehensible God than this God, who goes about among us like a man, *as* a man, without ceasing to be truly God, the completely Other, the Eternal, Immortal and All-Powerful. In his epiphany this God has lost nothing of his incomprehensibility; on the contrary, he has become even more incomprehensible. Only now do we begin to suspect how far divine omnipotence reaches into reality. Thus there can be no more profound worship than Christian worship, when it is authentic.

What, then, in the face of this God, is the significance of the world, with all the people around us, with all our activities and busy work? It is not God in any shape or form, and hence it is in no way to be worshipped. It is worldly, creaturely, and it is wrong to say that all created reality as such contains an uncreated divine spark at its deepest level. Otherwise we should have to worship ourselves. All the same, is there not something true in this idea that something divine lies at man's innermost core? As Christians we must say "Yes": every man has something divine in him, but not by nature, not by the fact of being created but by God's grace, which designates, chooses and calls all men to be children of the Father, brothers of Jesus and bearers of God's Holy Spirit. Many, probably the majority, know nothing or very little of this vocation; they live at the level of passing things, as if they had nothing eternal in them. So they can see nothing other than the worldly dimension, not even in their fellowmen. They do not see that, in Christ, their fellowman is a child of the Father, who loves him because Christ has stood surety for him and made him his brother. We can even say that Christ has made him the brother whom the Father so loves, of himself, that he gave up his Son, Jesus Christ, for his sake. Thus, as the Apostle says, God has paid a very high price for this love of his. People ordinarily see nothing but their own likeness in their fellowmen, one chance specimen among millions. "Man is man" (*Mann ist Mann*—title of a play by Brecht); basically every man can be replaced by someone else.

Only the Christian is able to see something unique in each person he meets. In him he sees a being who is known by God not in a merely generic sense, or as a chance specimen, but whom God loves in his uniqueness and irreplaceability. This is only possible because of Jesus Christ, the Only Son, who gives something of his uniqueness to all his brothers and sisters.

If this is really the case, what does the Christian see when he looks at his fellowman? Not a questionable, cheap and highly imperfect specimen of humanity in general but someone whom God himself loves with a love that is unique to him, however mired and obscured the image of God within him has become. And the divine love that loves this person is worthy of worship. We are not saying that men should worship each other, for that would be ridiculous; what we are saying, however, is something quite serious and implying very definite consequences: every person should be to others an occasion for epiphany, stimulating them to worship God's presence in each individual.

So we do not need to erect a wall between the moments we

keep for prayer and worship and our everyday life in which we have quite different things to think of. Of course, if in our daily round we do not reserve a single moment for thinking of God, such thoughts will never occur to us when we encounter each other in the everyday hurly-burly of life. But once we have penetrated to the worshipful love of God through pondering the mystery of the epiphany, we shall have no need to abandon this attitude of worship in the midst of our daily work; not only are we constantly surrounded by this mystery, but each encounter with another will make us more deeply acquainted with it.

When a person is able to see and treat the world from this point of view, we say that he is living in the presence of God.

Many people think it takes long preparation by way of meditation and technical exercises to attain this attitude. I do not believe that. It is enough if we simply recall our Faith, which receives its visible seal on Christmas night: "God so loved the world" and each one of us "that he gave his only Son" for it and for each of us. Before our very eyes we have this Son, given for us. We see him before us here at Christmastide, but equally we see him on the Cross, and on Easter Day, and on every ordinary day of the Church's year.

How Rich the Poor Man Is

As soon as God is in the world and has become one of us, everything belongs to him. He does not even need to take it; it is enough that he is there. He is the King "to whom all things live". He is there as the Lamb "who was slain . . . worthy to receive power and wealth and wisdom and might and honor and glory and blessing". This is the song of heaven, but it applies to earth too.

What is poorer than the newborn child who clings to his mother's breast? All the same, he reaches out for her breast as if it represented all the treasures of the earth. The "kings" throw open the door and set gold, incense and myrrh before him, symbols of the treasures of the earth, which now belong to the Son of God. They are only symbols, and the Child does not know what to do with them—they are not even toys. What he does desire is his Mother's milk—that is quite a different treasure. This is something that wells up, fresh, straight from her heart, something that can be taken up immediately into his heart.

The example of the human mother explains in a quite simple way the Christian mystery that had begun to seem almost threatening. When God appears among us, we are dethroned, we belong to him, all our treasures are his. But when any child comes into the world, his mother belongs to him and he can make demands of her. And this glorious milk is not only something she has *for* the child: she has received it *through* the child. Her riches have no other cause and no other raison d'être but the child. But God himself becomes a Child: so in his case, too, this is not only a metaphor but highly concrete Christian reality. This Mother is both things at once: she is a human mother like others, with her child and her milk; and she is also the unique Mother of the unique divine Child, who has his Mother and, implicitly, all the treasures of the world, at his disposal. He disposes of everything both supernaturally, since he is the Son of God, and completely naturally, since everything converges on him, both because of his own nature and because of the nature of things themselves.

So we should not make a fuss when it comes to offering our little bit of value to the Lord and making it available to him. In itself, of course, it is just as worthless as the magnificent and unusable gifts given by the "kings". But perhaps, if the Mother takes over our gifts, she can turn them into something that will delight the Child and be of use to him. What Mother Church takes up of the gifts we offer her—the hard bulk she is able to transform, by her care, into fluid love—she can infuse into the Child. The gifts' precious external appearance is lost, but they are rendered useful. And since the poorest person, who has no gold, incense or myrrh to give, can offer his very poverty, his poor love, no one is poor before the Lord. The poorest man can become the richest. Poverty is not a value in itself, nor is gold worthless in itself, but poverty enables us to have a clearer, more transparent love; where there are no windowpanes, the light can stream in unhindered.

Blessed are the poor. Not simply the have-nots but the poor in spirit, those who realize and affirm their essential poverty. This essential poverty is threefold: the poverty of the needy creature over against the riches of God; the poverty of the sinner who has lost the love of God within him; and the poverty of the Christian who, as a result of the royal sovereignty of incarnate Love, has been dispossessed of all his own property in favor of the King. Thus it is not difficult for him to acknowledge his threefold poverty and ratify it in a single act whereby he hands over his own self. It is this act, ultimately, that is the essential requirement, and anything else he might have to offer, even the most brilliant achievements in whatever field, would remain unusable and in vain.

There are people who, when they give presents, evaluate them according to the pleasure they themselves find in them. My favorite thing is a particular harpsichord recording of music by Bach, and so at Christmas I give everyone this same record. In a way it is touching, the way people give away what is dearest to them. But surely it would be more touching if I were to get to know the recipient's taste; he might put a high value on quite different things. Indeed, he might value highly the very things I find repugnant. To our way of looking at things, the good God has strange preferences. Gold, incense and myrrh do not mean very much to him. Yahweh is not one of those gods who draw nourishment from the smell of the roasting animals sacrificed to them; he himself has told us as much. So we should not press such things on him. He wants what he can use, that is, the love that springs from our poverty. This is something that is related to him, for he became poor for our sakes. We could also say that, as God, he is so unimaginably rich that our riches mean nothing to him; and at the same time, in his innermost self—and Rilke got a hint of this in his *Stundenbuch*—he much prefers being poor to being rich. In becoming a man, poor unto death, he not only took upon himself something totally alien to him but also yielded to a most profound longing of his heart. In himself he does not know what to do with all his royal treasures, like King Solomon. That is why King Solomon leaves his six hundred wives and concubines and goes out into the vineyard to love the poor, dusky Shulammite. That is something he cannot find at home. And the strange thing is that the Shulammite is not ashamed of her poverty. She does not even refer to it. She is loved: that is enough; she *is* lovable to the King: why should she wonder who and what she is, or what, apart from this love, she might be? She is an ineffable jewel to the King, and she has no intention of robbing him of this joy. Perhaps King Solomon disguises himself so as not to be recognized and not to frighten the girl. Perhaps it is an exciting, romantic episode for him. But God does not disguise himself in becoming poor with us and for us. He carries our threefold poverty in himself, once and for all, irrevocably. So let us give him what he needs, and what he has already taken as his; for he really wants to receive it as a gift from us. The Christian life is a marriage in poverty, and the cross is the marriage bed. This is easily said; the doing of it is very hard, and it can only be understood by those who have tried it at some point or other. Such people will also understand that they have nothing to offer God, except precisely what he wants of them. They will understand that the only way of being "beautiful" for God is by being just as he wants them to be, that is, people whom he can love. "I am black, but comely!" I am poor and beggarly, and yet I am the richest, because God himself loves me, because I am important to him.

In those whom God loves, the whole world becomes lovable

to him. The Son on the Cross suffices the Father; he is so incredibly beautiful that, as the Father gazes at him, all that is connected to him, the whole world, seems wonderfully beautiful. With all its fragility, its sin, its murdering of God, it has still brought about the most beautiful thing of all, namely, the dying, squandered love of the Son of God. The Father's heart, wounded by all the arrows of this love, must capitulate to it. It may be that we never love more profoundly and definitively than at the moment when we forgive. When the Prodigal Son returns, his appearance does not matter. He is back, and nothing else counts. Creation is whole again; it rests in God once more; it has emerged from the nightmare in which both God and the world felt estranged from one another. The nightmare is past, and it is as if it had never been, nor will it ever return.

Baptism of Jesus

The Nature of Christian Vocation

Even the most critical biblical scholar has to admit that the event of Jesus' baptism is as firmly authenticated as his death on the Cross. But just as, in the case of his death, we learn of many external details and yet scarcely gain any insight into the profound abyss of this tortured man's interior experience, so it is with his baptism: the accounts we have of it are, as it were, only approximations, presenting us with different aspects that are hard to harmonize. What did the Baptist know of the person and mission of Jesus? Who actually saw the heavens open and the dove descending, and who heard the Father's voice? And why did Jesus allow himself to be baptized at all, since baptism was a washing that presupposed a confession of sin and an inner conversion? Surely this baptism only had a meaning with a view to his coming, so that as far as he was concerned—and basically the same applies to the ceremony of circumcision—it was totally unnecessary? Questions such as these seem to place a distance between us and the event. In fact, however, what the event shows us ought to give us the very opposite experience: we should feel that we are being presented here with a magnificent total picture of which we are most definitely a part.

God's word was in the world right from the beginning of creation, and emphatically and urgently so ever since the Old Covenant; it was both present and to come. By instructing the individual hearer, it always pointed forward to some final and future coming, to someone who would be called "God with us". Where will he come from? From heaven or from Israel? From both: the Spirit of God overshadows the Jewish girl. Again: Will he come down from God as an embodiment of his Spirit? Or from below, from the sinful nation that had always tried to turn back to God and yet continually fell away from him, and that is now urged to repent by the greatest of its prophets, John the Baptist? Again the answer is: both. He rises out of the waters of the Jordan, in which he allowed himself to be baptized along with the multitude of his guilty brethren, in solidarity with them, with their guilt and their attempt to find their way back to God; and as he does so, heaven above opens, the Spirit descends upon him to remain with him henceforward and the Father's voice resounds: "This is my beloved Son, with whom I am well pleased" (Mt 3:17).

"This" Son is the link established between earth and heaven. All his life long, and for all eternity, he will be the Son of the Virgin Mary and of her forefathers but also the Son and the seed of the Father, brought by the Spirit into an earthly womb. All his life long, right up to the Cross and for all eternity, he will be the one who wills to bear the sins of his human brothers. And at the end of his mission, this symbolic act of repentance will take on the most terrible form, because his mission from above, which is given to him on account of his Sonship and his possession of the Spirit, will enable him, the Lamb of God, in all reality to bear sins away. Thus, and only thus, can heaven and earth meet, and God the Father's being "well pleased" rests upon this meeting of God and man in the one "beloved Son".

The meeting is about to take place, for just as Jesus rises out of the water, from below, the Spirit descends on him from above, and in this twofold movement the Son is sent out upon his mission that will decide everything. For the first time the two sister sacraments of baptism and confirmation meet; in the giving of the mission, confirmation builds on the foundations laid by baptism in the rebirth of those who are reborn of God. The eternal Son, born from all eternity from the womb of the

Father, would not need rebirth except to provide a blueprint for all his sinful brothers in the future. For this purpose, his coming forth from the Father, his *processio*, must expressly take the form of his mission, his *missio*; thus he no longer sends forth the Spirit of love together with the Father (as in eternity) but obediently allows this Spirit of love to come down upon him and rest upon him as the Spirit sent by the Father to instruct him. Henceforth, following and *driven by* the Spirit, he will exclusively perform the Father's loving will. Now the Spirit rests *upon* the Son, for this is what the mission requires: mission always comes from above; man never takes it for himself. Naturally, however, the Spirit also rests *in* the Son, who performs the Father's will out of his innermost depths and not as some externally imposed law; for he is always the one born of the Father, the Child familiar with the Father's heart.

So the *beloved Son*, who in his mission joins heaven and earth and has brought the kingdom of heaven to earth, will be the presupposition for all Christian existence and action, and in his forthcoming work and suffering he will live it out in model form. For the present, we shall not follow the path of his mission any more closely—the Church's year will unfold it—but dwell a little on the idea that it is precisely the Christian mission, and the carrying out of it, that brings earth and heaven together.

In themselves, both sides of creation have been fashioned by God to correspond to one another and to be there for one another. But sinful man has turned away from heaven in order to exist for himself alone, and in this way he has created a split in creation that was never intended. God in heaven has never distanced himself or alienated himself from man. So we can say that, while there is a distance from earth to heaven, there is none from heaven to earth. In the Old Covenant we can see how the distance between below and above is gradually diminished in a movement from above to below. The manifestations of God in the making of the Covenant with Abraham (Gen 15) and on Sinai are gracious condescensions on the part of heaven, but in their terrifying aspect they make man aware of his distance from God. This distance could be overcome if he could follow God's gracious precepts, but the abyss yawns every time he fails to follow them, with the result that, for him, the flame of heavenly love turns into a flame of anger. God's anger, of which the Old Testament speaks so much, is the zeal of his spurned and violated love. God's word is already there as an offer, and there are attempts to follow it, but it is not recognized, in its innermost substance, as pure love. And wherever men try to keep it by grasping for it, regarding it as their own property and attributing it to themselves, this love that calls for surrender is pharisaically destroyed.

All the attempts and failures of the Old Covenant were the preliminary stage of what would eventually come to fruition; they were signposts along the way, pointing from all sides toward a reserved place in the center. The people of the Old Testament already know what is meant by word and precept, mission, obedience, personal poverty; somehow they even have a grasp of what it means to be a son of God, a bride of God. But only now, when the water is joined by the Spirit, the Spirit who has already overshadowed the Virgin in the selfsame event, is the mission truly successful. Only now are the Father's will and kingdom and name realized on earth as in heaven. In the fulfillment of this mission the distance between earth and heaven is obliterated. True, we still think of heaven as something that only concerns us seriously after death, as the "beyond". But we are mistaken; for the union, the New and "everlasting Covenant which will never be forgotten" (Jer 50:5), has already been achieved in Jesus Christ and in what, through his life, he has given us. God's law is already written in our hearts (Jer 31:33); we no longer need to teach each other about God, but all of us have been taught by God (Jer 31:33; Jn 6:45).

Let us beware, however, of taking possession of the will of God as if it were our own. Let us not lay claim to any ethical autonomy. For that, in pharisaism, was the real and irreconcilable opposition to Jesus. He could get on with the tax collectors and prostitutes, for there was the possibility of their being converted and becoming children of God. But when someone wields God's mission as if it were his own, grace is frittered away to no purpose and the love that resides in the divine will goes unrecognized and is swallowed up in the abyss of the self. The more piously this autonomy conducts itself, the further it is from the Holy Spirit. In such a case the Spirit seems to have been absorbed *into* the pious mind and heart, but he is no longer the Spirit of mission resting *over* the obedient man. How closely the two spirits can resemble each other! And yet the one brings heaven and earth together, and the other actually widens the gulf between them. The Crucified will have to endure this gulf too; peace between heaven and earth will only finally be concluded in his blood (see Eph 2:13–18). Thus the water and the Spirit must be accompanied by a third, the blood, making a full, triune witness (1 Jn 5:8), so fulfilling the mission of the *Beloved*.

Obedience to God's loving (and often incomprehensible) will imparts to us on earth a heavenly freedom. It can seem to turn things upside down: Jesus, the Son of the Father, is subject to his parents, a no doubt uneducated carpenter and his wife. Jesus, in whom the New Covenant is already under way, wishes to receive the baptism of the Old Covenant. It is taken aback: "I need to be baptized by you, and do you come to me?" The answer is: "Let it be so now, for thus it is fitting for us to fulfill all righteousness" (Mt 3:14–15). The Old Covenant attempts to *perform* righteousness; the New Covenant brings it about: *fiat*. This is its primary act. And again, finally, we have the ultimate paradox: Jesus obeys the Spirit, yet the Spirit proceeds from him too, as if he were—and he *is*!—the pure transparency of the Father's will. This is possible because the Son's divine, autonomous will always was, and always remains, the pure, spontaneous echo of the Father's will.

The entire ethics of Christian activity lies hidden—and manifest—in these depths.

Week of Prayer for Christian Unity

A Hint for the Ecumenical Movement

In this Sunday's Gospel we encounter the Baptist's words about Jesus: "Behold, the Lamb of God, who takes away the sin of the world" (Jn 1:29). A tremendous utterance, unveiling in advance the ultimate meaning of Jesus' mission and pointing ahead to the end, so terrible and yet so full of grace, of his earthly path. We do not need to delay over whether it was possible for this pronouncement really to be made at that time or whether the Holy Spirit later inspired the Evangelist to write it down as being the right expression for the situation. Why should not the mighty forerunner of Jesus, whom Jesus described as the greatest of those born of woman, have been permitted an insight into the true nature of the Person he was announcing? Let us take the word as it stands, in its indivisible and alarming magnitude.

It points to the very heart of Jesus' mission; it hits the nail on the head. The task of Jesus cannot be compared to anyone else's in world history. Wise men have tried to show us a way in which we can keep ourselves from being entangled in the sin of the world, or purify ourselves from it, but where is the wise man who would claim to be able to take the entire sin of the world on his shoulders? The prophets of the Old Covenant went further than the sages and spoke of the mercy of Yahweh, who can purify the nation from its sins and forgive them by his divine omnipotence. And then, right on the periphery, not really understood by anyone, there appeared the puzzling figure of a nameless person, atoning—unacknowledged—for the sins of the nation, and indeed for all mankind, brought to the slaughtering block "like a lamb that does not open its mouth".

Here we are given a preview of the most profound Christian mystery: God cannot restore order in man unless man, with whom God is in a Covenant relationship, participates in the process. Of himself, however, sinful man cannot do anything toward this reconciliation; but if an entirely pure man is sent from God, embodying God's presence among men, he can atone for his brothers and lift their sins from them, so that, relieved of this burden, they are able to turn to God and accept his offer of reconciliation.

This is the innermost heart of the Christian Good News. The most ancient profession of faith that has come down to us in the New Testament is from St. Paul, and he says that he is handing on something that was entrusted to him by the first Apostles, in Jerusalem or Antioch, as the quintessence of the Faith. This profession says that "Christ died for our sins in accordance with the Scriptures, that he was buried, that he was raised on the third day in accordance with the Scriptures, and that he appeared to Cephas, then to the Twelve" (1 Cor 15:3–5). The scandal of the Cross, which was something the disciples could neither grasp nor bear, is given its meaning from the vantage point of the Resurrection: evidently Jesus, who, while he was alive, lived for everyone, did not die a meaningless death: on the contrary, his death was full of meaning, and he bore away the sins of all. This is not one interpretation among others—as many theologians nowadays would have us believe—but the only central and satisfactory interpretation. All other ideas on the Passion of Jesus converge upon it. It is the only interpretation, and became the normative teaching of the primitive Church; Paul, who was converted three or four years after the death of Jesus, found this teaching already in existence and gave it a place of honor in his powerful theology. No one has the right to try to go behind it or relativize it.

My dear Brothers and Sisters: we are in the Octave of Prayer for the unity of the Christian churches. It is right, therefore, in view of what we have just said, to reflect upon our lamentable situation in the churches. And on the basis of the biblical testimony we must do so in a way most of our listeners will not expect. It is true that the issues in which we differ as Christians, Catholics, Protestants, Anglicans or Orthodox are not unimportant, and the disagreements between us have their roots in particular passages in Holy Scripture itself. For instance, should Peter have a successor for all time, and if so, what should his powers be? Or, how are we to understand man's cooperation with God's grace, and what does it mean when Paul attributes everything to grace and yet calls himself and his colleagues "fellow workers" (*synergoi*) with God? Or, what is implied when Jesus offers us bread and wine as his Flesh and Blood? These and similar questions, which all arise from Scripture, have caused the differences of opinion that persist to today, and we are bound to regret most deeply the practical effects they have produced. But I would like to speak not of these things but of the way we should respond to the Baptist's words: "Behold, the Lamb of God, who takes away the sin of the world." For, according to all the New Testament writings, from Paul and the other Epistles to the Synoptic Gospels and the Johannine writings, this is acknowledged unanimously to be the very foundation of Faith, as the ancient Creed bears witness when it says "for us men and for our salvation he came down from heaven and was crucified for us". Everything depends on this assertion: that is, the fact that Jesus is God's eternal Son (for a mere man cannot bear away the sins of the world); the fact that God is eternal Love (proved by the Son's surrender, through the Father, out of love for the world); the fact that God shows himself to be the hope of a dark and terrible world by raising the crucified and buried

Christ and so giving us a promise of our own resurrection. Anyone who tries to dislodge these central affirmations will find that all the major truths of Christianity threaten to collapse; he will be left with the pitiful remains of what was once a whole.

What we see, however, is that in all churches there is a strong party striving to relativize this central affirmation, to weaken it to such an extent that nothing tangible is left. Leaving the Orthodox aside, we find today that Catholic theologians vie with Protestant and Anglican theologians (and they in turn spur on those engaged in preaching) in marginalizing the fact that Jesus lived, suffered and rose from the dead "for us". They do this primarily by using techniques of exegesis to discover (as they think) earlier levels in the Gospels, levels at which this affirmation was still unknown. The liberal-rationalistic disintegration of the gospel on all sides, its reduction to a one-dimensional religious humanism, seems to me to be the greatest danger facing the ecumenical movement; encountering and agreeing with one another on this level would seem to have no wider significance for Christianity.

What are the arguments that liberal theology everywhere adduces against the tenet "died for our sins"? Primarily the fact, allegedly established by exegetical research, that during his earthly life Jesus probably never, or hardly ever, spoke about his coming Passion, or, if he did, never attributed to it any atoning significance for the sins of Israel, let alone for the whole world. It seems as if he did not foresee his death on the Cross at all, or only at a late stage. It was the post-Easter Church, supposedly, that gradually imported this idea into faith in Jesus in order to explain away the stumbling block of the Cross.

Here, naturally, we cannot go into the very complex arguments used to support this view; we must content ourselves with a few summary thoughts. In the first place we can say this: it would have been tactless for Jesus, whose whole efforts were devoted to the conversion of Israel, to announce to the people beforehand that they would not be converted but rather would reject and crucify him. The people must be left the opportunity of conversion. But this does not stop Jesus' knowing about his forthcoming rejection. In the case of all the great prophets before him, when they were chosen and sent out with their mission of conversion, it was made clear to them at the outset that their task would fail; it did not stop their putting all their strength into their mission. Furthermore, it cannot really be proved that Jesus' words to his disciples regarding his impending suffering do not originate from him, at least in their basic substance, not even when he explicitly describes this suffering as an atonement suffering (as in Mk 10:45). The words of institution at the Last Supper, "my Flesh which is given for you and my Blood which is shed for you", emphatically say the same thing. Who could have put such words into the Lord's mouth after Easter?! We must conclude that, during his earthly ministry, Jesus did speak about his future, albeit very discreetly, but he left the details of that great and terrible hour to the Father.

Nor can the evangelists' repeated assertions that, prior to the Resurrection, they did not understand Jesus' references to his death and rising again be dismissed as mere invention. They sound completely sincere; and we must say, in fact, that the disciples *could* not grasp the definitive Word of God in its entirety, that is, Jesus Christ, before its last syllables had been announced. These last syllables were the most important ones: the dying and rising of Jesus. Only where the complete Word had resounded did complete understanding become possible.

All this has far-reaching consequences for ecumenical endeavors. A real uniting of denominations can only take place from the very kernel of faith. Provided this kernel has been guaranteed intact by each side, the dependent layers, the flesh, so to speak, can wrap around it, and agreement can be sought at these levels also. But there can be absolutely no progress on the opposite path, that is, unity in relatively secondary matters while bracketing out the primary issue. Uniting one watered-down version with another will never produce something fresh, vigorous and radiant—and this is what Christianity must be. Christian faith stands or falls with the belief that God has set up a "pillar of atonement" (as Paul says) that proves effective. God does not continually show two faces, as in Israel: judging and saving, threatening and pardoning. God is absolutely clearly the God and Father of all; he grants forgiveness to all who accept it and, through their own forgiving of others, show that they have accepted it. What the Sermon on the Mount requires of Christians is presupposed by the Cross: Jesus will show us how to "turn the other cheek", how to "love one's enemies". Otherwise, how could he require us to do the same?

Christianity is the religion of thanksgiving. We give thanks not only for existing, for having been created, but also for being reconciled with God without any merit on our part. We gratefully accept this gift of reconciliation and try, by our lives, to help others to grasp it. If we do this, we shall have taken the most important ecumenical step together. All the questions that still separate us will be seen and solved in the light of this thanksgiving. In conclusion let us ask God:

Lord, let us never forget that we owe everything to you, the triune God, who has perfected the work of redeeming the world in Christ. May we all unite in praising you for this redemption, as we also ask that you will give us full unity in professing our faith, through Christ, our Lord.

Lent

Love Provides a Last Chance

In the Song of Songs we read: "Love is strong as death; jealousy is cruel as the grave" (Song 8:6). Jesus sometimes says things reminiscent of this, things that do not fit in at all with the sweet and sickly picture many people draw of the Man from Nazareth. We must be prepared for this kind of ruthlessness as we listen to today's Sunday Gospel. Here it is:

> There were some present at that very time who told him of the Galileans whose blood Pilate had mingled with their sacrifices. And he answered them, "Do you think that these Galileans were worse sinners than all the other Galileans, because they suffered thus? I tell you, No; but unless you repent you will all likewise perish. Or those eighteen upon whom the tower in Siloam fell and killed them, do you think that they were worse offenders than all the others who dwelt in Jerusalem? I tell you, No; but unless you repent you will all likewise perish."
>
> And he told this parable: "A man had a fig tree planted in his vineyard; and he came seeking fruit on it and found none. And he said to the vinedresser, 'Lo, these three years I have come seeking fruit on this fig tree, and I find none. Cut it down; why should it use up the ground?' And he answered him, 'Let it alone, sir, this year also, till I dig about it and put on manure. And if it bears fruit next year, well and good; but if not, you can cut it down' " (Lk 13:1–9).

Two truths confront each other in these words of Jesus. The first concerns the political atrocity of the Roman governor, but also the disaster at the Pool of Siloam, the collapse of a tower that buried eighteen people alive. Should such catastrophes be interpreted as retribution for the guilt of those who perished, as the Pharisees were inclined to believe? Jesus says a categorical "No". The second truth concerns the same episodes and then is made clearer by the parable of the fig tree. Are those struck by misfortune innocent then? No, says Jesus, they were just as sinful as you who are asking the question, and you are just as open to punishment, just as much in danger of punishment, as those who have already been overtaken by it. The only profitable lesson you can take from these reports, from these newspaper columns headed "crimes and accidents", is this: be converted, change your life, turn around 180 degrees. Not some time in the future, either, when it suits you, when the recession gets worse and food gets scarcer, but now, because this is God's time and, as John the Baptist says, the axe is already laid at the root of your tree. It is high time for the fig tree to bear the fruit for which people have been waiting impatiently; even the vinedresser, requesting a postponement of drastic measures, has to agree that next year may be too late, indeed, surely will be too late, if the tree remains without fruit any longer, a parasite using up the soil.

There can be no question of saying that God's love is not to be seen in this Gospel. In fact, it appears in many forms, but as a love that is so stretched by man, as it were, that it seems to have reached the end of its patience and is obliged to assume the form of a warning.

First of all, Jesus says that God does not simply treat sinners according to their deeds, and that the suffering that overtakes them is in no way an indication of the magnitude of their guilt. Others may have more against them and yet be spared.

Second, he offers his questioners an opportunity. The very misfortune of their fellowmen should be a warning to them: they should take it as a sign from God that they should change the course of their lives. Notice how urgently Jesus speaks of "all the others who dwelt in Jerusalem", those who, if they do not turn about, will all perish in the same manner: he can foresee the imminent, terrible ruin of the stiff-necked city.

Third, according to Jesus, it is in the nature of the fig tree that it should bring forth fruit. God has given it an inbuilt capacity for good, for being useful. In the same way man only needs to follow a natural instinct, and he will respond to God's requirement of fruitfulness.

Fourth, there is the goodwill of the vinedresser who asks for a final postponement and who is prepared to do his utmost, by digging and manuring, to elicit fruit from the recalcitrant tree.

And fifth, there is the Lord who yields and grants this last postponement.

Love is quite definitely present, therefore; it shines out from all the cracks, but, in the face of men's tepidity and lack of love and their habit of accusing others of sin and excusing themselves, it has to assume the features of a ruthless and resolute power. "Love is strong as death; jealousy is cruel as the grave." Eventually there comes a point at which God's longanimity is all used up, when man will not take advantage of the time remaining to him. Then God's love has to resort to other methods. But please understand that I am talking of God's *love*. I am not saying that God's love is inwardly limited, by his justice, for instance. This is how many people think of it. But none of God's qualities is limited, least of all his love. Nor is his justice, either, or his mercy. All these qualities totally interpenetrate. We cannot say that God is unjust when, in the parable of the laborers hired to work in the vineyard, he pays the latest-hired man the same as those who have worked from morning. The fact that justice and love coincide in God was one of the most felicitous discoveries of little Thérèse. It is true, however, that after a certain point has been reached God's love must use severe measures in order to achieve its goals. The judgment that all sinners must undergo, and from which they will not emerge without being purified, after a shorter or longer time, this judgment must be unyielding. It must be completely irrevocable, precisely because what is at stake is access to ultimate pardon.

It is worthwhile dwelling for a moment on this idea of

judgment. Catholics believe in the existence of purgatory, a period of purification. Paul explicitly speaks of it in the First Letter to the Corinthians:

> Each man's work will become manifest; for the Day will disclose it, because it will be revealed with fire, and the fire will test what sort of work each one has done. If the work that any man has built on the foundation survives, he will receive a reward. If any man's work is burned up, he will suffer loss, though he himself will be saved, but only as through fire (1 Cor 3:13–15).

There we have it exactly, this ruthlessness on the part of love. But now, instead of being in the form of a warning in the dimension of time, it actually begins to take measures on the threshold of eternity. Purgatory is nothing other than a dimension of judgment; it is the undergoing of judgment, in which we are measured against the unyielding norm and conformed to it, as we must if we are to be allowed into the kingdom of eternal love. For that is our destination. So the fire of the divine love must burn up everything in us that does not correspond to it. And, depending on how we have lived here on earth, this can be more or less painful; indeed, it may involve appalling pain. Then it may come about that all our earthly superstructure, all we thought we had to identify ourselves with here on earth, will go up in flames, and the burning ruins will fall on us like the tower of Siloam. "He will suffer loss", says Paul, he will grieve over the futility and perversity of his life, and in shame and disgrace he will have to sit down among the dunces to learn the ABCs of real love. Up to now all he knew (and that by heart) was the ABCs of egoism. What can divine mercy do with such a person? He would not even understand it; he would not even know how to accept it. The sinner needs a kind of brainwashing to make him grasp the ideas that lie behind God's love. In the end, however, the ideas God has are the only true ones, and ultimately we simply have to submit to them. In judgment and the fire that goes with it we shall have to walk slowly toward the final, all-embracing idea, the final notion of God's inventiveness, namely, the crucified Son of God. He is the truth, and I must allow myself to accept this truth. The truth of sin: that is your contribution. The truth of grace: that is what God has done for you. Conversion is always a painful and lonely process. No one can do it for me, and I must learn to love things I previously disliked and renounce the very things I previously held dear.

But now let us leave purgatory and return to the world. As Christians we cannot interpret suffering in the world in any other way than as divine love veiling its face when confronted with the world's terrible sinfulness. It may seem to us that those who are less sinful have more to suffer. In that case, no doubt, their suffering is on behalf of the others. The Galileans mentioned in the Gospel were actually having their sacrificial animals slaughtered in the Temple when they themselves were butchered along with them. Compared with others, they were God-fearing sinners. The least guilty can be imprisoned in concentration camps or banished to the Gulag Archipelago. This arises from the Cross of Christ: the better can suffer on behalf of the worse. Or rather, let us say, "are privileged to suffer" on their behalf. And this suffering can be genuinely harsh and pitiless. This is something for us to remember if, in our suffering, we reach the end of our patience; it will support us and prevent us from becoming bitter.

Above all, however, we ought to hear the urgent note of warning in Jesus' words: "Unless you repent you will all likewise perish." This "unless" implies the possibility of averting disaster. Jerusalem could have repented. All of us could repent, and then our future would look different. The axe is laid to the roots of the trees, but many respond to the Baptist's words, are converted and baptized. The fig tree could bear fruit next year—its last chance—and so escape destruction.

We can apply all this to our own country. If God had found ten righteous men in Sodom, the town would have been spared as Abraham requested. Who knows how many righteous people, interceding for their fellows, are left among us? One thing is certain: there would be more if *we* were to be converted; perhaps there would be enough then to save our country. One suspects, however, that today there are probably fewer than in former times, when people prayed more, did more penance and believed with greater hope. In those days less paper and print were produced (by synods, episcopal offices and all manner of committees) to go straight into our wastepaper baskets, but there were a more genuine Christian atmosphere and outlook in our parishes. In those days there was not the destructive dispute between the mindless left and the ossified and embittered right. Then, in the last war, we were aware of the protecting hand of our interceding Abraham, St. Claus, our country's patron saint, blessing and preserving our native land. "By grace you have been saved through faith" (Eph 2:8). We should remember this, nor should we assume we will be saved by grace the next time round. "I tell you, No", says the Lord, in his "I tell you" showing his full power as Judge, "but unless you repent you will all likewise perish." Just as millions have perished, to the north, to the south, to the west and east of us. We have a good life; our land is full of gold that people send here for safekeeping, and we look after it for them and for ourselves. But it is doubtful whether this gold is the manure of which the Gospel speaks, helping us to bear fruit. The same could be said of all the prosperity that has formed our life-style and has become the almost unconscious goal of our work and efforts.

For the present we are still free; we have what, for the modern world, is unheard-of freedom, and we must use it responsibly for ourselves and for others. But among us there are those, and their numbers are increasing, who lust for the fleshpots of Egypt, of the slave house, and who would dearly like to wallow along with the multitude, as our own Carl Spitteler puts it. They are not prepared to learn any lesson from those trees of Europe that have already been felled and have lost their freedom to bear fruit. *They* are no longer parasites on the soil: they themselves are being bled dry. For *them* the system that bleeds them dry, the system of the Egyptian slave drivers, no longer holds any attraction or fascination. The pears rot from within; you can only see it when you cut them open. Who can do anything to stop the rot among the intelligentsia of our country? Once it has spread far enough, it will hardly be worth stretching out a hand to protect it.

But we have no intention of being fatalists like those still under the spell. We must affirm that the personal attitude, personal conversion, can be the decisive factor in everything. "Let it alone, sir, this year . . . if it bears fruit next year, well and good; but if not", then—in God's name and for his greater glory, so that he can make room for other and better things—"you can cut it down."

What Is Required in Witnesses

The account of the transfiguration of Christ on the high mountain is given a human context by the very first word, "*Assumpsit*": Jesus took the disciples up with him. The three he chose, Peter, James and John, did not ask to accompany him to the Mount of Transfiguration, nor do they personally have any special qualities or characteristics enabling them to see him transfigured. Nor does Jesus take them *seorsum*, aside, with him into the mountain retreat on the basis of some inclination of theirs for solitude and contemplation. Rather, it is solely and exclusively his will, his free choice; and this, in turn, is not some unfathomable divine arbitrariness but something that corresponds precisely to the needs of the Christian economy of redemption. Jesus, who has now set out on the path to his Passion, *must* first be transfigured; it must be revealed who it is who is thus going into darkness on behalf of all men; it must be made plain from what heights he comes to descend into such depths. Furthermore, he *must* be seen by the Church, he must have witnesses and they are the same three witnesses he will take with him later on to experience his hour of darkness on the Mount of Olives. By the light of the transfiguration, therefore, they will be able to realize the whole import of the mortal anguish of the Son of Man, the Lamb of God; and if they had not fallen asleep on the Mount of Olives, they would also have been able to grasp why the conversation between Jesus and Moses and Elijah on the high mountain circled around this hour of darkness.

So he must have witnesses, even if these witnesses on the Mount of Transfiguration will get the wrong end of the stick, like Peter, who wants to build booths for the transfigured Lord; even if they will be thrown to the ground by the radiance of his glory and, as Luke says, are overpowered and heavy with sleep; even if they will be seized by extreme fear at the sight of the enveloping cloud (for ultimately it is the same somnolence, the same fear, that subsequently will come upon them on the Mount of Olives). Because of all this, they will also give witness to the fact that both aspects, the sublimity of transfiguration and the depths of the night on the Mount of Olives, exceed the capacity of human testimony, just as ultraviolet and infrared radiation do not register on human organs of perception.

All the same they are witnesses, albeit necessarily unequal to their task, and when, later, the time of the Church and her proclamation comes, Peter will be able to take his stand on the fact (as indeed he must). He will describe himself as "a witness of the sufferings of Christ as well as a partaker in the glory" (1 Pet 5:1) and even more explicitly as "eyewitnesses of his majesty. For when he received honor and glory from God the Father and the voice was borne to him by the Majestic Glory, 'This is my beloved Son, with whom I am well pleased', we heard this voice borne from heaven, for we were with him on the holy mountain" (2 Pet 1:16–18).

Here, in giving his witness, there is no mention of the state

Peter was in on the mountain or of the shameful way he, the witness of Christ's sufferings, denied and betrayed his Lord; the human conditions have become totally unimportant, as, basically, they always were. The only thing now that is really important, the only thing that counts, is the fact of having been a witness: these three were there; they have "heard and seen and touched the Word of life". That is what God needs. And that is what man needs.

In the end that is what Jesus succeeded in doing through these three disciples, because, with all their weakness and vacillation, he could count on them. They had irrevocably committed their lives to him; they had followed his call and gone with him without any reservations, leaving behind all they had. They made no conditions, and even when they were asked to accept things that were hard and almost unbearable they did not leave him: "To whom shall we go? You have the words of eternal life."

This is the timber from which Jesus carves his witnesses. Now we can draw the consequences, and they are pretty important.

It can be said that this decides everything; it decides between true and false Christianity. These are the criteria for discernment.

The witness of Christ is not someone who has undergone something and gives an account of his internal and external experiences. Many people experience many different things, and at the level of experience many have far more astonishing and fantastic things to relate than the witnesses of Jesus. Experience in itself does not make a witness.

The witness of Christ is not someone who has acted correctly, bravely or outstandingly in the situation to which he is testifying; it is not someone who has passed the examination with the best marks. There are many who have passed God's tests with flying colors (or think they have), but this cannot be said of Peter, James and John—for even John fell asleep on the Mount of Olives and was overcome by drowsiness on the Mount of Transfiguration.

The witness of Jesus is not the spiritually cultivated, polished and cosseted personality, beautified, refined, smoothed and painted up with all the techniques of spiritual cosmetics, but the poor devil who is nothing and has nothing because once and for all he has handed over and entrusted all that he has—and above all his own self—to God in the hope that, if he seeks for God, all these things will be added to him.

Here indeed there are decisions to be made. Anyone who is concerned about the Christian personality and its self-realization will always be anxious, willy-nilly, about his own growth, whereas the witness of Christ par excellence speaks thus: "He must increase and I must decrease." Sooner or later, openly or covertly, and whether he is aware of it or not, anyone who is concerned about Christian personality will sooner or later find the idol of psychology on his altar where the word, God's theology, ought to be. Ethical man, moral man, the man with a cultivated religiosity, is still but a man, a holy ego, a *sacro egoismo*.

Jesus needs witnesses for the Church. He needs people who have become totally unconcerned about themselves because they have seen and heard, on Tabor and on the Mount of Olives, "what no eye has seen, nor ear heard, nor the heart of man conceived, what God has prepared for those who love him": namely, what takes place in the heart of God and what he has granted his chosen ones to see, to hear and to sense. Only people who have totally forgotten and lost themselves, who have become detached from themselves, to be found by God, have any effect on others as witnesses of Christ. Paul was such a person, and psychology cannot get anywhere near Paul, for it is no longer he who lives, but Christ who lives in him. Is Christ, are the Holy Spirit and the grace of God, are faith, hope and love psychological data? But it is precisely the fact that the Christian datum ultimately bursts the categories of depth psychology and psychiatry (however diligently they are applied) that convinces people of its power and truth. This man is different: Why? What makes him tick? He is only waiting to tell us, if we are prepared to listen: "Christ has died for all, that those who live might live no longer for themselves but for him who for their sake died and was raised" (2 Cor 5:15). "I count all things as refuse, in order that I may gain Christ and be found in him . . . that I may know him and the power of his Resurrection and may share his sufferings" (Phil 3:8–10). If the lives of Christians do not witness to the truth of Christianity, that is, that Christ is God and man, who has died for our sins and risen again, what use are sermons and catechisms and all the libraries of theology? Christianity is intended to be true not *in itself* but *in us*: we ourselves, in our lives, in our believing, hoping and loving, in our suffering and victory, are meant to be the Lord's witnesses.

Jesus needs witnesses for the Church. He also needs them for himself. Not everything in Christianity can be reduced to social and caritative terms. There remains that surplus, that excess that, to the annoyance of our age of rationalization and rationing, just will not go away. In fact, this connection between *ratio* and ration is highly comical. Where *ratio*, calculating reason, governs everything, everyone has to be satisfied with the ration thus rationally apportioned to him; if technology has the last word today, communism will have it tomorrow. Christianity, however, is the religion of freedom for God, the freedom that God brings and that is God. Love cannot be reduced to any calculation, not even the calculations of the Church herself and of caritative organizations. Calculation misses the most important thing: the heart's free impetus toward God, above all prayer, adoration, thanksgiving, the heart that gives itself entirely to God. That is what the Lord calls the *one thing necessary* and what can never be entrapped in the mesh of statistics. I am not saying that all statistics are of the devil, although that was the view of the Old Testament: God's anger was directed at David because he conducted a census of the people, so that he could bask in his royal power and in the thought of how far the kingdom of God on earth had progressed. Let us be honest: we can have a statistical assessment of the number of confessions and communions, but we would still need to know *what kind of* confessions and communions these were, that is, to what extent they were a genuine expression of the love of God. The "one thing necessary" is for people to bear witness to the glory of God's love for the world, witnessing through adoration and adoring through witness. From ancient times Tabor was the name and the place of contemplation, of beholding God in his glory, for his own sake. At the Lord's transfiguration three men are chosen for this beholding: people are chosen for the contemplative life. No one enters a monastery to become "perfect". No one enters for his own sake but for God's sake. No one enters because he wants to but because he knows he must, and so for that reason he *does* want to. Contemplative monasteries are like the spires of the earthly Church, like a pennant high up blowing freely in God's wind, proclaiming the love of God over all the land. If Christians today wonder what is the use of contemplative monasteries, others tomorrow will ask what purpose is served by all these churches and cathedrals that cost the state so much to maintain. And the day after tomorrow, perhaps, others will ask what good are poets, artists and all scholars who are not chemists and physicists. They are superfluous and uneconomical: we do not need them.

Christ is transfigured on the Mount, and so he needs witnesses. Witnesses who put their whole lives into their vocation of bearing witness, and whose raison d'être is simply to testify to the light on the mountain, the city set on a hill, the mountain's God-given freedom. Being a witness of this kind is more a burden than a dignity. It calls for a life familiar with the air of the mountains, the air of the heights, and prepared to extend it to others. There is no substitute for this; there is no "artificial sunlight" or "ozone spray" to replace holiness. It is either genuine or not there at all. Ultimately everything depends on a straightforward choice: one way the lines lead to the ego, the Christian personality; the other way they lead to God and the witness of faith, to the simple words "Behold, I am the handmaid of the Lord; let it be to me according to your word", and "Father, not as I will, but as thou wilt." Christianity is no more difficult than that.

Still the First Commandment

"I am the Lord your God, who brought you out of the land of Egypt, out of the house of bondage. You shall have no other gods before me" (Ex 20:2–3).

The great literary texts of history cannot be seen in isolation from the contexts in which they first appeared. And if this particular text has a validity that persists over time, so has the historical event out of which it arose. The context of the giving of the law on Sinai is that of a Covenant between God and his people, established in virtue of a saving act that made the people into a people: the deliverance from Egypt. In all probability the form of the Decalogue we have today comes from a thanksgiving celebration of the Twelve Tribes in the Covenant shrine of Sichem, where the event of the deliverance was recalled and solemnly reenacted. "*We* are those whom the living God has redeemed! We are privileged to have him as our God. We have no need to run after false idols. Our relationship with God is that of exclusive, bridal-conjugal love; to go after other gods would be adultery, fornication against God, as the prophets say."

What we have here is an awareness of being endowed with grace, of being chosen, in an exclusive relationship with the living God, whom we, the redeemed, are privileged to love. This and nothing else provides the basis for an understanding of the Ten Commandments, and particularly of the first. Where this awareness is lacking, the Decalogue sinks to the level of a code of general moral requirements, in which case it cannot be understood as what, historically, it was and what it still is; its marrow would have been sucked from its bones. And where the living, religious relationship with God has disappeared, the general moral ethos will not survive much longer; it will become mere convention, a tradition of which no one grasps the full implications.

The Covenant with the people of Israel has expanded in Christ into a Covenant between the Father of grace and all mankind. Whether we are aware of it or not, whether we want to or not, all of us belong to this New and eternal Covenant, which was sealed by the atonement achieved through the Cross on behalf of the whole world, through the redemption of the world in the Resurrection and the hope of eternal life. "Look, this is what I have done for you", says the eternal Father to each one of us: "I have handed over my only Son to suffering and death; I, God, have staked the ultimate in terms of love in order to prove my love to you. I have struggled with my very heart's blood to possess you, my child; how, therefore, from henceforth, could I renounce you and your love, how could I allow you to run after false gods, since you belong to my love, that is, you belong, quite simply and absolutely, to love?"

God does not say, "*If* you keep the Commandments and know no alien gods, I will make a Covenant with you", but, "I *have made* a Covenant with you; you are already endowed with grace; you have already been adopted into a relationship of intimacy with me; since you are so close to me, therefore, act as a child of my household!" We fail to understand the very first thing about Israel if we view the Commandments as something purely juridical, to be followed in the New Covenant by the Commandment of love. No: everything rests on the prior redemptive act of the loving God, who, because of his Covenant of faithfulness and love, is bound to banish the alien gods. That is the basis; that is the fulfillment brought by Christianity; that is the only way the Decalogue can mean anything to man—including modern man. Since God has bestowed maximal grace, he can expect those who are his to live a life of love and gratitude that is expressed in a minimal demand! These minimal requirements of the Ten Words (to which, if we are to understand their spirit aright, we need to add many other Old Testament instructions on how men should treat their fellows), these minimal requirements are intended to fashion a man who is worthy of God and hence worthy of man; in this sense they really are Commandments of a genuine *humanity*, a most original proclamation of public and private human rights and—in consequence—human obligations. The fact that those who scornfully transgress these Commandments incur punishment and, in religious terms, a curse, an anathema (even capital punishment for idolatry), will be understood by anyone who reflects even for a moment on the immense good represented by righteousness and holiness, by the untouchable, conjugal love that God himself jealously guards. There can be no fooling about with God.

A plausible objection can be leveled at this first Sinai Commandment, to the effect that it addresses a very particular historico-religious situation, and one that has been long superseded. After all, it presupposes a widespread belief in the existence of other gods, that is, polytheism. True, even for a good half-millennium after Moses, Israel un-self-consciously took it for granted that other nations had other gods; the First Commandment does not say that there *are* no other gods, but "you shall not worship any other gods besides me". Only in the time of the prophets does the awareness assert itself that these other gods are either demons or nothing at all.

Precisely because the two questions are not the same, however, the Commandment loses none of its relevance for us. Israel—and this applies also to the New Israel, Christianity—must not practice worship of any kind, high or low, besides that of its true, living, grace-bestowing and judging God. Its whole heart, its entire love, must be devoted to the One. "You cannot serve two masters", Jesus will say: you cannot split your heart into two parts without bringing ruin upon yourself;

you cannot give it to your God and at the same time—in case he does not exist or has not power enough to save you—enter into a secret pact with some other, some worldly god. You cannot enter the kingdom of God both by the front door and by the back.

There are always plenty of "gods" with which we make pacts. They are always a reality whenever we do not love the Lord our God with all our hearts and serve him alone. What else is it when we venerate and worship all kinds of supposedly neutral "sacred" things besides him who alone is holy: for instance, the personality of a Socrates or a Goethe or a Mao, or of some dictatorial genius? What else are we doing when, beside him who has said, "I am who I am", we worship the "being of all being" ("*Sein des Seienden*") or "lightness of heart" ("*die Heitere*") or Hölderlin's gods, which have been rehabilitated with such enthusiasm? Or when, perhaps, as well as the God of love, we worship the god of Picasso, the minotaur in whatever form (bearing more than a distant resemblance to the gods that became a temptation for Israel); or when, like Saul, we pay a nocturnal visit to the Necromancer of Endor and engage in a little spiritism? Or perhaps we liven up our Christianity with a dash of anthroposophy or yoga or metempsychosis? Or perhaps we quite simply pay homage to the ever-youthful god Mammon in one of his countless incarnations and avatars; or, even more simply, we place the beloved god Ego—also called "the self"—in our domestic shrine and offer incense to it by day and by night. This is the sacral cult of the "I" writ large, and worship of it is far more dangerous than any of the Old Testament fetishes. Similarly the cult of the "we", where "we" means we men, alone in empty space where God is long dead. Or the cult of nihilism, of the *nothing*, to which we offer melancholy and ardent worship, sacrificing to it our living, real, beating hearts. But

I am the Lord your God, the God of the living and not of the dead, the God of grace and not of judgment. . . . A new heart I will give you, and a new spirit I will put within you; and I will take out of your flesh the heart of stone and give you a heart of flesh. And I will put my Spirit within you, and cause you to walk in my statutes . . . and you will loathe yourselves for your iniquities and your abominable deeds. . . . I will cause the cities to be inhabited, and the waste places shall be rebuilt. . . . Then they will know that I am the Lord (see Ex 3:6; Ezek 36).

Palm Sunday

Hosanna—For Which Liberation Theology?

Jesus' entry into Jerusalem was a many-sided, kaleidoscopic event; its ambivalence is most painfully obvious in view of what happened a few days later, where Jesus was rejected by the people and by the Jewish and Roman authorities and condemned to the Cross.

There are many layers here. First, there is the Old Testament prophecy that the Messiah would not establish the reign of God by force of arms but would come "humble and riding on an ass . . . [to] cut off the chariot from Ephraim and the war horse from Jerusalem; and the battle bow shall be cut off, and he shall command peace to the nations" (Zech 9). Second, there is the expectation of Jews at the time—multitudes of them, assembled for the festival—that the new prophet from Nazareth would set up this messianic kingdom, as the crowds cry out in Mark: "Blessed is the kingdom of our father David that is coming!" (Mk 11:10). What they are expecting is a final and definitive reign of peace, as the crowd's words make plain: "We have heard from the law that the Christ remains forever. How can you say that the Son of Man must be lifted up? Who is this Son of Man?" (Jn 12:34). We can see here that the people, understandably, had no notion of what was at stake. As John tells us, they had heard of the raising of Lazarus (Jn 12:17): this played on their imagination, causing them to conclude that the expected kingdom was about to begin.

If, third, we ask what the disciples were expecting (and

several times they had heard Jesus speaking about his forthcoming suffering), we must say that their expectations were little different from those of the mass of the people. Even after the Resurrection they ask, "Lord, will you at this time restore the kingdom to Israel?" (Acts 1:6).

Fourth, what was going on in the mind of Jesus amid all the uproar surrounding this festival? No doubt he prayed to the Father that this perpetual, ineradicable misunderstanding would be set aside once and for all as a result of the terrible suffering that was in store for him; no doubt he prayed that he, whose kingdom is not of this world (Jn 18:36), would penetrate beyond the hour of darkness and of hell and, through his Father's power and the operation of his Holy Spirit, would enter into his real kingdom, a kingdom that would be eternal, never to pass away.

Then, on top of the layers of ancient prophecy, popular expectation, the expectations of the disciples and Jesus' own prospects, there is the fifth layer: that of the mind and heart of today's congregation as it celebrates this event, in other words, the Church of Jesus, which, in her liturgy, shouts her hosannas as she goes to meet the King at his triumphal entry. What are *her* expectations? (*If* she still actually expects anything crucial to happen, anything that will decisively change the course of history, as the prophets, the Jewish people and the disciples of Jesus expected. *If*, that is, this feast means something more to Christians than a recurring annual custom that gets swallowed up and lost in the plethora of other celebrations!)

Nowadays we have more reason than ever to inquire into what the Church expects, what Christians expect. The Old Testament looked toward a messianic kingdom on earth, a realm of peace in which "they shall beat their swords into ploughshares, and their spears into pruning hooks" (Is 2:4). And did not the last Council direct the Church to exert herself on behalf of the world's future and help to bring about a "kingdom of justice, love and peace" of which the Preface of Christ the King speaks? But how can we attain earthly justice for the oppressed against the oppressors except by first of all creating order—which can only be done by using force? It cannot be done without discerning the spirits and acting on the basis of such discernment, which will involve abandoning the general, comfortable lukewarmness in which our rich nations live. "Liberation theology" is the widely accepted watchword at present. We can even quote the Lord's words in support of it: "Do not think that I have come to bring peace on earth; I have not come to bring peace, but a sword. For I have come to set a man against his father" (Mt 10:34f.), that is, the younger generation against the older. And there is that other mysterious saying prior to the Passion: "Let him who has no sword sell his mantle and buy one" (Lk 22:36). Obviously, Jesus is not interested in setting up a new kingdom of political power as envisaged by the Israel of old—that is, one that would dominate the other nations of the earth—but a kingdom in which the poor and humiliated of this earth, whom Jesus called "blessed", would finally share in those goods to which they are entitled. Thus, by creating justice among nations and classes, or rather, through abolishing the barriers between classes, something analogous to a kingdom of love and peace will become possible. Clearly, this kind of liberation theology, fighting, sword in hand, for eschatological peace, is very closely related to those secularized forms of the Jewish hope of redemption that have such a powerful influence worldwide today in the form of Marxism and all its derivatives. Is this what Jesus had in mind?

In the first place, it has been proved conclusively that Jesus himself was not a political zealot, and that the sword he wanted to bring to the earth was the spiritual sword of an interior decision—for or against him. "He who is not with me is against me, and he who does not gather with me scatters" (Lk 11:23). When the first Pope draws his sword to strike an enemy of Jesus, the rebuke he receives applies not only to him but to all who will come after him: "Put your sword back into its place, for all who take the sword will perish by the sword" (Mt 26:52). So, both in Latin America and in the East, the correct approach is taken by those who press for a spiritual decision, who set up a Christian banner by engaging in spiritual and nonviolent resistance, which can lead to imprisonment and torture. Such action will be more effective, in the long term, than high-profile revolutionary campaigns, because it contributes to the inner transformation of conscience and undermines the tyrants and those who wield authority—whether they call themselves atheists or Catholics—and points out the only way in which anything like a kingdom of love and peace can come into being here on earth.

But oh, how infinitely fragile and threatened such a kingdom will always be as long as there is in man the evil urge for power, the urge to dominate the weaker! In this context, then, let us turn to the mind and ultimate aim of Jesus as he enters Jerusalem. He knows what is in store for him: the crowd's "crucify him!" and his appalling death amid Israel's mocking ridicule: "He saved others; he cannot save himself. He is the King of Israel; let him come down now from the Cross, and we will believe in him" (Mt 27:42). And he also knows that, by enduring this suffering in atonement for the world's guilt, he will be creating access for human hearts to God's mind and heart, to his kingdom. Through the Cross, and only through the Cross, the gates of the kingdom will be opened. Only through the Cross will the sharp swords in the hearts of men be beaten into ploughshares, and the wickedly designed spears of their plans and ambitions be made into pruning hooks in the service of a fruitful harvest.

What, therefore, will the program of Christian activity in the world look like? In discipleship of the Lord, which must be the foundation and essence of the Christian life, it is only through death that we can look toward the kingdom of God. What does this mean? In my view it means three things. I will mention each one briefly, to provide material for further reflection.

First of all there is natural death. None of us can avoid it; it stands, menacing, behind every day of our lives; our modern anticulture suppresses it, and, as a result of this suppression, our entire perspective on the future is distorted. No human future will be able to get rid of death; mankind is a race, that is, an infinite succession of generation, birth and death. We should draw up our plans as those who are ready to work while it is day, in the knowledge that tomorrow comes death: thus we should conduct ourselves with dignity and freedom, and not with cowardly fear, in view of the end that awaits us; we should work to improve conditions, using the time allotted to us soberly and responsibly. Not so much for the sake of some uncertain tomorrow, but for the today in which we live and can exert an influence on our surroundings. Beware of futurology!

Second, there is something much more important to be considered: the death of Jesus Christ was and is the event in which the fate of human existence, to which death belongs, has been overcome, opening up salvation and eternal life to us. Since we have been sealed by the sign of this death—for baptism, according to Paul, signifies that we have died, been buried and risen to new life together with Christ—we are in a position to show the world a road leading out of the futility of all earthly things, a road leading to a kingdom that treasures and cherishes the abiding harvest of all man's efforts throughout world history. This is not the cowardice of transposing the ultimate result of human toil into a beyond that cannot be manipulated and that could eventually prove to be a huge illusion; on the contrary, it is the courage shown by Jesus Christ when he rode into Jerusalem to meet his crucifixion, to bear fruit only after having undergone the Cross; *in* history, but going out *beyond* history and entering into eternal life. "Unless a grain of wheat falls into the earth and dies, it remains just a grain of wheat; but if it dies, it bears much fruit" (Jn 12:24). This is precisely the Christian paradox: the man who fashions his inner attitude and orients himself toward the eternal kingdom according to the instructions of Jesus, that is, who is gentle, merciful, peacemaking, pure of heart, thirsting for God's righteousness, inwardly poor and humble—such a man can have a deeper and more lasting effect on world history than the magnates to whom nothing is more important than the exercise of power. It is precisely what *cannot* be manufactured on earth by political, economic and social programs, in other words, what comes from the kingdom of God and its righteousness—for which, according to the words of Jesus, we must strive before all else (Mt 6:33)—that indicates to us everything that has genuine, valid substance and creative power on earth.

The third point simply arises from this. As Christians we not only have to look, together with Jesus, toward the everlasting kingdom beyond death and to proclaim it, we also have to go further and, together with Jesus, realize the necessity of the cross for us and "in our flesh complete what is lacking in Christ's afflictions for the sake of his body, the Church" (Col 1:24). All who suffer in this world, the sick and incurable and dying, those in prison and tortured, the oppressed and those who are hopelessly poor, must know that, in their situation, they are not condemned to total powerlessness: if they unite their hopelessness with that of the crucified Son of God, they will do more to build the real kingdom of God than many an architect of earthly happiness. Of course people, and Christians in particular, should do all they can to minimize mankind's present and future misery. But, while they are doing this, they should not forget the Beatitudes uttered by Jesus as he looks through the suffering and the Cross to the fruit that lies beyond:

> Blessed are you poor, for yours is the kingdom of God. Blessed are you that hunger now, for you shall be satisfied. Blessed are you that weep now, for you shall laugh. . . . But woe to you that are rich, for you have received your consolation. Woe to you that are full now, for you shall hunger. Woe to you that laugh now, for you shall mourn and weep (Lk 6:20f., 26f.).

This is how the Lord speaks, with almost unbearable harshness, in Luke's Gospel. What is the status of our rich, sated, affluent and addicted society in the face of words such as these?

If, today, therefore, we join in with the jubilant crowd and shout our hosanna to the Messiah, let us seriously remember that, as Christians, we know only one King and Messiah, who was rejected and crucified by everyone—including us—and who alone knows and opens up the path to the kingdom of God. Now that this path has been blazed for us, we can and should follow in his footsteps.

"Simon Peter said to him, 'Lord, where are you going?' Jesus answered, 'Where I am going you cannot follow me now; but you shall follow afterward' " (Jn 13:36).

Holy Week

Bought at a Great Price

"You are not your own; you were bought with a price. So glorify God in your body" (1 Cor 6:19f.). This is unpalatable news! Is man, then, not free and autonomous? Does he not belong to himself? Can he be compared to something for sale on the market, that does not care whether it is expensive or cheap or by whom it is bought? Is he in someone else's possession, a slave, bound to serve his buyer and master with all that he has? Who would not protest against a religion of this kind, which seems to rob man of his self-determination and totally alienates him from himself? What chances does Christianity have in an enlightened humanity that has come of age? Let us examine them together.

"You are not your own"—on the contrary, is this not the most welcome news we could ever receive? Is it not a fact that man's true happiness lies in surrendering himself to a cause that is worth his efforts, to a beloved to whom he can give himself as a present? At the highest level, when love has reached its zenith, he gives himself once and for all, for better, for worse, in a lifelong marriage; he can also give himself, maybe, in a friendship that is not tentative but sees itself as definitive and final. Is it not the case that man actually acquires a sense of his life's value when he becomes valuable, not to himself but to something or someone else? And what if this Someone is the eternal God, who is not just anyone but the One whose judgment and evaluation give all things their true significance? It is ridiculous for us, tiny, evanescent beings that we are, inhabiting this planet in millions, to regard ourselves as important; our attributing of eternal value to each other is both tragic and comic, and it is hardly credible that God takes us seriously, not simply mankind as a whole but each individual, you and me—or rather, it is not something we can know; it is something we have, quite literally, to believe. We can only believe that he has chosen us to be his children, adopting us in all seriousness and giving us a right to all that is his. Nor is "adopted" the right term, either; it sounds like a legal formality by means of which he has granted this race of beggars a right to his royal inheritance, whereas in reality, though we cannot understand how, he takes us worthless men up into his inner divine nature and causes us to be reborn from his eternal womb. As John says, we receive power to become children of God, born no longer of the urging of the blood, the will of the flesh, the desire of the man, but of God. "How is this possible?" asks Nicodemus. "Jesus answered, 'Are you a teacher of Israel, and yet you do not understand this? . . . Do not marvel that I said to you, "You must be born anew." . . . That which is born of the flesh is flesh, and that which is born of the Spirit (of God) is spirit' " (Jn 3:6, 10).—"You are not your own."

Let us join the teacher of Scripture and ask how this is possible. The answer is "You have been bought at a high price". Christianity, which, alone among all the religions, attributes such dignity to man, can only back up this affirmation by pointing to a further one, that is, what it cost God to make this divine sonship available to man. Indeed, God made men so free that he could not stop them laughing in his face and renouncing all obedience to him. All his attempts to reason with them were to no avail: they killed the messengers he sent to them one after another, as Jesus describes in the Parable of the Vineyard. We can even say that the more God exerted himself to reconcile them, the more stiff-necked they became and the more despicable and hateful his divine love seemed to them, since they had turned away from him. Can God do anything against the finite freedom he himself has created if it stubbornly gives him a "No"? And the whole mystery of this week lies in the fact that we can say, "Yes", he can. Christianity stands or falls with this mystery, which we can only profess: we cannot explain it. It is mystery coming from the heart of God, and we cannot explain God. "God so loved the world that he gave his only-begotten Son", says John, and Paul makes it clearer when he says, "He made him to be sin", he caused him to bear man's "No", he caused him to bear the world's alienation from God and abandonment by him. Whether we like it or not, whether we can imagine it or not, that is the fact. Those who champion autonomy are indignant and regard it as theft on God's part, a violation of our freedom. To them it is like anaesthetizing a man and cutting some organ from his body without his permission.

But is this comparison valid? Is sin, man's refusal to be reconciled with eternal, absolute Goodness, really an organ essential to life? Is it not much more like a spreading cancer? Can we say that God is robbing man of anything by restoring his health? Furthermore, if a man has become locked in a syndrome of refusal, if he refuses to keep faith with God, can he free himself from his own obstinacy? He may think he can, but in reality he becomes a slave of his "No" because there is only true freedom when we are in contact with the Good, in the atmosphere of love—that is, of God. This is something that has to be shown, from within, to the person who has turned away. What is taken away from sinful man through the surrender of the Son of God is nothing other than his alienation from the Good; what is given to him is nothing other than inner access to the Good, that is, true freedom. He is liberated both toward himself and toward God.

"Bought at a great price." The first Christians were well aware of this when they put these two little words, "*pro nobis*", at the heart of the Creed. It was "for us" that the Son came down from heaven, "for us" that he was crucified, died and was buried. And this means not only "for our benefit" but also "in our place", taking over what was our due. If this is watered down, the fundamental tenet of the New Testament disappears and it looks as if God is always reconciled, sin is always forgiven and overcome, irrespective of Christ's self-surrender; then the Cross becomes merely a particularly eloquent symbol of God's unchangeable kindness, only a symbol, indicating something but not effecting anything. There would no longer be a Lamb of God who takes away the sins of the world. No longer would God "reconcile the world to himself", as Paul explicitly says, "through his Son". Without noticing it, we have become like the men of the Enlightenment, aware of God's kindly disposition but refusing to countenance his anger over sin, of which Scripture speaks so insistently, because it does not fit in with our enlightened concept of God; in the end we make it all into an anemic, transparent philosophy. Then, as a result, what Grünewald endeavored to portray in his crucifixion seems to us to be a tasteless medieval exaggeration. And the high price becomes a cheap price; costly grace becomes cheap grace.

By sleight of hand the modern world has caused death to vanish from its everyday awareness: let us make sure that we Christians do not, by equal stealth, remove the tremendous drama of the Cross from our Christianity. Or, if we still speak of it in our church services and catechesis, let us beware lest we fail to realize what we are dealing with. Many people think that it is simply up to them to reconcile themselves with God, and that many do not need such reconciliation at all. Meditative techniques are all they need to get in touch with themselves and hence, so they think, with God. They have no conception of the flames necessary to burn up all the refuse that is within man; they have no idea that these flames burn white hot in the Cross of Jesus. There is a cry that penetrates all the cool pharisaism of our alleged religiosity: "My God, my God, why have you forsaken me?" In the darkest night of the soul, while every fiber of his body is in pain, and he experiences extreme thirst for God, for lost love, he atones for our comfortable indifference.

And what is our part? Are we to be simply observers; are we

simply to appropriate what has been done for us without our deserving it? This, again, is not what is expected of Christians. It is true that the essential and decisive thing has been given to us as a gift. But we have to do something with this gift. "So glorify God in your body", as the Apostle concludes his exhortation to the community. And this means more than a hasty "thank you". God has paid a high price for us, the highest price he could ever pay. Not only has he *canceled* our huge debt (as the master did for his servant in the parable), for it is not simply a matter of money that we cannot pay: he has *borne* our guilt or given *himself* for us as our "ransom". For the point is that we cannot free *ourselves* from our alienation from God. Now that we have received the gift of Christian freedom from him, we express our gratitude by really making it our own, which means putting it into practice, demonstrating its reality. This is freedom to embrace the Good, freedom to dedicate ourselves, freedom no longer to belong to ourselves but to God and our neighbor, to the kingdom of God that is to come to earth from heaven. To glorify God with our whole being means exercising the freedom of the children of God in being concerned for God's purposes in the world.

The flames that envelop him in white heat on the Cross are bound to touch us too as we undertake this mission. It is written of Jesus that "zeal for thy house will consume me", when he purged God's Temple with a whip, but ultimately this zeal consumed him on the Cross. If we are zealous for God's cause on earth, we should not be surprised if it does not stop at a little apostolic activity and that a particle of the Cross is allotted to us. It is well for us to recognize this and accept it with thanksgiving. "Remember the word that I said to you", says Jesus as he bids farewell to his disciples: "A servant is not greater than his master. If they persecuted me, they will persecute you" (Jn 15:20). There are other words, too, to the same effect; and this discipleship is seen in the scourging of the Apostles, Peter's death on a cross and the countless sufferings of Paul.

But whatever we have to suffer in our following of the Lord, we can never add it to his suffering, as if it took the two together to make up the full sum. Rather, we know that whatever suffering comes our way flows from the overflowing fullness of his Cross, in which we are privileged and ennobled to participate. "Where I am, there shall my servant be also; if anyone serves me, the Father will honor him" (Jn 12:26). The Son burned for our sake; by contrast we always burn on our own account, but through his grace it can happen that we also burn on behalf of others, in a way known only to God. Even in the Gospel there are some who stand under the Cross not in order to look and see him suffering but in order to *be with him*.

Good Friday

The Scapegoat and the Trinity

Nearly two thousand years ago a trial took place that resulted in the death of the condemned man. Why is it that, even today, it will not allow mankind to forget about it? Have there not been countless other show trials down the years, particularly in our own time, and should the crying injustice of these trials not stir us up and preoccupy us just as much as that ancient trial at the Passover in Jerusalem? To judge by the constant and even increasing flood of books and discussions about Jesus, however, all the horrors of the extermination camps and the Gulag Archipelago matter less to mankind than the sentencing of this one innocent man whom, according to the Bible, God himself championed and vindicated—as is evident from his Resurrection from the dead.

The question is: Was he the one, great and final scapegoat for mankind? Did mankind load him with all its guilt, and did he, the Lamb of God, carry this guilt away? This is the thesis of a modern ethnologist, René Girard, whose books have attracted much attention in America, France and recently in Germany. According to this view, all human civilization, right from the outset, is constructed on the principle of the scapegoat. That is, men have cunningly invented a way of overcoming their reciprocal aggression and arriving at an at least temporary peace: thus they concentrate this aggression on an almost randomly chosen scapegoat and appoint this scapegoat as the sacrificial victim, in order to pacify an allegedly angry god. According to Girard, however, this divine anger is nothing other than men's reciprocal rage. This mechanism always needs to be set in motion again after a period of relative peace if world history is to proceed in any half-tolerable way; in this context it reached its absolute peak in the general rejection of Jesus by the gentiles, the Jews and the Christians too: Jesus really did take over and carry away the sins of all that were loaded onto him, in such a way that anyone who believes this can live in peace with his brother from now on.

Girard's ideas are interesting; they bring the trial of Jesus to life in a new way. But we can still ask why this particular murder, after so many others, should be the conclusive event of world history, the advent of the end time? Men have cast their guilt onto many innocent scapegoats; why did this particular bearer of sins bring about a change in the world as a whole?

For the believer the answer is easy: the crucial thing is not that this is an instance of our wanting to rid ourselves of guilt. Naturally, no one wants to admit guilt. Pilate washes his hands and declares himself guiltless; the Jews hide behind their law, which requires them to condemn a blasphemer; they act in a pious and God-fearing way. Judas himself has remorse for his deed; he brings the blood money back and, when no one will take it from him, throws it at the high priests. No one is prepared to accept responsibility. But precisely by attempting to extricate themselves, they are convinced by God that they are guilty of the death of this innocent man. Ultimately it is not what men do that is the determining factor.

The crucial thing is that there is Someone who is both ready and able to take their guilt upon himself. None of the other scapegoats was able to do this. According to the New Testament understanding, the Son of God became man in order to take this guilt upon himself. He lived with a view to the "hour" that awaited him at the end of his earthly existence, with a view to the terrible baptism with which he would have to be baptized, as he says. This "hour" would see him chained and brought to trial not merely outwardly; it would not only tear his body to pieces with scourges and nail it to the wood but also penetrate into his very soul, his spirit, his most intimate relationship with God, his Father. It would fill everything with desolation and the mortal fear of having been forsaken—as it were, with a totally alien, hostile and deadly poisonous substance that would block his every access to the source from which he lived.

It is in the horror of this darkness, of this emptiness and alienation from God, that the words on the Mount of Olives are spoken: "My Father, if it be possible, let this cup pass from me." The cup of which he here speaks is well known in the Old Testament: it is the cup full of God's anger and wrath, which sinners must drink to the dregs; often it is threatened or forced upon unfaithful Jerusalem or enemy peoples like Babylon. The cry from the Cross is uttered out of the same horror of spiritual blackness, the cry asking why God has forsaken this tortured man. The man who cries out knows only that he is forsaken; in this darkness he no longer knows why. He is not permitted to know why, for the idea that the darkness he is undergoing might be on behalf of others would constitute a certain comfort; it would give him a ray of light. No such comfort can be granted him now, for the issue, in absolute seriousness, is that of purifying the relationship between God and the guilty world.

The man who endures this night is the Innocent One. No one else could effectively undergo it on behalf of others. What ordinary or extraordinary man would even have enough room in himself to accommodate the world's guilt? Only someone who is a partner of the eternal Father, distinct from him and yet divine, that is, the Son who, man that he is, is also God, can have such capacity within him.

Here we are faced with a bottomless mystery, for in fact there is an immense difference between the generating womb in God the Father and the generated fruit, the Son, although both are one God in the Holy Spirit. Nowadays many theologians say, quite rightly, that it is precisely at the Cross that this difference becomes clearly manifest: at this precise point the mystery of the divine Trinity is fully proclaimed. The distance is so great—for in God everything is infinite—that there is room in it for all the alienation and sin of the world; the Son can draw all this into his relationship with the Father without any danger of it harming or altering the mutual eternal love between Father and Son in the Holy Spirit. Sin is burnt up, as it were, in the fire of this love, for *God*, as Scripture says, *is a consuming fire* that will not tolerate anything impure but must burn it away.

Jesus, the Crucified, endures our inner darkness and estrangement from God, and he does so in our place. It is all the more painful for him, the less he has merited it. As we have already said, there is nothing familiar about it to him: it is utterly alien and full of horror. Indeed, he suffers more deeply than an ordinary man is capable of suffering, even were he condemned and rejected by God, because only the incarnate Son knows who the Father really is and what it means to be deprived of him, to have lost him (to all appearances) forever. It is meaningless to call this suffering "hell", for there is no hatred of God in Jesus, only a pain that is deeper and more timeless than the ordinary man could endure either in his lifetime or after his death.

Nor can we say that God the Father "punishes" his suffering Son in our place. It is not a question of punishment, for the work accomplished here between Father and Son with the cooperation of the Holy Spirit is utter love, the purest love possible; so, too, it is a work of the purest spontaneity, from the Son's side as from the side of Father and Spirit. God's love is so rich that it can also assume this form of darkness, out of love for our dark world.

What, then, can we do? "Now from the sixth hour there was darkness over all the land until the ninth hour." It was as if the cosmos sensed that something decisive was going on here, as if it were participating in the darkness invading the soul of Christ. For our part, we do not need to experience this darkening, for we are already estranged and dark enough. It would suffice if we held onto our faith in a world that has become dark all around us; it would be enough for us to be convinced that all inner light, all inner joy and security, all trust in life owes its existence to the darkness of Golgotha and never to forget to give God thanks for it.

At the very periphery of this thanksgiving to God, it is legitimate to ask that, if God permits it, we may help the Lord to bear a tiny particle of the suffering of the Cross, of his inner anxiety and darkness, if it will contribute to reconciling the world with God. Jesus himself says that it is possible to help him bear it when he challenges us to take up our cross daily. Paul says the same in affirming that he suffers that portion of the Cross that Christ has reserved for him and for other Christians. When life is hard and apparently hopeless, we can be confident that this darkness of ours can be taken up into the great darkness of redemption through which the light of Easter dawns. And when what is required of us seems too burdensome, when the pains become unbearable and the fate we are asked to accept seems simply meaningless—then we have come very close to the man nailed on the Cross at the Place of the Skull, for he has already undergone this on our behalf and, moreover, in unimaginable intensity. When surrounded by apparent meaninglessness, therefore, we cannot ask to be given a calming sense of meaning; all we can do is wait and endure, quite still, like the Crucified, not seeing anything, facing the dark abyss of death. Beyond this abyss there waits for us something that, at present, we cannot see (nor can we even manage to regard it as true), namely, a further abyss of light in which all the world's pain is treasured and cherished in the ever-open heart of God. Then we shall be allowed, like the Apostle Thomas, to put our hand into this gaping wound; feeling it, we shall realize in a very bodily way that God's love transcends all human senses, and with the disciple we shall pray: "My Lord and my God."

Easter

We Walked Where There Was No Path

Let us translate what happened into terms of our everyday life: a friend of ours is dying. We visit him; we watch him becoming weaker and weaker; we hear his final words and exhortations, his last will and testament; we see the no longer intelligible movements of his lips; we are privileged to be present, embarrassed and weary, at this sacrament in which another person is stripped to ultimate nakedness of soul and body; we hear the long drawn-out rattle that finally subsides in a terrible gasp as the stony weight of existence collapses upon its broken carrier and buries it. We deal with the cold corpse, wash and anoint it, wrap it in cloths and bandages according to ancient custom, lower the coffin into the ground, throw the shovelful of earth on top, fill in the grave, slide the gravestone into place, seal the grave and set a guard. We go home and crawl around like disoriented, half-dead flies, like beings whose present is submerged in the past and to whom the future blows as down a drafty pipe.

The next day the man we buried stands before us and greets us as if he has just come back from a journey. For our part, we do not know whether to laugh or cry; nothing like this is anticipated within the range of human experience and emotion, within the limited spectrum of our comprehension between the boundaries of bearable pain and bearable joy. Thus, while the event explodes upon us and reveals such vast dimensions that we dare not trust ourselves to it or believe it, because to us mortals it seems inhuman, he shows us his hands and feet and side—just as one might show souvenirs of some journey—in order to prove that he really was there (and was not, for instance, hidden in the house all the time), really was in the land of death and of shadows, the land of cold and of imprisonment without hope, of which the four coffin planks are only a symbol. He really was in the land where all life is of the past and where the soul is robbed of every hope that seemed justified here below, like losing a watch and not knowing when or how one lost it. He really was among the shades of Homer and Virgil, in the land of shadows of the Psalms and the Book of Job and the Wisdom literature, among the shadowy figures like Samuel when the Witch of Endor conjured him up for the doomed Saul, who, on the morrow, would be just such an insubstantial shadow himself, without hope, incapable of looking to heaven for help and deliverance, for heaven is more tightly closed than the Iron Curtain, and even if the whole world or hell were to burn, it would not melt this curtain; anyway, who knows what is behind the curtain, someone or no one.

From this realm, therefore, he returns and shows his wounds. The open wounds allow us to see through, as it were, to what *was*, a past that, as such, is past; they also allow us to see what was—what, evidently, now is—and what will be.

But now, listeners, let us imagine something even more difficult, something even more fantastic. Let us assume, for argument's sake, that the dead man of whom we have been speaking is actually the "Logos", as understood by the received religious and philosophical wisdom of the late ancient world. It is not at all enough to translate it as "world reason", "world soul" or "cosmic reason": we must speak here of divine reason indwelling the world, mirroring and expressing itself in the universe; we must speak of a divine meaning informing the world, human existence and all things, a formal and material logic on which depend the truth and validity of all individual statements made by men and that forms the basis for the (albeit rather imperfect) continuity of our everyday life. If, for the sake of argument, we accept this presupposition, what would follow from it? As a result of the death of this person, the meaning of our personal existence and of the world's existence, of the whole of nature and the whole of history, would have gone to the grave with him. Not just in the way that every death brings the world to an end and signifies an irreparable loss that puts a question mark over the meaning of life as such. No. For in such a case all other people go on living and believing in some meaning to existence; they presuppose it in order to go on living at all. But there is more: we need to go further and imagine that, after some indefinable period, this world meaning comes to life again on the celebrated "third day"; and now it acquires a meaning, a logos, a logic, that is no longer of this world, no longer transitory, but directly divine, eternal, so absolute and fulfilled in every respect that its meaning could not be or become fuller.

This is the supposition made by the Christian Faith. The world's ultimate destiny—as nature and as the history of mankind—is summed up both really and symbolically in the historical destiny of the man Jesus Christ. *Ecce homo*: behold man! Behold life destined for death! That is his destination; thither his destiny draws him, to a profound abyss of oblivion. And the shadow cast by this end covers everything with horror and chill, confusing all the threads of reason. But with the Resurrection *from* the dead, of whom the man Jesus Christ is the firstfruits, man comes forth from God, new, eternal. On the other side of death he begins his immortal life. And thanks to the death on the Cross on the part of the one man Jesus Christ, who was God's Son, expiating sin and death's doom on behalf of all, this eternal Resurrection life reflects a brilliant light onto the whole of our doomed existence. "Death, where is thy sting, where is thy victory?" Death is still there, and yet it has been superseded. The Cross is there but has turned into Easter. All the questions that guilty existence is bound to ask are still there, and yet "whenever our hearts condemn us, God is greater than our hearts, and he knows everything".

This brings us to the decisive question: What is it that takes place on Holy Saturday? What kind of a day is this on which, as the old hymn says (and it is followed here by Hegel and Nietzsche), "God is dead"? The world's meaning, the purpose of existence, is dead and buried; the object of our faith, our hope and our love is stolen from us, so that, literally, we are cast down and left alone in an unspeakable void, disappointed and forsaken: "Are you the only visitor to Jerusalem who does not know the things that have happened there in these days . . . concerning Jesus of Nazareth. . . . We had hoped that he was the one to redeem Israel. Yes, and besides all this, it is now the third day since this happened." In between came the day of death, the day when life had no being. Not merely a day when life and its meaning faded for a while, when hope had become somewhat sleepy. Not merely a day when a few strands of the world reason had become tangled while the rest of its machinery, the majority of its moving parts, had continued to function tolerably well. Not merely a day when certain components of rational thought were not properly evident, while the underlying laws of formal logic remained unshaken, seemingly unaffected by the events in Jerusalem. No. On this day the world's meaning died and was buried without any hope of the resulting hiatus ever being bridged: there was no hope of ever closing the rift opened up by this death. For the Resurrection effected by God upon his dead Son is an act of such perfect freedom and grace that it has no connection with anything that is of the world; it originates beyond death, beyond this absolute hiatus, this rift and rent, this collapse, this world's end, at some point that no rationality, no creature, can envisage. There is a total end and there is a total beginning, but . . . what comes in between them? Is death, for instance, "being dead", the neutral, persisting background against which the foreground events of dying and rising again take place? And, if this cannot be, what *is* it that persists between death and Resurrection? What links them together so that, all the same, they are the history of a single being, dying, dead and now rising again? A single world meaning, which has passed away and gone, to acquire new, eternal reality, presence and future in God? This is a problem of theological logic; perhaps it is *the* problem that the theologians have never attended to and that, if it were taken seriously, would threaten to throw into confusion all our beautiful Archimedean drawings on paper. And yet it is what is called the *Logos tou staurou*, the word and the message of the Cross, by Paul, who, in Corinth, renounces all other worldly and divine wisdom because God himself "will destroy the wisdom of the wise, and the cleverness of the clever. . . . Where is the wise man? Where is the scribe? Where is the debater of this age? . . . I decided to know nothing among you except Jesus Christ and him crucified." Risen too, of course, the "firstfruits of the dead". Yes, he, he is the continuity for which we have been looking, the connecting thread linking ruin and rising, which does not break even in death and hell. He it is who walks along paths that are no paths, leaving no trace behind, through hell, hell which has no exit, no time, no being; and by the miracle from above he is rescued from the abyss, the profound depths, to save his brothers in Adam along with him.

And now there *is* something like a bridge over this rift: on the basis of the grace of the Resurrection there is the Church's faith, the faith of Mary; there is the prayer at the grave, the faithful watching and waiting. It is a lightly built bridge, and yet it suffices to carry us. What it spans, however, is not some indifferent medium but the void of everlasting death. Nor can we compare the two sides as if from some higher vantage point; we cannot bring the two together in some rational, logical context by using some method, some process of thought, some logic: for the one side is that of death in God-forsakenness, and the other is that of eternal life. So we have no alternative but to trust in him, knowing, as we walk across the bridge, that he built it. Because of his grace we have been spared the absolute abyss, and yet, as we proceed across the bridge, we are actually walking alongside it, this most momentous of all transformations; we do not observe it, but can only be seized and pulled into it, to be transformed from dead people into resurrected people. May the sign of this transformation be found on our Janus destiny. May its mark be branded on each of our works, those that come to an end inexplicably and those that, inexplicably, are resurrected through grace. Their two faces can never meet; they can never behold each other, and we can never link up the two ends because the rope across the chasm is too short. So we must put it into God's hand: only his fingers can join our broken parts into a whole.

Eastertide

The Heart of Stone Beats Again

We are men. More than that, we are modern men, and that means men who are meaninglessly overstretched by things that are meaningless. There is so much hustle and bustle. What we can contain in our heads is so little, and the more that forces its way in, the less we can hold. A constant stream of images passes through us, appearing and disappearing. What do Good Friday, Holy Saturday and Easter mean, when tomorrow it will already be Low Sunday, soon to be followed by Pentecost, Advent and Christmas? These feasts, too, race past us, and we race past them.

But where is everything hurrying to? Where is all this insubstantial activity of ours going? As far as we are concerned, it is destined for the grave: that much is certain. And since that is certain, whereas the value of all our activity is uncertain, would it not be reasonable to extend what is certain to what is uncertain, and—if dying is the last word of our life—allow death to affix the seal of meaninglessness to everything? Between birth and death there are all kinds of significant fragments, as it were, islands of meaning, but all is encircled by a roaring sea of doubt. What is worse, meaninglessness does not stop at the borders of life: it penetrates its most delicate textures. I love this person, for instance, love him sincerely, selflessly; he could be everything to me, and I would wish to give him everything: but what does this mean if tomorrow he can be (indeed, *will* be) snatched away from me? In this case is it worth fanning the flames of real love, of love's fiery adventure, rather than merely toying with love's fireworks? People tell each other, "I will love you forever", but death grins over this "forever". We know only too well, if we are honest, how precarious our love is, how little we can rely on our feelings and how the passing of time can reveal their transient nature and, maybe, their falsehood. We may be prepared to sacrifice much of what we regard as ultimate, as "forever", to some more genuine, greater truth; we might even be prepared to let go of some affection, of a love, if we knew that it would be better this way—for both parties, but at least for the beloved (I will not tie him down and hold him back; he must be free, must be allowed to be himself). Deep and painful as this renunciation may be, however, it has not said the last word about the love that men are capable of. Real faithfulness cannot be superseded; real love, through all the confusions of emotions and all the misunderstandings to which hearts are prone, really does intend nothing less than eternity.

That is why many religions, in an attempt to resist this meaninglessness and these contradictions, have affirmed some kind of immortality. We sense that, in doing so, they are simply expressing what is in man's heart, which cannot bear the contradiction. Death simply cannot be the end of everything. But there is no way of getting beyond this idea, which is in fact only a negative one ("it cannot be"); it is only the creature crying out inarticulately, a gesture entreating protection. Every projected solution disintegrates, all the windows are stubbornly sealed and there is not even a crack to admit the least light. Spiritism and a belief in the transmigration of souls yield nothing but uncertainty and, as far as their revelations are concerned, disappointment. Better nothing than that!

Ancient peoples possessed a great strength of heart that enabled them to embody their hopes of a life beyond in magnificent mythical images or dramas and so find peace. We cannot tell whether it was these images that calmed their hearts, or whether their hearts themselves had such a sure grasp of the correct laws of being that they produced the images unconsciously and naturally. This is true of Babylonian, Egyptian, Greek, Etruscan, Roman and Germanic images, but also of African, Aztec and East Asiatic images. They have practically all disappeared, and it has become such a twilight world, the laws of being have become so obscured, and our hearts have become so profoundly confused, that we no longer know what our life's destination is, unless it be ineluctable death.

The only surviving image of real power—and for Christians it is more than an image—is the tangible reality of resurrection from the dead. One man has come back, not as a spiritist phenomenon but in flesh and blood: "Touch me and see; for a spirit has not flesh and bones as you see that I have." He did not come back as a projection of the living faith of his disciples, for he came when none of them had the least idea of such a possibility, and he had a hard battle against their stubborn unbelief. This One Man brought back with him from the realm of the dead the hope and the certainty of eternal life for all. He brings us the very thing we need, although we cannot see how, namely, a continuing life that is not simply a continuation of the old life. (Not that, please, at all costs! We have already had enough of that!) A continuing life, but not *totally* new and different either—a new form of cosmic life on some other planet, for instance—for that would be no solution and we would no longer be ourselves. It is both things at the same time, therefore, and in a way that is beyond our imagining: both a transition into God's eternity and at the same time the transfiguration and fulfillment of all that remained hopelessly unfulfilled and unfulfillable on earth. *This* wonderful, unique, earthly life, purified of all its slag, of all its inadequacies, is to be lifted up to the plane of the eternal. Of all the religions, only Christianity holds out this opportunity that goes far beyond our intellectual grasp. It is such a beautiful vista that many people falter at this point, like the disciples of Jesus, who "still disbelieved for joy": it seems too beautiful to be true.

Those who bring tidings of the Resurrection testify that it *is* true. Let us allow ourselves to accept it: this is our chance. Here, and only here, is there a way out of the cosmic prison of time, space and death. Here alone are we enabled to return to our everyday life, after the days of celebration, and instill a significance and radiance that anticipate eternal life even into the most boring, most meaningless, most futile drudgery and servitude. For our works—that is, the world as transformed by us—will follow us into eternity (Rev 14:13). The new earth that will one day come will result both from man's endeavor and from God's act in raising it up to a final and complete form. For the present, everything, man and his work, is subject to death. But in the power of the believing heart we can imprint the significance of eternity upon it all, even today.

Once we have summoned the courage to open and entrust ourselves to this hope, however, how can we live, practically and in detail, on the basis of it? How can we apply it? First let us realize that something as great and mysterious as this cannot be like a simple doctor's prescription. It is not something we can try out for a few days and then throw away as useless if it seems to be of no immediate help. Rather, the power of hope grows within us by battling against meaninglessness and futility. The vast regions of unbelief all around us; all the mortal weariness of our culture (behind its superficial noise and clamor); the absurd with all its powers of persuasion, soliciting us with its monster advertisements and drawing us into the devouring whirlpool of instant success, immediate comfort, tangible pleasure and the satisfaction of desire: all this must first of all be negated, constantly, by our hope. Our hope must beat it down, switch it off, lay it to rest; it must continually say "No". The essential thing is not that, not in that way, not to be found there. You are only obscuring and covering over and burying the delicate mystery more and more. It is all quite different; you are looking in the wrong direction.

Will hope not be worn out by this kind of battle, day in, day out? No. It can steel itself against it. This is the role for which hope was designed. Hope only exists, in fact, as "hope against hope". And the fact that it is looking in the right direction is confirmed daily. In the first place it realizes more and more that it alone holds the key to the meaning of life: the more mature hope becomes, the more clearly it perceives the utter nonsense of a mere existence running toward death. Second, however, hope is continually being confirmed in little, outwardly insignificant but irrefutable ways. How? In the sparks that flash forth in love's response. Summoned by love, hearts recognize each other now here and now there; they work to extricate themselves from all the pretenses involved in frantic activity; for whole moments someone lifts his closed visor, pierces the artificially cooled atmosphere with spontaneous warmth, so that everyone knows immediately: that's it! That's what makes life worthwhile. This is a spark from the immense fire that burns somewhere, whether near at hand or far away, in its unapproachable center. The fact that such sparks do jump—and they do!—confirms our hope. Hope would not exist if it did not come from the immense fire at the heart of things, if eternal love—contrary to appearances—were not the meaning of life.

The Christian, together with everyone who has genuine hope, fights his way through the meaninglessness of the world. He establishes cells and islands of conspiracy, networks of hope in the kingdom of the dark lord of the world. Right from the beginning Christianity was seen as a total, highly dangerous revolution. Why else was it so persecuted? It is meaning's revolt against the meaninglessness of dying, which casts a shadow of absurdity on all that lives. It is the revolt of Resurrection against the finality of bodily disintegration. The revolt of love's absoluteness against any resignation on the part of the heart. Everything depends on the power of faith, love and hope. All culture depends on it too. There was a Germany once that believed in love: the Germany of Claudius, Herder and Novalis, of Eichendorff, Brentano, Runge and Richter. It has sunk and been lost, but why should its heart of stone not begin to beat once more and produce new forms of love in concrete experience?

God's Interpreter

Brothers and Sisters in the Lord, first let us listen to the words of today's Gospel:

> Jesus said to his disciples, "Let not your hearts be troubled; believe in God; believe also in me. In my Father's house are many rooms; if it were not so, would I have told you that I go to prepare a place for you? And when I go and prepare a place for you, I will come again and will take you to myself, that where I am you may be also. And you know the way where I am going." Thomas said to him, "Lord, we do not know where you are going; how can we know the way?" Jesus said to him, "I am the way, and the truth and the life; no one comes to the Father, but by me. If you had known me, you would have known my Father also; henceforth you know him and have seen him."
>
> Philip said to him, "Lord, show us the Father, and we shall be satisfied." Jesus said to him, "Have I been with you so long, and yet you do not know me, Philip? He who has seen me has seen the Father; how can you say, 'Show us the Father'? Do you not believe that I am in the Father and the Father in me? The words that I say to you I do not speak on my own authority; but the Father who dwells in me does his works" (Jn 14:1–10).

What amazing words in the whole of world history and literature! And at the same time they are as limpid as stream water, words that everyone can understand, no mystical stammerings about God: three fundamental assertions that everyone who recognizes Jesus for what he is can grasp through faith in him. And it is important to Jesus that people shall recognize him for what he is; that is why, in his third point, there is a certain regretful tone: "Have I been with you so long, and yet you do not know me?"

Jesus does not start by declaring who he is: he begins by doing things. He comforts anxious, despairing hearts by promising them the ultimate that any heart can hope for: to be eternally with God, enjoying salvation, with all its wishes and longings fulfilled. But how can the heart arrive at this inaccessible spot on the other side of the abyss that separates it from God? It is Jesus who sets out to walk across the chasm, to build a bridge over it. That is the significance of the farewell that is in front of him: he can reach God, not primarily for himself but in order to prepare a place for us with God. And not only that: he will return to help us cross the bridge and come home. But how can there be a path across this abyss that separates man and God, earth and heaven? How can Jesus, who is about to die, find this path? This is the great riddle for the disciples. At the end of his first words Jesus lightly adds, almost with a smile, "And you know the way where I am going." They do know it, for they know Jesus; and yet they do not know it, because they have not yet realized that he himself is the way.

Hence their helpless question, "Lord, we do not know where you are going; how can we know the way?" Who can know where someone goes when he dies? It is hidden from all human eyes. Is it the underworld? Elysium? Nirvana? Pure nothingness? All we can see is a black abyss; how could we know anything of a way across, a bridge?

Now, since what he does is not understood, Jesus must speak of what he is. He himself is the way. Prior to him there was no way. He has provided it, this bridge to God, by his death. And, dying, he does not sink into an unknown, fathomless realm: his dying is a form—the highest form—of living. "I am the life." Nor are these two things an illusion, the product of an inflamed imagination, but the most reliable reality: "I am the truth." These three words, way, life and truth, belong together, particularly so in view of the impending death of Jesus. As we have said, prior to him there *was* no way: it is made available through the dying of Jesus. The other religious founders in world history all believed they could point to a way that already existed. It existed, but men were not aware of it. They, the founders, Buddha, Zoroaster, Lao-tse, found it and are able to describe it for the benefit of others. Thus none of them would have dared to describe himself as the Way. But as for the ways they indicate, they lead either to an unknown region or they fail to lead beyond the world. They lead to a cosmic law, a cleverly balanced Tao. Or, with Mohammed, to a paradise containing all earthly delights multiplied many times. They do not lead to the innermost dwelling, the heart of the divine Father. Only one way leads there, and it is not a neutral or an already existing path, but a Someone: "I am the way." I, the bridge builder between God and man. And in order to be such, he must come from God, from the life of eternity. If we are to attain to eternal life once again, a purely finite, mortal life is insufficient. Hence: "I am the life", that is, life in an absolute sense, not one living person but the origin of all that lives—and its destination too. That, furthermore, is why he is "the truth": whereas all that is transitory passes away and fades in a twilight of half-truth or falsehood, he stands in the full light of perfected reality: a God who underpins and comes to succor his world, a man who knows and returns to his origin and goal, namely, God. Everything is irradiated with the holiness of him who is manifest, unconcealed.

If Jesus is the Way, he could not arrive at the ultimate origin in order to prepare a place for us there if he himself did not come directly from that same origin. So, logically, he goes on: "If you had known me, you would have known my Father also; henceforth you know him and have seen him." The disciples imagine they can grasp the way of Jesus without knowing or seeing his destination. But the Way is not just one stretch of the way; it is the Way from beginning to end.

Consequently it is a Way that must come to us from its end, from God, who is its beginning. Earlier in the Gospel Jesus had said, "Truly, truly, I say to you, we speak of what we know, and bear witness to what we have seen. . . . No one has ascended into heaven but he who descended from heaven, the Son of Man" (Jn 3:11, 13). Heaven, the Father, is the origin. Anyone who really knows the way will find that the truth and the life are plain to him; he will know the origin, the Father. This is what Jesus says in his second point.

But here comes another disciple with his naïve request: "Lord, show us the Father, and we shall be satisfied." Thus Jesus has to begin his third explanation, which really only draws the consequences of what he has already said, and yet it sheds an even more profound light on the mystery between Father and Son, the triune mystery that is the linchpin of our Faith. What we must understand is that Jesus, as the way, the truth and the life, comes directly and visibly from the origin; therefore we should be able to recognize the origin, the Father, in him. Anyone who sees him sees the Father. But what no one could have understood is the unimaginable intimacy between Father and Son, the way they exist in one another and indwell each other. At this point, words and concepts are no longer adequate; here the divine mystery holds sway, unmediated. Jesus, the Way, who comes into the world from God, does not thereby distance himself from the Father: when he lowers himself to man's level, to be the servant of all, the Father also lowers himself; we see the humility of the divine heart, which is willing, through the Son, to prepare a place for all men in this heart of his. The stupendous intimacy of Jesus' words comes from the most intimate regions of his Father's heart: "The words that I say to you I do not speak on my own authority"—it is the Father speaking to them through Jesus. And these words are not mere words, but deeds, works: "The Father who dwells in me does his works." The foot washing, which these words accompany, is already past, that act of perfect self-surrender on Jesus' part, kneeling down before his disciples to wash the dirt from their feet, to take it upon himself. "The Father who dwells in me does his works." The foot washing, too, is a work designed to reveal the Father's heart; it does so, most effectively. God is like this, says the Son, as he carries out these actions, as he heals the sick, forgives sinners and eats with tax collectors and prostitutes.

Let us stop here for a moment and try to reflect. Is not this central affirmation, "He who has seen me has seen the Father", so paradoxical as to border on insanity? Here we have a man—for Jesus is a man, after all—saying that anyone who sees him, really sees him, actually sees God. At the beginning of the Gospel we read: "No one has ever seen God; the only Son, who is in the bosom of the Father, he has made him known" (Jn 1:18), or, in Greek: *autos exegesato*, he has given us the interpretation, the exegesis, of God. But is God not ineffable, does he not live "in unapproachable light", does he not blind our weak eyes with the result that we cannot look at this light unscathed? Is any representation of the divine possible within our limited, narrow world? Certainly none of us would adopt the role of interpreting God—unless he were out of his mind. But let us put the question the other way round: Can we refuse to allow God to reveal himself to the world if he wishes to? And not merely to communicate certain information but to manifest his own nature to the world? To deny him this ability would be to imprison him in his glory as in a golden cage. In any case, has not the Creator of this world already begun to reveal something of his wisdom, greatness and beauty "through a glass, darkly" (1 Cor 13:13). Why should not he be able to go further and let his own features shine forth in the countenance of a man? "He who has seen me has seen the Father." That is, he who has seen how I squander myself for men, in my teaching, my miracles, and all the toil I engage in for their sake, in all the suffering I load on myself as coming from them: anyone who sees this can read it as God the Father's attitude toward men, toward his creatures. Jesus tells the Parable of the Prodigal Son; everyone who hears it is moved by it. What is the point of it? "That is what the Father is like." Not only can you understand this attitude without any difficulty: through his grace you can even imitate it and make it your own. "Be merciful, as your Father is merciful" (Lk 6:36). If the Father has forgiven you such a great debt, you can easily forgive one another your little debts.

The strange thing is that Jesus not only gives us a portrayal of God: he actually lives out God's attitude toward us in all that he is and does. He does so in his phenomenal sublimity—"no one ever spoke like this man! A new teaching, set forth with authority!"—and at the same time he does it in his equally phenomenal humility, patience and humiliation, not only making himself the servant of all but also allowing the most wicked injustice to be perpetrated against him. What terrible things God must continually accept from his creation. He is despised, spat upon, pronounced dead and finished. And let no one think that God does not feel this, that he does not allow it to touch his very heart. "He who has seen me has seen the Father." Anyone who sees how mankind rejects, mocks, scourges me and nails me to a cross can also see what it does to my divine Father.

The high point of Jesus' interpretation of God is the time (although time stands still here) that the Son on the Cross is forsaken by the Father, when everything between heaven and earth is dark and void. Here, certainly, Jesus is the man who takes away the sin of the world, and God can only turn his face away from the monstrous proportions of this sin. But is this God who has turned his face away not also a forsaken God? "He who has seen me has seen the Father"—he who has seen my forsakenness has also seen the Father's forsakenness. So far does Jesus' transparency go, allowing the Father to shine through him; and this is true at every moment of his life, in the darkness of Golgotha just as much as in the light of Tabor. For the Christian believer this transparency is the aspect of God that is really beyond comprehension. What baffles us is not that we cannot validly say anything about God but that his inner, triune life of love, the mutual indwelling of Father, Son and Holy Spirit, could be revealed in the world in such a way that anyone who sees Jesus with the eyes of faith has seen God; that in worshipping Jesus he can worship God. Yes: he is the Way to God, and anyone who embraces this Way has eternal life; furthermore, anyone who lives in this Way lives in the truth and knows it.

The Logic and Ethics of the Forty Days

The Passion and death of the Logos in this world, even if they involved an agony and a death on the part of logic, still seemed somehow expressible in this-worldly words. But what words can we use to describe the logic of the Resurrection? For, of its very essence, it bursts the bounds, the grave wrappings, of our concepts; it explodes our ideas of time and space; it sovereignly walks right through the doors of our closed categories. It is so spiritual that it suspends all the laws of matter, and yet it is so material that the Son of God not only appears and speaks but lets himself be handled and felt, and eats and drinks with his friends. The Word-made-flesh has proven entirely divine while remaining entirely human. And this humanity, which had always been an expression of his divinity and now is taken back into the heavenly sphere, is so credible as a natural, earthly humanity that no distance separates it from this world: the Son's entire earthly past, summed up, as it were, in the wounds he shows to his disciples, enters with him into the truth of eternity. His scars are more than an external sign, a kind of distinction awarded in virtue of the suffering he has undergone; they reach over the abyss between dying and rising again (an abyss that reaches to the very bottom of hell): they are the identity of the subject in the identity of his consciousness. It is always he who has undergone this life, this Cross and this death. "See my hands and my feet, that it is I myself" (Lk 24:39).

It was Bonaventure who most consistently followed this christological logic, which is based on the principle of the Incarnation but is developed most daringly in death and Resurrection. Christ becomes "the logician's exemplary syllogism since, from the major premise of his divinity and the minor premise of his death on the Cross, he draws the only possible conclusion, and one to which all logic tends. . . ." The theologian contemplates the return (*reductio*) of all things to God and the world's total reconciliation (*universalis reconciliatio*) with God; for him, Christ, through his eternal blessedness, becomes the eternal Mediator, for "all blessedness is mediated through the Lamb seated in the center of the throne". In this way Christ is "*logica nostra*". An unknown author (Kilwardby?) similarly spoke of the God-Man as the *medium enuntiabile*, since he

> unites and mediates the infinitely remote extremes in the simplicity of a single Person, whence theology goes beyond every other science, because no other science can discover a principle of mediation of similar power. It unites things that nature could not unite; it brings into harmony things that were most alien, Virgin and Mother in a single woman, God and man, Creator and creature, the simple and the compound in the simplicity of a Person.

In the framework of this Resurrection logic there is a special logic of the Forty Days, the laws of which—precisely because of the tangibility of the Risen One—mock all attempts to formulate them. With the Ascension, this logic is also transported into heaven, and yet it is given to the Church as a mode of her experience; the eyewitnesses had this experience, and believers can share in it according to the measure of grace distributed to them. From the reproved Thomas' touching and worshipping of the Lord there is a direct path—both exclusive and inclusive—to those who do not see and yet believe. The same is true of the resistance the Lord offers to Mary Magdalen, who wants to touch him (right in the middle of Easter's concreteness): there is a path that both excludes and includes, leading to all those who, like her, must not "hold" him but must allow him to "ascend". This means that the mystery of the Ascension is already present in the mystery of Easter—just as the Pentecost mystery of his breathing the Spirit into the Church is already a reality at Easter (Jn 20:22)—and this in turn proves that the state of the Logos at Easter will become part and parcel of the context of Ascension and Pentecost; that is, all the concreteness of seeing, hearing, touching, sharing meals and walks (Emmaus) will enter subsequently into the rapture characterizing the life of faith. And then all that the Logos was on earth—the child, the youth, the man, the whole multiplicity of his experiences among us—will also become part of the experience of believers.

The Resurrection-Logos arises from the miracle of the Father's demonstration of power, integrating everything that he was on earth in order to snatch it up and translate and elevate it into the sphere of this miracle. He preserves continuity with the realm of history solely by affirming and creating it anew on the basis of this new beginning. In his radical newness this Logos cannot be understood in the categories of the former context. "The unspiritual man does not receive the gifts of the Spirit of God, for they are folly to him, and he is not able to understand them because they are spiritually discerned. The spiritual man judges all things, but is himself judged by no one" (1 Cor 2:14–15). Here Paul steps in with his teaching that the believer is buried with Christ and has risen with him, indeed, that he has ascended to heaven with him. Thus the believer is given, in addition to the "formal" articulations of Christology ("Christ-logic"), the ability to understand something of the content of this logic. Where these articulations are concerned, the less we rely on things that are familiar to us from any other source, even if only for the purposes of analogy, but rather draw everything from the unique and nondeducible activity of the incarnate Person of the Word, which becomes the "syllogistic form" of Christian thinking and living, the more profoundly we become aware of the truth.

Of course the Father has implanted within nature metaphors of the unique event that surpasses nature. Jesus uses these images (in the Parables of the Seed and of the Dying and Fruitful Grain of Wheat), and the Apostle takes them up and develops them (1 Cor 15:35f.); but these metaphors only find their full meaning in Christ, who is unique and as such recapitulates everything. That is why he (along with the Apostle) demands that the believer undergo a serious, not merely intellectual or symbolic death, burial, resurrection and ascension together with Christ, in order to participate as a "member of Christ" in Christ's destiny and truth. It is a being "built up in Christ" (Col 2:7), a "coming to fullness of life in him" (Col 2:10) through being "buried with him in baptism, in which you were also raised with him through faith in the working of God, who raised him from the dead" (Col 2:12), since our "trespasses", "the bond that stood against us", has been canceled and "nailed to the Cross" in him (Col 2:14). Thus "one has died for all" (2 Cor 5:14), or, what comes to the same thing, "one man's act of righteousness leads to acquittal and life for all men" (Rom 5:18). To "die with Christ to the elemental spirits of the universe" (Col 2:20) means that we have already "been raised with Christ" and "seek the things that are above, where Christ is, seated at the right hand of God" (Col 3:1–2). So we exist in a process of transition that Christ has carried out and (solely thereby) has made available to us: "Put off the old nature with its practices and put on the new nature" (Col 3:9). This new man, however, does not become a gnostic or a contemplative remote from the world but develops through concrete, active participation in the role and activity of Christ: "Put on then, as God's chosen ones, holy and beloved, compassion, kindness, lowliness, meekness and patience, forbearing one another and . . . forgiving each other; as the Lord has forgiven you, so you also must forgive. And above all these put on love, which binds everything together in perfect harmony" (Col 3:12–14).

Thus ethics springs from the logic of death and resurrection, for this logic enables the organs to recognize and follow it. The "new creation" (Gal 6:15), the "new man" (Eph 2:15; 4:24) on the "new and living way" (Heb 10:20) receives not only a new spirit but also new senses, so that he can lay hold of the Risen One and his spiritual-bodily reality through commandment, word, sacrament and life: new wine in new wineskins (Mt 9:17). Only the new man has a receptivity spacious enough to accept the word of Resurrection. He needs to be capable of responding to it in all its concreteness and tangibility, without spiritualizing it, and at the same time he must not "hold it fast" but must allow it to take whatever form of "ascension" and spiritual being it wishes. Indeed, in this process, he must continually allow his senses to be refashioned and his whole self to be spiritualized.

Since he himself is not yet risen bodily from the dead, however, he can only participate in the Resurrection by the *daily* "wasting away" of his "outer nature" (2 Cor 4:16). He can acquire the necessary space only by being newly molded, every day, by grace. People with earthly minds often do not recognize the risen Lord at all; they are entangled in conversation with him without realizing who it is that is speaking to them. Resurrection eyes are not implanted like a natural organ: they are imparted through the act of seeing itself, through the event in which the old tomb is burst and the new truth streams forth. Mary Magdalen does not simply speak to the angels through the curtain of her tears; she "turns round" —and even the first time she still does not recognize Jesus, either by his voice or by his appearance, and thinks he is the gardener (Jn 20:14). Only when she "turns" a second time (Jn 20:16) and the Resurrection word is directly addressed to her does the veil of Holy Saturday fall from her. The hearts of the disciples on the Emmaus road burn within them as Jesus explains the Scriptures to them, but it does not suffice to burn away the scales from their eyes; only as he "vanishes" does the Word strip the blindfold from their eyes and ears. The fishermen by the lake go further in that they not only reply to the One who stands on the shore and gives them instructions but also expressly obey him; yet their understanding too is obscured, and this darkness is only removed—and then not completely—when the miracle is performed; then, at breakfast, "none of the disciples dared ask him, 'Who are you?' They knew it was the Lord" (Jn 21:12). They know, yet in a suppressed awareness that hovers between familiar, unspoken, mutual understanding and a fearful sense of strangeness. Those fishing from Peter's boat act with an obedience that is given and underpinned by the Risen One; it rests calmly and constantly in the depths of their souls; but it does not penetrate into their consciousness with the same constancy. The senses and thoughts of the outward, world-oriented person dwell on the Resurrection world only for brief, flickering moments. Thus the disciples doubt the message of the women, Thomas doubts the testimony of his fellow Apostles, and even on the mount in Galilee, where the Lord bid them meet him and, ratifying their obedience, appeared to them, "some" of the Eleven "doubted" (Mt 28:17). This is an "inability to believe" in the midst of faith, be it from shock and fright (Lk 24:37), as once before in the storm on the lake, or from the overwhelming weight of visual and tactile evidence granted them ("their joy was so great that they still could not believe it, and they stood there dumbfounded" Lk 24:41).

When the Church fails to respond to the Resurrection word, she attracts the Lord's reproach. In Mark there is so much confusion—the women are so frightened that they do not carry out the Resurrection command (Mk 16:8), the "mourning and weeping" Apostles do not believe Mary Magdalen (Mk 16:10–11) or even the disciples returning from Emmaus (Mk 16:13)—that the Lord, appearing and interrupting their meal, "upbraided them for their unbelief and hardness of heart, because they had not believed those who saw him after he had risen" (Mk 16:14). He reproaches the Emmaus pilgrims with similar words of judgment, formerly applied to people of fleshly minds: "O foolish men, and slow of heart to believe all that the prophets have spoken!" (Lk 24:25). The joy and nearness of Easter call at the same time for a word of judgment—precisely in order to confirm this joy and nearness—such as we find, ultimately, in the Book of Revelation: sitting at God's right hand, to the end of the world, the Word, as Bridegroom, judges his Bride, the Church, with the sharp, two-edged sword. The entire function of judgment, of "dividing" judgment, of accepting and rejecting, is conducted within the love relationship itself, in the purification by fire that presupposes that the Sword-Bearer has in his hand the "keys of hell" (Rev 1:18). Thus the Church, in all her differentiated historical forms, is continually being newly patterned on the Word and assimilated to him. Here we see what ecclesial grace, including its ontologico-sacramental side, involves, namely, a decision to embrace the Word in response to the Word's definitive commitment to the Church.

The sovereign superiority with which the Risen One reveals himself to those who are his gives further confirmation of Origen's doctrine of "accommodation". The latter says two things: the Lord is free to be seen when he wishes to be seen, whereas material things in this world of the senses are not free: they cannot avoid being seen; and, in appearing, he is free to adopt whatever form he wishes. "Physical and sensory things make no contribution to their being seen by some other thing. By contrast, higher, divine beings are not perceived unless they wish it, even if they are present, and it depends upon their free decision whether they are seen or not." Everyone could see the fleshly body of Christ. "But they could not see what made him Christ. Only those Jesus deemed worthy of seeing him actually saw him." "It may be that the Word of God appears in different glories, depending on the receptivity of the individual souls that behold him." The manifestation stands in a fundamental relationship with the subject to whom it is manifested. The expression Mark uses in the case of the Emmaus disciples substantiates this view: "After this he appeared in another form [and with Luke in mind, we might translate it "in disguise"] to two of them, as they were walking into the country" (Mk 16:12). But in each case it is the real, risen Man-in-God who is manifested, and even his choice of appearance arises, in part, from the integration of his real, lived, earthly existence into the glory of God.

Although the Resurrection can only be a resurrection into the Father's heaven, and to that extent contains the Ascension within it, the word does present it as a separate event. It is an event that newly defines not so much his relation to heaven as his relation to the world. It brings to an end the period of Forty Days in which the Resurrection experiences had a special tangibility; this period, together with the rest of the Lord's earthly existence, is transposed to heaven. It would be imprecise to term this process a "spiritualization", at least if we are thinking of the human spirit rather than the Holy Spirit; it is the final "divinization" of Jesus' completed mission, its passing over into the Father's eternity; in it, the whole cycle of doing and suffering is taken up into the sphere of God, not as a turning away from the earthly or an alienation from it but as a constant relationship, no longer bound to particular times and places, high enough to relate all places and times to itself. If there had been no Ascension, it would inevitably have seemed as though the Word of God that resounded between years 1 and 33 of the new reckoning of time were subject to the laws of historical cause and effect. It would seem, for instance, as though the land where Christ appeared on the scene were quite seriously a "holy land", as though having been to Palestine conferred an advantage on a Christian over other Christians, as though it mattered in whose political hands the "holy places" are. Or as if those who were privileged to be Jesus' contemporaries had an advantage over others; or as if those who were closer in time to primitive Christianity were more fortunate, since an idea's historical influence is a radiating series of concentric circles, gradually fading as it spreads out.

The Ascension, however, was not a vague process whereby the mission of Jesus faded away into infinity; it was a sharply outlined event, historically exactly ascertainable, which took place during a walk from the town to the Mount of Olives. It followed a particular conversation in which Jesus gave his disciples a mission and promised that he would be with them all the days, right to the end, and would then come again visibly. The tremendous event was in three dimensions, fully available to the senses, particularly as regards the cloud that received him and the way in which Christ's words were succeeded by the words of the angels, who now appear to take up the word that is fading from the world of sense and translate it into the new mode: the word of the Church. There is no farewell atmosphere about this: sadness, the old leaven, was swept away at Easter, and the unbelieving Thomas was a laggard; the Ascension leaves a "great joy" (Lk 24:52) in the disciples' souls. Chronologically speaking, grief at the Lord's departure belongs to the period prior to the Passion; now the disciples' sorrow is like that of the woman whose time has come, and the Lord consoles them with the thought that his going away is good for them (Jn 16:6–7). "So you have sorrow now, but I will see you again and your hearts will rejoice, and no one will take your joy from you" (Jn 16:22). This is Easter, and they have seen the Lord again, and the Easter joy is not upset by the Ascension. For it heralds the outpouring of the Holy Spirit, which can only take place if the Word, having returned to the Father, causes the Spirit's outpouring within the internal relationship of the Divine Persons to become a historical, saving outpouring in the world. This takes place through the human nature of Christ, which is drawn into the mutual relationship ("spiration", "breathing") of Father and Son.

In this way the Spirit can become the Word's regent, bringing his works to completion:

> I have yet many things to say to you, but you cannot bear them now. When the Spirit of truth comes, he will guide you into all the truth; for he will not speak on his own authority, but whatever he hears he will speak, and he will declare to you the things that are to come. He will glorify me, for he will take what is mine and declare it to you (Jn 16:12–14).

Anything like a mood of "winding up" is outshone here by the sense of the momentous transition that is going on, in which the Word flows into something greater, something ultimate. There is an atmosphere of surprised amazement that what seemed the conclusive transfiguration has become yet another new beginning, the sending forth of a new divine hypostasis. There is no end in God, only a new setting forth on the part of what seemed finite and final. The "end" only shows that, right from the start, it was endless, infinite; and now it is not interpreted backward, but forward, prophetically.

With the sending of the Spirit the period of the prophetic interpretation of Scripture begins. Since the Spirit, who proceeds eternally new from Father and Son, interprets the word, there is no danger of the period of interpretation becoming merely derivative. No pall of resignation lies over the Church's history. Whatever "fullness", "height and depth, breadth and length" are to be found in the Son's word, the Spirit who "searches the deep things of God" (and thus is in his own element) will prophesy it, when and how it pleases him, "blowing where he wills". He will bring forth things that lie hidden in the narrow space of the letter like the tree that is latent in the seed, things that are hidden even from the Church, to whom the deposit of faith, all the truth-seed that is to be broadcast, has been entrusted. It is as if the truth of Christ, including the truth of his earthly life, suffering and death, can only come to full blossom if his humanity is transplanted into the life of heaven. What the Holy Spirit achieves in the Church is not an artificial transposition, for example, the drawing of morals from past history or from supratemporal, eternally valid truths. From the heavenly presence of the Word-Made-Flesh, from the constant unfolding of the Word's earthly existence on the eternal plane, the Spirit can read off what he has to mediate to the earthly Church at any one time. Thus "he will take of what is mine" without any fear of ever saying the same thing twice, right up to the end of the world.

The event of Pentecost is closely linked with the precise details of the Ascension. The disciples' gaze is held fast by the Lord's upward motion; without seeing him, their eyes follow him as he disappears into the cloud and proceeds to a destination beyond their imagining. But the heavenly dimension, embodied by the angels, is already on the ground "beside them", summoning the rapt disciples to their earthly task. As to the logic and ethics of this mission, the Spirit will instruct and train them.

Ascension

The Twofold Farewell

For us ordinary mortals the end of the life of Jesus Christ is very strange, primarily because the momentous farewell that, one day, each of us must take is repeated in his case; twice does he bid the world farewell: once prior to his death and a second time prior to his Ascension. Looking closer, we note that on the first occasion, before his death, he delivers his extremely detailed farewell address to the disciples, as if he is to part from them for a very, very long time, and then, after three days, he sees them again! On the second occasion, however, when he is about to leave them for the entire duration of world time, he disappears from their sight without really saying good-bye at all, only making reference to the coming Holy Spirit and their mission of bearing witness to the ends of the earth. The auspicious farewell celebrations with the solemn words and deeds he bequeaths to them, the institution of the memorial meal, the ultimate symbol of the foot washing showing what they should do for one another—all this basically applies to both farewells. Whereas, when the Risen One is transported to the Father without any farewell, it is because the human farewell situation is already behind him; it means that he is not at all leaving them for some remote and inaccessible place.

No doubt the scene at the Last Supper is overshadowed by the horror of his impending death on the Cross. This applies not only to the disciples, who, uncomprehendingly and helplessly, sense the approach of the inevitable—"Let not your hearts be troubled" (Jn 14:1), "You have sorrow now" (Jn

16:22)—but also to the Lord who comforts and strengthens them: "Jesus was troubled in spirit, and testified, 'Truly, truly, I say to you, one of you will betray me' " (Jn 13:21). And the parting gift of his flesh and blood is given within the context of this anguish in the face of imminent death: for it is a gift of flesh already offered, blood already shed. It is with an eye to the death that is threatening him that he hands the memorial to his disciples, so that later, when they think of him, they will always recall his love-death as well: "The Lord Jesus on the night when he was betrayed took bread, and when he had given thanks, he broke it, and said, 'This is my body which is for you. Do this in remembrance of me.' . . . For as often as you eat this bread and drink the cup, you proclaim the Lord's death until he comes" (1 Cor 11:23–26). So Christians should recall that hour, they should real-ize, re-present, the hour in which the horror of death enveloped both the Lord and the disciples. Christians too should celebrate the Mass with death in mind, *with a view to* death and not simply *in the wake of* it; they should always be moving toward the Cross, not be always simply coming from it; they should be moving toward their own bodily death, the death of all temporal and earthly things, the death of their relations, of their fellow-countrymen, of their civilization, toward the death and end of the earthly Church and of the world in its totality. This is not something that can be short-circuited. Otherwise we should be robbing the finitude and transience of our existence of the vitality and salt that give it its seriousness and its attractiveness, its profundity and its baffling spell; we should be like balloons hovering over a no-man's-land, neither earthly nor heavenly beings. Jesus wept at the grave of his best friend, together with the man's sisters and other friends; thus, as far as he himself and his own experience were concerned, he stood *under* death and not *above* it. In like manner it is appropriate for the Christian not only to weep at the grave of his loved ones but also, recalling the Lord's dying gift and receiving it from his hand, to experience his trouble of soul.

All philosophies and religions have been driven to try to

palliate the ill of death, to circumvent it or perhaps to deny it completely. Death is seen as only a superficial appearance, merely the butterfly's shedding of the cocoon, not really an end but a transformation, a liberation from the body (the body that was a grave); thus death becomes, in fact, a resurrection from the grave. This will not do, however. Even if people have always sensed something consoling over and above the horror of death, something ultimate and all-embracing that they could not articulate, they were still always confronted with a closed door, and all were bound to weep. And only in this way did Jesus Christ overcome human death: by allowing the horror of death to penetrate his innermost, loving heart and showing that, dying, buried and descending to the underworld, he had a longer breath than death and hell. He did not conquer this last and most wicked enemy by fleeing from it, but, symbolized by Jonah, he was swallowed up by the monster and overcame it from within. Jonah, in the Jewish parable, came back the same man from the jaws of hell; he went on living as a mortal man and eventually had to face the monster waiting to devour him after all. But Christ arose from the jaws of hell with an immortal life and left the monster, death, slain. Thus, following in the footsteps of Christ and in the power of his death, men only become immortal by walking through death with him and so conquering it.

Historical man only exists as mortal, moving gradually toward what will infallibly overwhelm him. Creature that he is, not vegetating like plants and animals but awake to a sense and a vision of the totality of being, of the world as a whole and of God, it will overwhelm him. It will overcome him, though he be able to love another being completely and forever and consequently cannot be compelled to regard bodily death as setting bounds to his love. This is how Dante loved Beatrice, with a love that knew it was eternal and that traversed all the kingdoms of the world, hell, purgatory and paradise in order to find his beloved for eternity in the realm of love. He knew that he possessed a right to that eternity.

All peoples have tried in one way or another to break open

the odious door, and many a hero such as Orpheus seemed almost to succeed in bringing back his lost Eurydice. Human love, at its fullest measure, has a greater goal than earthly life. All human existence is oriented to this fullness of love.

All the same, man only exists as a mortal being and hence as an absolute contradiction that no philosophy can resolve. Trying to resolve it, he is bound to dissolve himself, proclaiming himself to be either pure spirit alienated into matter or pure matter, a higher animal, for instance, acting as if it possessed spirit. He will do a great deal to conceal this contradiction from himself, to cover over the humiliation he feels that he, the ruler of the world, who can do everything, cannot even fulfill his own self. In the ancient world, imagination was assiduous in developing myths: sidereal migration, palingenesis, judgment courts of the dead, tests that, if passed, allowed entry into Elysium; it was possible to win the favor of the heavenly beings through magic. But however "the ancients depicted death" [title of a treatise by G. E. Lessing (1729–81) —TRANS.], very many people remained sceptical. Nowadays the world of mythology has become unfashionable, but it has been replaced by a frantic activity designed to cover over entirely the question as to the totality of man's being or to trivialize it. New mythlike ideologies in East and West are joining hands for this purpose: the world must be kept happy —even as far as the individual is concerned—without any regard to death. But have there ever been as many suicides as there are today?

Jesus is troubled as he faces his death. And in this state he surrenders his very self, in a state—torn flesh, shed blood—that explicitly envisages death. Does he also see death as a mere transition? This is a difficult question. We could say "Yes", since he says he will see his friends again. But at the same time we must remember that, man that he is, he by no means glosses over the finality, the timelessness, the abyss signified by all death in general and his own death in particular. He who will carry the sin of the world will doubtless also bear the intolerable contradiction in human nature, just as, alienated from God, he can become available to the sinner's experience. Everything is falling apart, and the synthesis of these parts is practically unreal to his consciousness at the present time; the entire foreground is occupied by the significance of words such as "no longer" and "no more on earth". "I tell you I shall not drink again of the fruit of the vine until that day when I drink it new with you in my Father's kingdom" (Mt 26:29). Then the background synthesis will fade more and more until his imminent death takes up the whole stage of his soul and seems utterly unbearable to him: "My soul is very sorrowful [*peri-lypos*], even to death." It is filled with grief and a sense of "unease" (*ademoneo*, Mt 26:37) and "great distress" (*ekthambeo*, Mk 14:33). Humanly speaking, it seems that he cannot walk down the path he has been shown: "Father, if it be possible. . . ." But it is not possible, and the contradiction must gape even wider until it reaches the proportions of his being forsaken by God, when all hope of full human realization is at an end.

Jesus must sense all this approaching him when he takes his first, lengthy farewell. He will have to undergo all the naked brutality of a death that *in itself* has no way out; experiencing the extreme of human desolation, he will render the ultimate, divine-human surrender of himself to the Father and to men. This is the only way he can go through death in its entirety and create a way out of a situation that has no way out. He experiences this death of his as the death of his brothers, sinners, estranged from God; yet he embraces it in very truth out of a love that surrenders itself thus. As such, his death is already a work undertaken on our behalf and in our place, and (according to John) a work of glorification. Consequently, Jesus brings this state of utter self-surrender with him as he emerges into Resurrection, into heavenly, eternal existence.

However God fashions our own death, something of this mystery is bound to cling to it in our discipleship of Christ. Our hope for totality can only be fulfilled through death; our ascension can only take place on the basis of some kind of journey to hell. Only the man who loses his soul—who survives the state of losing and having lost—will gain it. Only the man who builds all his earthly edifice with an eye to the fire of the Day of Judgment can hope to see his work and that of his brothers, and the entire work of creation, survive the purifying flames. The white heat of death allows no pacts. What applies here is not just the worldly wisdom that says that we must "die" in order to "become"; but such wisdom can acquire a Christian sense if by "dying" here we mean the whole seriousness of christological death, if our everyday renunciations are marked and fashioned, right from the outset, by the tremendous, ineluctable "dying" that the eternal Father has to require of his incarnate Son. If this is at least the horizon of faith to our everyday little deaths—and our experience of this horizon can never come to an end—we shall ultimately learn how to let go once and for all, clinging neither to things of this world nor to things of the world beyond (as if we *could* cling to *them*!); then, stripped of all security of our own, we shall learn how to fly in the realm of love. And if we do not manage it ourselves, death will show us how; death, gently violating a life that resists in the belief that it is virginal. For Brother Death has been entrusted with the task, sooner or later, when we have to leave everything, of making us like him who left everything for our sake. Objectively speaking, death is love's "Yes" to God; as to whether man will repeat the "Yes" or resist this truth right to the very end, that is a mystery reserved for the divine Judge. We can only hope that all will utter their "Yes"; for the Son of God's full self-surrender on behalf of all men could not be illustrated more graphically, under the conditions of this world, than through his death, which as such was the expression of a life that was alive to the highest degree. "For this reason the Father loves me, because I lay down my life, that I may take it again. No one takes it from me, but I lay it down of my own accord. I have power to lay it down, and I have power to take it again" (Jn 10:17f.). The very fact that he has *power* to lay down his life implies that he takes our death into his own, with all its fear and hopelessness. Thus the Apostle can say: "And he died for all, that those who live might live no longer for themselves but for him who for their sake died and was raised" (2 Cor 5:15).

All mankind's attempts to get beyond death weigh less than a feather compared with this fulfillment that has made death the locus of the most living life: death's poison tooth has been extracted, since living love has filled death with its own reality and reinterpreted it in love. "Death, where is thy sting? Where is thy victory?" The devouring aspect of death, drawing all life into itself irresistibly and with increasing speed, like the waters of Niagara, becomes, in Christ, the irresistible attraction of love for God, bursting all bounds—even (and particularly) the bounds of death—and foaming on into eternal life. Only he can do this, of course, not we; we can only go through this door in a spirit of humiliation; life must be violated if it is to yield its love mystery.

Now let us look back to the beginning, to the strange double farewell. First we have the long farewell discourse and shortly afterward the Lord's reunion with the disciples. Then we have the short, almost repressed farewell, followed by his disappearance for thousands of years. He utters his long farewell discourse in the face of death and its devouring superior power. All of us have to walk one day beneath this shadow, which darkens not only the body but the soul too. We feel the cold breath of the lightless underworld as it casts its long diagonal evening shadow in advance over a life that has begun to chill. "The scenery is a farewell." Again and again, in our troubled state, we must listen to the words of consolation uttered by Jesus in his trouble of soul; we shall never outgrow these words, as long as death exists. But then, when the Risen One who announces the fulfillment to us—the earth, soft and fragrant, bathed in God's sunlight—when he disappears from among us, how little we feel abandoned! How little we mourn for him, for the one who has gone *to prepare a place for us*, who has gone away in order to come again, who has disappeared without becoming remote from us: "Lo, I am with you always, to the close of the age." "Where two or three are gathered together in my name, I am there in the midst." He is just so far away that our heart's longing is kept alive, and just so near that this longing, satisfied, can give birth to further, vibrant longing.

The Exalted Lord's Care for the World

Christians celebrate a special feast today, the Ascension of the Lord, but how many of them are really glad that he has left us and has returned to heaven? In all probability they are not sad about this farewell either; the event is so distant that it is more or less a matter of indifference to them. But for the person who knows why he calls himself a Christian, none of the events in the life of Jesus Christ can be of no consequence. All of them concern us and have a mysterious and profound significance and relevance today. If we first consider what the Ascension of Jesus means for him, we shall be in a better position to see what it means for us.

In the Upper Room, where Jesus is together with his disciples for the last time on the night before his Passion, and where he gives his highly moving farewell discourse, the atmosphere is gloomy and full of fear. He senses this and tells them: "Let not your hearts be troubled, neither let them be afraid. You heard me say to you, 'I go away, and I will come to you.' If you loved me, you would have rejoiced, because I go to the Father; for the Father is greater than I" (Jn 14:27–28). First, therefore, there is no reason for sorrow. Second, there are reasons for rejoicing: Jesus is returning to his Father, who is greater; also, in going away, he will come to them, to believers. For these reasons his departure is to be a feast, the very feast we celebrate today. We shall examine the two reasons Jesus gives us why we should and must rejoice, why we are privileged to do so. But he also mentions a condition that must be fulfilled if what humanly speaking seems like a painful farewell can be celebrated as a joyful feast: "If you loved me". That is easy to understand. We do not celebrate for our own sakes but for someone we love or value, someone to whom something joyful has happened. We are glad because someone has passed his exams, received some honor or promotion, or because a child has come into the world and we want to share in the joy of the parents. Even if those who are celebrating are all in a festive mood and are enjoying their own rejoicing, the deepest reason for their joy is selfless: they are rejoicing over the joy of someone else and want thereby to heighten the other person's joy. So Jesus wants us to enter into his joy, and for the reasons he gives.

The first reason is that he is going to the Father, who is greater than he. For the moment he does not dwell on how dark the path of this return to the Father will be—through all the stations of the Passion right up to being forsaken by God, right up to his descent into the realm of the dead. He focuses not on this but on the fact that this is his way home, home to the bosom of the Father, where he has dwelt for all eternity (Jn 1:18). For the Father is his home and his perfect security, and he has left these things temporarily in order to proclaim the Father's being and the Father's love. "I came from the Father and have come into the world; again, I am leaving the world and going to the Father" (Jn 16:28). And "the Father himself loves you, because you have loved me and have believed that I came from the Father" (Jn 16:27). However much he expressed his solidarity with this terrible, guilty world, even to taking upon himself all its sinfulness before God, for him to leave his Father's bosom was, all the same, a setting out into an alien territory. True, this world belongs to him, for all that the Father has belongs to him, but the world, though it belongs to him, does not *want* to belong to him: "He came to his own home, and his own people received him not" (Jn 1:11). This world that he was to teach, with which he had to struggle and suffer, was a petty, self-seeking, narrow-minded and blind world; at all points he came up against its disappointing and wounding sharp edges. How would he *not* rejoice to return to the Father, who is "greater than I", in whom there are no limits, no differences of opinion, no divisions and splits! The Father is the infinite realm, both immeasurable and utterly familiar. He is not an empty void, not a nirvana, but a totality that, right to its foundations, is the Son's origin, lovingly affirming him. In the Father there is nothing beyond this eternal "Yes" to the Son, nothing he keeps to himself and does not share with the Son; the Son dwells in the Father's absolute, boundless self-surrender to him; he is the result of this self-surrender; indeed, he *is* it. His is the fathomless bliss of being begotten, loved and affirmed by the entire abyss and bottomless ground of Being. And now, in addition, the Son returns to this pure realm of eternal love, in which he has dwelt for all eternity as God's Son, as the *Son of Man*: from now on his humanity may participate in this happiness, a happiness that is superabundant because it is divine.

But is it possible for a finite little man to live at all in the fire of this eternal love? Must not this fire suffocate and devour him in an instant? If we did not know of the Ascension of Jesus, we might incline to this view. He, however, has been accustomed to this fire from all eternity; it is his element (like the Salamander of mythology), and he takes his human nature with him right into it, for this nature, which is inseparably and eternally his from now on, must be able to be wherever he is. This, then, opens up vast possibilities for us: Perhaps we too are destined to. . . ? Is it possible that we too might be able to exist in this blissful fire of love beyond the narrow confines of mortal life? Let us hear what Jesus says: "In my Father's house are many rooms; . . . I go to prepare a place for you" (Jn 14:2). In the infinite realm of the origin there is room for us, but this room must be prepared through the Son's Ascension. How else would we get there? He is the Way, the only one who, at the end of the road, can open up to us all the space, in God, we could ever want. Only in the revelation of Jesus Christ does the eternal, blessed goal of our dark and baffling life on earth become a really credible possibility. And so our selfless joy at his return to his Father who is greater (for the origin is always superior, as such, to what springs from it) is redoubled by Jesus' farewell gift to us, namely, that we shall share *his* joy. "And when I go and prepare a place for you, I will come again and will take you to myself, that where I am you may be also" (Jn 14:3).

Jesus has given us a further reason why we should rejoice at his return to his Father. When he says, "I am going, and I will come again", this coming to us does not mean the hour of our death, when he will come to meet us, or the end of the world: it means, quite simply, that his care for us, in response to the Father's will and together with the Father, will be intensified. Putting it differently, he can say that he will send and implant into our hearts, from the Father, the Spirit who is common to both Father and Son. "I tell you the truth: it is to your advantage that I go away, for if I do not go away, the Counselor will not come to you; but if I go, I will send him to you" (Jn 16:7). And both Father and Son come to us in the Spirit who is common to both: "We"—I and the Father—"will come to him and make our home with him" (Jn 14:23), that is, with the man who loves me.

Thus there is an aspect of Jesus' care for the world that depends precisely on his Ascension. Paul puts this in his sovereign fashion:

> He who descended is he who also ascended far above all the heavens, that he might fill all things. And his gifts were that some should be apostles, some prophets, some evangelists,

> some pastors and teachers . . . we are to grow up in every way into him who is the Head, into Christ, from whom the whole body, joined and knit together by every joint with which it is supplied, when each part is working properly, makes bodily growth and upbuilds itself in love (Eph 4:10–16).

Here, suddenly, we have a totally different perspective on the Feast of the Ascension. By going away, Jesus comes to set the world aright and mold it according to its destination. He appears to turn away from the world, but by this means he actually turns toward it in the fullest possible sense. Paul uses a metaphor to explain it: Christ is elevated to the position of Head, Head of the Church and of all creation, and from this position of preeminence he reorganizes the entire body that is subject to him. Only now are the individual members, such as we are, given their precise functions. Only now do we learn why we have been placed in the world and what we have to do here. What we are engaged in is not some passing project; we are not like cogs in a vast and possibly pointlessly running machine; rather, it is a ministry that is given its meaning from and in eternity.

This is particularly the case in the visibly ordered Church of Christ, which is always compared to a meaningfully organized body with its many functions. The Church too, for instance, has the meaningful function of suffering, meaningful and productive just as Christ's suffering was for us. Thus—and only thus—the many sufferers in the world can be shown the positive, indeed indispensable significance of their pains, renunciations and powerlessness. There is also, for instance, the meaningful function of dying, which, undertaken in a Christian spirit, is an act of pure self-surrender in which we allow ourselves to be taken hence. Then there is the meaningful function of prayer: seen from the world's point of view this seems to be a futile occupation, but from the point of view of the Lord it is completely indispensable for the health of the body; it is like lifeblood, circulating through all the members and rendering their lives fruitful through being part of the whole. Then, of course, there are all the various gifts of grace and offices and ministries, in which everyone shares according to his capacity and according to God's choice.

We can be sure, however, that the Lord who has suffered for all men and is now elevated to the Father's height addresses his care not only to the Church but also to all those outside her. Ultimately his body is mankind in its totality; indeed, it is the entire cosmos together with mankind; for we read that the cosmos groans for redemption, groans to be set free from the thralldom of corruption along with the children of God. We cannot say how this much vaster body will be organized by God with a view to its redemption; it is enough that we have a sure hope in that regard.

Now all this gives us a new insight: not only will Jesus meet the individuals who believe in him when they come to die, in order to bring them whither he has prepared a dwelling for them; he also is causing the whole world to mature into its full shape like a vast body, so that it may attain its goal in God, that is, to exist in the fire of eternal love of Father, Son and Spirit. If the world did not have this goal, to be attained through the Ascension of Jesus Christ, we should have to say that it had no ultimate meaning. There could be meaningful moments in the life of the individual and in the history of mankind, but they would be merely islands within an ocean of meaninglessness. Atheism, of course, endeavors to construct a total meaning in the process of world history toward a better future. But this is bound to shatter hopelessly when confronted with the meaningless suffering of the countless people who die along the utopian road without contributing the least spark of meaning toward the process.

Yet again we must marvel at the power of the Christian Faith to bring together earth and heaven, man and God, the world beyond and this world, in a single framework that gives meaning: the Word comes from God and becomes flesh; God's announcement of salvation assumes a human form, and as Jesus, the Word of God, returns to God, he draws the Church, mankind, the cosmos with him to prepare a place for them with God. This heavenward direction is also what creates order on earth: the Ascension seems to turn its back upon the world, but in reality it is the exalted Lord's turning toward it: thus heaven takes the highest interest in earth.

In conclusion, therefore, we see how profoundly the Feast of the Ascension is woven into the totality of Christian celebrations: it is the conclusion and result of Jesus' entire earthly activity, from his conception and birth, via his public ministry, to his Passion and Resurrection. At the same time it heralds the period of his presence, in his Holy Spirit, in the Church: the Ascension is a direct prelude to the Feast of Pentecost, which fulfills the promise of God's program for the world. "I will not leave you orphans", says Jesus (Jn 14:18). Orphans would be those, too, who see nothing in Jesus but a great religious genius: they possess only a few heirlooms of his inheritance. If we are believers, possessing his Spirit, we have him and the Father present in us.

This presence may be veiled in the thick fogs of this world's eon, and there may be many forceful objections and refutations of our Faith. We only see the reverse side of the carpet with its tangled threads; we do not see the pattern they make on the other side. But we have the Lord's word. Read these words in John's Gospel for yourself, and ask yourself whether there is anything in the whole of world literature—and that includes religious literature—that can remotely be compared to the power and profundity of these words.

The Threefold Presence of Christ

Today the Lord leaves this world and returns to the light of the eternal Father. But nothing could be further from this Feast of the Ascension than a mood of resignation. In the almost precipitate succession of feasts between Easter and Pentecost and on to Trinity and Corpus Christi, the Feast of the Ascension is one of the most joyful. The Lord himself bids us rejoice with him as he returns to the Father; to do so, as he says, would be a sign of our love, "for the Father is greater than I" (Jn 14:28). But we can also rejoice because his going away itself promises us a home: "I am going to prepare a place for you", for "in my Father's house are many rooms" (Jn 14:2). Nor is that enough: there is a further reason for us to be glad, and we shall devote this present reflection to it. The Lord says to us, mysteriously, that his going away and disappearing will also be a coming and an appearing: "I am going away, and I will come to you" (Jn 14:18). And to help us understand that his going away and his coming are one and the same, he puts it even more clearly: "I will not leave you desolate; I will come to you. Yet a little while, and the world will see me no more, but you will see me; because I live, you will live also. In that day you will know that I am in the Father, and you in me, and I in you" (Jn 14:18–20). His disappearance from the world begins with his Passion and ends with his Ascension. For since he was laid in the tomb, no worldly person, no one who lacks the Spirit of Christ, has seen him anymore. His coming to us, however, starts on Easter morning, where he meets one disciple after another; it continues throughout the Forty Days and is brought to its fulfillment at Pentecost, when he pours out his Spirit over the Church and thus fills her with his own innermost being. It is not that his presence changes into his absence; what changes is the mode of his presence.

For there are many modes of being present. Two stones may lie side by side, or two trees may stand next to one another: they are present to one another, but in a totally external and incomplete sense. They do not know of one another, they are of no concern to each other and in spite of their proximity they are alien to one another. Presence in a real sense only begins where two beings know one another with mind and heart, where they meet at the conscious level. In this case each one is capable of carrying a kind of picture of the other in his soul, whereby the other being acquires a secondary existence inside the one who carries it. And if this kind of presence remains pale in the case of the countless people we encounter every day, it can attain to powerful reality where people know and love each other: the picture they have of each other is infused with reality. Even when alone, such people can share conversation with one another. Of course, this presupposes that they share a common "spirit", a kind of communion that includes their objective attitudes and their subjective experience of life, so that the other person can share and be present in all that happens to them externally and internally. It also presupposes something else: there must be no fear of being overpowered on either side. Each person must trust the other and allow him freedom, freedom to come and go within a constant keeping of faith, freedom to have different opinions on the basis of a mutual understanding. Perhaps this ideal model of the mutual presence of two people may offer some grasp of the presence of Jesus Christ as, today, he leaves us, saying that he will come to us in a new and deeper way?

As Catholics we can try to view this new presence from three angles: from God's point of view, from Christ's point of view and from the Church's point of view.

In the Creed we say, "He ascended into heaven and is seated at the right hand of the Father." Thus the humanity of Christ has been placed at the heart of the Divinity, and where God is, heaven is too. Now this humanity, immersed in the being of God, can also participate in God's attributes, as a red-hot iron participates in the attributes of fire. God, however, is the One in whom "we live and move and have our being"; he dwells in each of his creatures and, as St. Augustine says, does so more profoundly than the creature itself. So it is quite impossible for the creature to be lonely: even when it thinks it is alone, at the very ground of its being it stands before its God and Creator. He is our soul's guest, who cannot be driven away, because, at a deeper level, it is our being and nature that are *his* guest. Since his Resurrection, Jesus Christ also participates in this "in-dwelling" of God in us. Again and again we hear this word, *in*, in Jesus' farewell discourses. "You will know that I am in the Father, and you in me, and I in you." "I am the vine; you are the branches. He who abides in me, and I in him, he it is that bears much fruit." "Abide in my love." "As thou, Father, art in me, and I in thee, that they also may be in us." "I in them and thou in me, that they may become perfectly one. . . . I made known to them thy name, and I will make it known, that the love with which thou hast loved me may be in them, and I in them." This "indwelling" has the same intimacy as God's indwelling in his creature. Not only does it objectively permeate soul and body, but it can also govern consciousness, thought, faith, willing, loving and feeling, so that it almost obliterates the distinction between the parties concerned. For the love with which we love God, in particular, is based on God's love in and for us, that love that Paul says is "poured into our hearts". Without destroying our nature as creatures and persons, there comes about such a reciprocal presence of the one to the other that human words cannot express it; we are permeated, and yet there is no confusion. Ultimately there is only one image that will do: that of the Holy Spirit himself, who is the unity of Father and Son without obliterating the distinct being of either. And that is why the mystery of the Ascension merges into that of Pentecost. In going to his Father, Christ breathes out the Holy Spirit. So Paul can say, "Even though we once regarded Christ from a human point of view, we regard him thus no longer" (2 Cor 5:16). The Christ whom Paul knows and alone wants to know is the divine, spiritual Christ who is omnipresent, sublimely above space and time like God himself, in sovereign power manifesting himself, as on the Damascus road, to those he desires to seek out, filling the hearts of those who are his chosen vessels so that it is no longer they who live but Christ who lives in them.

This, however, does not give us a sufficient grasp of the mystery of the Ascension and of Christ's new mode of presence.

The Lord shares in God's mode of presence; but he is not only God, he is also man for all eternity, with a human body and a human soul. Now this humanity explicitly participates in the new mode of his presence and indwelling. And this is the really astonishing and baffling thing: that this finite soul and this limited body can share in the limitless omnipresence and intimacy of God. His wisdom and love have brought this miracle about: it is called "Eucharist". It is not only a spiritual being-together in which the parties think of one another, nor is it simply the kind of presence whereby man is in God: it is an indwelling of the divine-human being of Christ, soul and body, in the whole person, body in body and soul in soul. "He who eats my Flesh and drinks my Blood abides in me and I in him."

This mode of presence began in the anticipation of his sacrifice at the Last Supper, but it had to continue in his Cross and death, to be perfected in his transfigured Resurrection and now in the Ascension, so that he can reach the "place" from which he can give himself prodigally to the whole world. Now he can prepare a special meal in which he freely transforms himself into the food he offers. Nor, in doing so, does he become a "prisoner of the tabernacle", for he who can walk through closed doors remains just as sovereignly free to give himself, body and soul, wherever he wishes. Catholics are acquainted with spiritual communion, which gives believers who yearn for the Lord an intimate union with him just as sacramental Communion does. Man's eucharistic indwelling and permeation by the Lord—or, to put it the other way round, man's incorporation into the eucharistic Lord—is, for the Lord, a concrete aspect of his own Resurrection and Ascension: one of his earthly members, for which he went to his death, has now entered into him and (as the Apostle says in Eph 2:6) has been made to "sit with him in the heavenly places". Again, what we have here is a mutual indwelling that does not cause the persons to become confused: Christ remains the Lord and the Head; the believer remains the servant, the friend, the member. Indeed, he experiences the same paradox that is always there when God draws near: the nearer he comes, the more profoundly we grasp how totally "other" his divine nature is, the more we realize that his nearness is pure grace, always beyond our comprehension. The more graciously God bends down to our level and enters into us, the higher his mystery "ascends" above us.

We must make a third attempt, however, to grasp the way in which Jesus, ascending to heaven, comes back to us. He is with us not only as God, not only as the eucharistic God-Man, but also, essentially, as Church. What we mean by "Church" comes into being as a result of his Eucharist, from the outpouring of his Spirit; the Church lives in the power of his being-with-us all the days, to the end of the world. The Eucharist, which was instituted prior to the Cross, has drawn his disciples from the very outset into his sacrifice on the Cross. Thus the Church cannot celebrate the sacrifice of the Mass without offering herself to be included in that sacrifice. She only genuinely receives the food Jesus offers if she shares his sacrificial mind. And on the basis of this eucharistic unity the Church is drawn into the mystery whereby the exalted Lord is present for the whole world. The Church, which is one individual entity within mankind, is given a share in the universality of Christ's body and spirit, which, while it was on earth, also constituted a single person. These words are addressed to the Church: "Lo, I am with you always, to the close of the age" (Mt 28:20). This applies also to the sacrament that is linked to his presence: it is given to the Church, to be carried out and administered. The Holy Spirit too, who is promised to us as the highest gift and pledge of this presence, is ultimately not promised and granted primarily to the individual but to the community of the Church; thus this community becomes the distinctive locus of his presence in the world. Only as members of the Church are we members of the body of Christ. Jesus spent the forty days after Easter with his disciples, preparing and furnishing this Church. Then it was that he gave authority, instituted offices, gave instructions. And the last thing he had to do once the organism had been fashioned was to breathe a soul into it. This soul can be none other than the Spirit of Christ. His disappearance as a single, visible person, his Ascension, is simultaneously his entry into the Church; in the future, this is where he will always be encountered. He who was formerly a historical individual now lives on tangibly in history as the soul of the Church. He is present in the mouth of those who preach him: "He who hears you, hears me." He speaks through the voice of his official priests: "This is my Body; this is my Blood"; "I absolve you from your sins." He is alive in the souls of those who believe in him, who have "put on Christ" and can say: "It is not I who live, but Christ lives in me." He suffers in the torments of his martyrs: "In my flesh I complete what is lacking in Christ's afflictions." He lives in the love of Christians for one another: "As you did it to one of the least of these my brethren, you did it to me." Indeed, this mutual love of Christians actually becomes the essential form of Christ's presence in the world: "We know that we abide in him and he in us, because he has given us of his own Spirit", that is, the Spirit of brotherly love. This becomes the real magnet, drawing down God's presence in the world with a kind of infallible attraction: "He who loves me keeps my Commandments", and he will love his neighbor, "and we will come to him and make our home with him." Love is heaven on earth.

Only thus is the mystery of the Ascension complete, in which the Son comes to us so that we may be where he is. He is with God, and God is love. And if we love, says John, we are with God and in God. This is expressed by the prayer in today's Mass when it says: "Lord, receive our offering as we celebrate the Ascension of Christ your Son. May his gifts help us rise with him to the joys of heaven" [the (Anglican) Book of Common Prayer is closer to the German and Latin: "Grant, we beseech thee, Almighty God, that like as we do believe thy only-begotten Son our Lord Jesus Christ to have ascended into the heavens, so we may also in heart and mind thither ascend, and with him continually dwell. . . ."—TRANS.].

Pentecost

God Is Open to Us

If the Spirit had not come, the world and the Church would never have understood that the whole story of the crucified Jew from Nazareth was more than a provincial and historically insignificant event. Nor could they have understood. This man's claim (or was it his disciples' claim for him?) to have reconciled the universe with God through his particular bit of suffering on the Cross—such as thousands of others have undergone—and to have liberated each individual person, from the first to the last, from his sins, from eternal death, and to have brought him home to the eternal Father: such a claim was too fantastic to be taken seriously. It would have meant standing everything on its head. For this man, as is well known, regarded himself as the head of the entire "body" of the world and the Church; ultimately he was not in the world, but the world was in him; he was the Father's first thought, and the world with all its boundless dimensions of time and space came second, made possible through him.

If this monstrous claim were true, it could never have occurred to the men who went about with him on earth. He was quite clearly one of them; someone special, certainly, regarded with respect, but after all a man with the same needs as others, dependent on the world and his immediate surroundings, on the past and the future, embedded, like everyone else, in a vast context. How could they even suspect that the universe is upheld by him, that every need in the world ultimately looks to him to fulfill it, that everything was created through him, in him and for him? He himself knew that he could not demand them to see things in this way, and so for the present he showed that side of him that—in the dimensions of promise and fulfillment—they could come to understand on the basis of their existing experience of the world. All life paths run on rails: his was no different, but the rails were broader in his case. They ran from the Old Covenant; his words were in tune with those of the prophets, his calls to action echoed the original law and his miracles, as simple people realized, could only be performed by someone sent by God.

But in that case, why the stumbling block? Why was he not recognized by those who had spent their lives studying the Scriptures in order to be able immediately to recognize the One who should come, when he actually came? Had his face so changed down the centuries, like that of the wanderer returned, who has been away so long that his friends, and perhaps even his relations, no longer recognize him? The papers are in order, but the face is unfamiliar. It is the same here: they had hoped for a radiant fulfillment and were faced with an almost impenetrable veil. Where they had hoped to encounter a familiar Thou, they were repelled by something strange and baffling in his features: dimensions were opening up of which the prophecies had indicated nothing. This is clear from his discourses in John's account: there is a Rembrandtesque obscurity here, a tension such as we find in El Greco, and what we begin to see is something frighteningly larger than life: he draws his nourishment from the Father's will instead of from earthly bread; all judgment has been given into his hands; he, with his flesh and blood, is food for the world, and no one who does not eat him will rise again at the end of time. He is the light of the world, he is life, Resurrection. At this point his hearers, even if they believed in him devotedly, must have been seized by dizziness. They could not understand it; at best they could only put it to one side, like some precious thing for which, at present, one has no use, but sometime maybe. . . . For as John says, the Spirit had not yet come. They had not yet made the tremendous leap from their inherited concept of the Messiah—however high the expectations of believers may have been—to the manifestation among us, in bodily human form, of the eternal God, something inconceivable for which no prophecy had ever prepared them.

What was needed for this explosion to take place? He had to give us his Spirit. He had to break through the limits set by creation between I and Thou, between man and man, and infuse something of his own "I" into our own "I". Like a blood transfusion; except that here it is not the case of infusing an essentially similar, physical element belonging to the same "blood type" but of infusing something that is totally dissimilar and foreign to our creaturely nature because it is a divine element, not physical but spiritual: the Spirit of Jesus himself, who is one with the Spirit of the Father. For the divine Spirit is especially skilled in such transfusions: proceeding from Father and Son, his role in God is already that of fusing what is most interior and personal to them: they give each other what is most their own. (When we speak of "the spirit of Goethe" or "the spirit of Mozart", we mean this utterly specific dimension that forms the core of their personality.) And behold: the Spirit of both is the same Spirit; all is giving, all is receiving; all is the same love.

Today this Spirit is poured out over the world in visible gestures and signs (although he is the Invisible One who cannot be held fast in "flesh"). On the Cross the Son of God's heart was pierced and there flowed out blood and water (the source of the sacraments); but in reality the spear pierced right to his soul, his "I", "right to the knot of the Trinity" (as Claudel puts it); now, therefore, God's Spirit pours forth into the world as from a leaking jar. This is a coarse image for something so fine, but it is meant to help us realize the very tangibility of what is going on. Even the "rushing mighty wind" and the tongues of fire were only metaphors for an elemental event, elemental as were only the events of creation (where we were not present) and of redemption, from crib to

Cross (which we did not understand). It is by no means the case that God remains God and man remains man, and that God, who in any case is everywhere in the world in virtue of his almighty power and essential omnipresence, shows himself in his domain a little more clearly than usual. Or that man, who already has a certain receptivity for the word of God, is now privileged, for once, to hear and see God in this remarkable form and shape. No. What happens is something that, ultimately, can only be compared to what takes place in God himself in eternity and continually in our here-and-now present (for it is one with it): man is enabled to share in the Spirit's proceeding from Father and Son. This participation is what we call the fullness of sanctifying grace.

> "What no eye has seen, nor ear heard, nor the heart of man conceived, what God has prepared for those who love him", God has revealed to us through the Spirit. For the Spirit searches everything, even the depths of God. For what person knows a man's thoughts except the spirit of the man that is in him? So also no one comprehends the thoughts of God except the Spirit of God. Now we have received not the spirit of the world but the Spirit that is from God, that we might understand the gifts bestowed on us by God (1 Cor 2:9–12).

Christians are accustomed to understanding the beginning of this passage as applying to eternal life in the world beyond, but what Paul means is eternal life here and now, which begins with Pentecost. We have entered into God's inner space, as it were, into his eternal self-awareness, in which he knows himself and is familiar with his depths and mysteries; we have entered into God's inner subjectivity, which in reality is a threefold intersubjectivity: a single spirit life shared by the divine hypostases in a single Godhead. Moreover this is the ambience in which the creature endowed with grace is privileged to live. And while not yet "beholding" but existing in the mode of "believing", the creature's understanding of itself and its own being is radically changed: now it may and can think with God's thoughts, just as it may and can love with God's love. The graphic term used for this, namely, "infused virtue", as it were, "the ability and capacity poured in through a funnel", expresses it clearly enough.

No one who has had this entry into God's inner realm opened up to him has any right, henceforth, to complain that he cannot grasp faith, that it is "too high" or "too hard" for him, whether in terms of understanding or of practical application. No one may act as if it depended on his own efforts, for in reality any ability he has is a gift, and any suggestion to the contrary is unfaith and ingratitude. God has put the instrument into our hands as well as the skill to manipulate it: Is it asking too much to require us to work with it?

But what have we to understand; what is to be done? Something entirely mysterious, we might think, something positively arcane, particularly when we read how Paul continues:

> And we impart this in words not taught by human wisdom but taught by the Spirit, interpreting spiritual truths to those who possess the Spirit. The unspiritual man does not receive the gifts of the Spirit of God, for they are folly to him, and he is not able to understand them because they are spiritually discerned. The spiritual man judges all things but is himself to be judged by no one (1 Cor 2:13–15).

Does that not sound as if Christianity is a kind of secret teaching, an esoteric club, firmly preventing any unauthorized person from taking it upon himself to enter and speak and act as if he understood what the initiated are about? We cannot deny it: Paul's incisive words clearly demonstrate the stumbling block, namely, that Christianity is not some common or garden truism; it is not something on which anyone can speak with authority even if he is uninvolved in it. Only the person who has entered into the inner realm, the *arcanum* (that is, who shares in the unity of faith and love), can understand. All worldly wisdom crumbles at this point: all that it has to say from the outside is necessarily inadequate, necessarily wrong. For no one can "conceive", not even by accident, what goes on in God's interiority: " 'For who has known the mind of the Lord so as to instruct him?' But we have the mind of Christ" (1 Cor 2:16).

All the same the mystery of Pentecost is not a closed mystery; it is not the mystery of a sect or a conventicle. On the contrary, it is a mystery of opening and making available to all. Thus the Apostles endowed with the Spirit go out and preach in all languages to all peoples. Thus on that day around three thousand people are converted, in spite of mockery and opposition. God's manifestation is addressed not to a few chosen ones but strictly and literally to all. The "few" who perceive that God's realm is open to them are only chosen so that they shall announce their insight to the others. The Church on earth *is* this opening, this openness of God to the world; she is the place where this opening takes place and becomes a known reality. If others are to know of it too, however, Christians must step forth from this inner realm as pure and clean as from a bath, their features shining with the sun that has irradiated them, their souls full of the music they have heard in heaven. They must be this opening of heaven for others. They must manifest something of that "effulgence of glory" (Heb 1:3) that the Son reflected from the Father. This radiance might only be the strangeness of the spiritual person whom no one understands, but it is not the sectarian huckstering of mysteries for their own sake. It is the fathomless scope of a love that does not ask why, does not count and calculate, and that represents a constant puzzle to the man of this world.

Trinity

God Is "Being With"

One by one the Church celebrates the great, world-transforming deeds that God has done for us. One by one the believer makes them his own, until at last he may raise his eyes to the blinding mystery of light whence all these shafts of radiance come. Nothing in creation or in Christianity can be understood apart from this mystery, the mystery of the divine Trinity, which is always presupposed; now, however, it is made the object of explicit reflection, praise and worship. Today's feast joins the others, not as the recalling of some particular, recondite mystery that needs to be brought to mind once a year but as the sum of them all—Christmas, Good Friday, Easter, Ascension, Pentecost—finally allowing us to see together, in a unity, what up to now we saw as a colorful spectrum of broken light.

The recurring meaning of all the feasts was "God with us"; but how could God be with us if the word *with* were not part and parcel of his own being and life? If this were not the case, however we might try to utter profound truths about a relationship between God and the world, between unity and multiplicity, between the absolute and the relative, we should never arrive at the intimacy of a "with" such as is affirmed by Christian faith and Christian living.

We can see this even from the primary datum of the *creation*. We may hold fast to creation—and refuse to accept that the multiplicity of things is a tragic lapse from some original unity, into which the supposed individualities should redissolve as soon as possible—like the Book of Genesis, we may acknowledge a Creator and Lord who is able to create a real world, a world that is "very good"; but even then we must ask ourselves whether there is not something unfulfilled and unfulfillable in this abiding dichotomy between the Almighty in heaven and created man on earth—however much contact there may be between them, as the making of the Covenant subsequently reveals. This comes unequivocally to light in orthodox Islam, which abhors any idea of a Trinity in God but for that very reason fails to attain to any ultimate regard for the created person. Judaism, by contrast, on the basis of the Covenant, became aware of adumbrations, inchoate forms, of God's triune life: thus God can send his divine word into the world so effectively that it does not return to him without bringing the fruit it has borne in the world (Is 55:10ff.). He can pour out his Spirit, his wisdom that indwells all creatures, into the whole of created reality, so that this Spirit may be in things without losing its divine nature (Wis 7–8). Late Judaism went even further and accepted that God's presence in creation was able to suffer along with the latter; that God's presence could go into exile along with Israel, with the result that, as it were, God was separated from God. But could this idea be seriously followed through without introducing a kind of tragic hiatus in God's unity or else reducing it to a pure metaphor, inapplicable to reality?

In other words, if God is to be truly with man, is not more required: Must he not suffer along with sinful man, alienated from God? Must not God become man? And would not such an Incarnation mean that the God who was together with men, in the dimension of time, would somehow have to stand *over against* the God who cannot leave his eternity and glory without ceasing to be God? It is in Jesus Christ that we first discern this "over against", and if we take his Godhead seriously (and how could a mere man claim to be the Word of God, how could he bear the sin of the world?), it presupposes some distinction within God himself. It presupposes a reciprocity that, far from vitiating the unity of the Divine Being, actually gives God his overflowing vitality. Moreover, if this reciprocity in God is not to show the least suggestion of tragic unfulfillment on the one hand or "mutual egoism" on the other, it must (without canceling itself out) be overtaken by a higher unity where love meets love, and for this, revelation can find no other term but "Holy Spirit". In the life of eternity, the Holy Spirit is the fulfillment of reciprocity, of "being with": he both presupposes it eternally (and thus does not obliterate it) and demonstrates it positively (in the mutual interrelationship of the distinct and "other" Persons).

Whether it is aware of it or not, creation lives by the mystery of this reciprocity in God. The very fact that creation exists is a manifestation of this mystery: creation is "the other" over against God. It is good that there is this "other", for it is eternally good that there is "another" in God; and this "other" does not separate but, in the Spirit, unites the two and fills them with life. So we need not lament the fact that we are not God, that we are eternally separated from him by the chasm of our creaturely nature; for *because* we are "other" than he, we can be his image. More than that, we are destined for a union with him that is inconceivably profound—deeper than any pantheism can imagine—precisely because it does not obliterate the difference between him and us. For that same reason the difference between the creatures themselves, and the fact that, in all their modes of union, they remain "themselves", can be held to be "very good"; even in the world of living things the union of things that are different and distinct brings forth the mystery of fruitfulness, not only in the sexual area but in every genuinely loving encounter in other areas too.

Only on the basis of the divine Trinity can there be something like *grace*. Grace is a "participation in the divine nature", which does not destroy the difference between God and man. Multiplicity could not participate inwardly in a monolithic One, in spite of all that the Platonists tell us: they feel something of the reality and necessity of this participation, but, with their presuppositions, they can never reach it. For the multiplicity, the mere "One" remains an inadequate yonder realm. God can only communicate himself, his inner life, if such distributing and communing are of the essence of his own life, that is, if God is "being for another" and in such an absolute sense that, in him, the Three do not stand over against each other, each subsequently communicating something of himself to the others: here these Three are themselves the fruit of such communicating. He in God whom we call "Father" is the "fruit" of his self-giving to the One we call "Son"; he exists as this self-giving, and the Son exists as receptivity, gratitude and giving-in-return. Again, this giving-in-return does not close the Two in on themselves but opens them to the fullness of the "with" (the "co-" of "communion"), which is made absolute in the Spirit who is common to both. Only in this perspective does grace become intelligible. The Father can give us the Son to be "with" us at a human level—the Son's eternal proceeding from the Father is continued in the dimension of time—but when the Son takes us with him into his communion ("being with") with the Father, he does so in a way that opens us to the cascading stream of life of the absolute "With", namely, the Holy Spirit. "If you knew the gift of God. . . . Whoever drinks of the water that I shall give him will never thirst; the water that I shall give him will become in him a spring of water welling up to eternal life" (Jn 4:10, 14). God is not a sealed fortress, to be attacked and seized by our engines of war (ascetic practices, meditative techniques, and the like) but a house full of open doors, through which we are invited to walk. In the Castle of the Three-in-One, the plan has always been that we, those who are entirely "other", shall participate in the superabundant communion of life. Whatever we regard as the ultimate meaning of human life, be it giving, creating, finding or being given, being created and being found; all this is fulfilled in the original prototype: in the life of the eternal "With".

However, the whole tragedy of the *alienation* that exists between God and us, the tragedy of sin and the sinner's inability to return to God by his own power, is undergirded by the Father's sending of his Son to be "with" us, even to the extent of being "with" us in our separation from God. Here the Apostle makes liberal use of the vital word *with*: we suffer *with* Christ, we are crucified *with* him, we die *with* him, to be raised *with* him and taken up into heaven *with* him. Thus Christian ethics means rejoicing *with* those who rejoice, weeping *with* those who weep, simply "being with" all those *with* whom God is. The fact that we did not want to be *with* the Son but crucified him is taken by our redeeming God and used in a deeper context, namely, that the Son took upon himself our refusal to be with him: he was "with" us in this very form. At this point the sinner's imagination must surely be exhausted; he is left breathless.

We have contemplated all these mysteries of creation, grace, redemption and our return to God as the Church's year unfolds. Now we have before us the presupposition that underlies them all. At the root of all being whatsoever there is the mystery of an interplay that both presupposes and actually produces a "being with". Indeed, being itself is nothing other than this mystery. It is the origin and end of everything that participates—however fleetingly and superficially—in being. Each of us, therefore, must join our voices in that ceaseless cry of the seraph in Isaiah, which reechoes through the Book of Revelation: "Holy, holy, holy, is the Lord God Almighty, who was and is and is to come! The whole earth is full of his glory."

Corpus Christi

Flesh Becomes Word

Today Catholics are celebrating a feast called Corpus Christi (in German, *Fronleichnam*). What does this strange, obscure word mean? *Vrôn* means "concerning the (divine or secular) Lord, belonging or consecrated to the Lord"; *Leichnam* means "body". So it means "the Lord's body", the sacred body of Jesus Christ. And that is what we are celebrating.

It is worthwhile reflecting on how strange it is to celebrate a body. It is primitive, archaic, something that goes back, perhaps, to the dawn of time. Is not the whole thrust of our civilization directed toward seeking salvation in the spiritual dimension, in the spirit's creative powers, its discoveries and projects? Is not everything moving in the direction of the spirit and the intellect, which, through research, is becoming more and more master of the body, able to look after it, operate on it and mend it like a machine that is to be oiled and repaired when necessary? Does not man increasingly understand the workings of this machine, which is losing more and more of its mystery? And does not man's "spirit"—the *really* mysterious factor—look down on the body/machine in almost the same way as it looks down on the perfectly functioning automobile and locomotive that man has built? Nowadays the body is secularized, functionalized, desacralized. Or is it? Is not the converse true? Is it not the spirit of modern man that has desacralized itself and made itself into a tool in the service of technology and now sees everything, the body included, through these particular spectacles? Surely what remains an impenetrably sealed mystery is the very fact that the spirit inhabits a body and is somehow dependent on that body? Who has ever explained why a man weeps when he is sad, smiles when he is happy, or, when making an agreement with someone, holds out his hand and looks into the other's eyes? Quite plainly, if the spirit is to express what is most essential to it, it must descend into its own flesh; this is something it finds both humiliating and rapturous, and in such moments its flesh is by no means a mere machine but a friend and an intimately related medium. Through the flesh, the spirit gets to know and savor the most precious and priceless things in life, be they joyful or sorrowful, experienced in solitude or in community with others.

Of course, our bodies are also working tools, instruments for maintaining life and coming to grips with it. But the flesh is far more. It is the path we continually tread as we relate with the world around us, from the most external and superficial contact, like offering someone a piece of fruit, to the most interior and fundamental relationship (as in sexual intercourse), which overwhelms us and exceeds our comprehension. And how many intermediate stages there are! All instances of intercourse between men—from the thoughtless, conventional performance of the most profound, symbolic actions to the ability to impart a miraculously personal character to actions that seem to be quite ordinary (a simple greeting or "goodbye", or the gentle touch of a hand)—can say more than whole volumes. Lending one's own body is one ultimate way of giving: by stepping in with our own body we can spare someone a laborious walk or a tiring journey; we can put up with a thrashing for someone else or, under certain circumstances, give our life for him. In this kind of giving the body is not just a useful tool; it is the only way we have of expressing our mind; thanks to the body's part, our intentions do not remain mere pious wishes but become active deeds. And, each time, it means that the spirit must descend from its proud, solitary height; that is precisely what produces the aspect of rapture. It is as if our way out to freedom is not in the very top story but down below, on the ground floor.

And now the feast has arrived. At Christmas the theme was

"God's Word has become flesh." Flesh, of course, means man. But man, in turn, really does mean flesh. "The Word has become Spirit"—that would be of no use to us. The Word can only really give himself to us in the form of flesh. What God has to say to us, he now says in bodily terms, with his flesh and blood. It follows, then, that this flesh and blood is a genuine communication, a word, a gift, a handing over of a very special kind, since it is a divine handing over. When Christians celebrate the Lord's Supper and receive the Eucharist, they often think no further than flesh and blood and forget that "the *Word* became flesh". They forget that what they are receiving is a word addressed to them from God. It is the most profound word possible, a word that is so all-embracing, so full of meaning, that it transcends our comprehension. It is a word that resembles expressions of genuine human self-giving in that it is a bodily word, a word bodily performed. But it is also a word that goes beyond all human self-giving and makes the impossible possible, that is, to give itself, himself, to me as an entire body, as flesh and blood.

It is easy to say "I love you". We need to prove it. The deeds that demonstrate our words are always bodily deeds. We do something for the beloved person; we take pains, go out of our way, give up some of our time. This is often a better proof than the sexual presents people give each other, for these, where men are concerned, are often nothing but veiled egoism, mutual self-seeking, and they need the other, soberly undertaken acts if they are to be inwardly purified and shown to be selfless. In interpersonal love too, therefore, the word must become flesh in order to manifest its truth.

Naturally, this love is bound to come up against the boundaries that will always separate us in this world: in spite of all means of communication, each man remains an island. Each soul has its own consciousness and cannot fuse with another; bodies can only touch externally. That is how we are: we are finite; we are not gods. Only God's Word, who became flesh and dwelt among us, only the infinite and limitless Word, can bring about the miracle of being in bodily form and yet transcending these boundaries: "Take, eat; this is my Body. Drink; this is my Blood." Take into yourselves what seems only to exist side by side with you; and just as I can transcend the boundaries, so let your boundaries disintegrate by taking me into yourselves. It is not that your self-awareness should dissolve into mine; you must not think that you are to become I. But, in me, God's Word-Made-Flesh, you are destined to be freed from your narrow confines to lead a new life, together with others and shared with them, a life of *communio*, a life as befits members of my body, nourished by the circulating blood of my all-embracing life.

This is God's offer to us today. It strikes us as baffling, perhaps even embarrassing, like an infringement of the sacrosanct sphere of our "I" that no one is supposed to invade. We have to put up with so much interference from outside; people ought at least to leave our inner life alone. But let us be clear that this need to be left alone by God is completely nonsensical. We would not even exist if we were not already in God from the very beginning. "In him we live and move and have our being", as the Apostle says. He is more interior to us than we are to ourselves, and if it is true that each person, in his interior space, is unique and solitary, it is only because each one is a unique "image and likeness" of the unique and sole God. Otherwise individuality would be something tragic and inconsolable. Now the Christian Faith tells us that God's solitariness does not mean that he is eternally closed in on himself, brooding upon himself. Eternally, he experiences a life of loving intercourse: from the very beginning the Word was in God, the Son was in the bosom of the Father, one with him in the communion of the Holy Spirit. There is an eternal harmony between solitariness and life in common. The Eternally-One is this: mutual interpenetration in a loving self-abandonment and self-surrender that exceed all that we can imagine. Therefore our "I" is always bathed in this all-embracing life; to close ourselves off is to go against the very law of being that underpins us.

How can we say such extravagant things? Certainly not on

the basis of some speculation or as a result of the mystical experiences of high-flying individuals, whoever they might be. We are empowered to say these things solely and exclusively because of the sober facts of the destiny of Jesus Christ. He proclaims himself to be the divine Father's Word to the world and proves this claim through his complete obedience to God and his total self-surrender to and for the world. Love, as we have said, is only proved by deeds of flesh and blood. Here the deed consists in the body of Jesus being broken as he suffers for all the world's sin and in his blood being poured out for all the world's self-asserting egoists. This pulverizing, atomizing of the bodily form takes place for our sake; it takes place within us, flooding past the defensive dams our egoism has raised.

Whether we will or no, God is always the milieu in which we live, move and have our being. In the liquefied body of his incarnate Word he invades us, to liberate us from our supposed loneliness and isolation and bring us back into his community. Thus (and only thus) he fits us for genuine community among our fellowmen. This is the purpose and work of the Lord's body, Corpus Christi, the bodily Word.

By Water, Blood and Spirit

What are we celebrating today? The answer is to be found in the Gospel—a simple, clear answer, in the words of Christ: "Take, eat; this is my Body", and "Unless you eat the Flesh of the Son of Man and drink his Blood, you have no life in you." These are tremendous and solemn words, and it is obvious that there are only two alternatives: either we accept them as they are and give up trying to understand how such a thing might be possible, or we must reject them as intolerable, as the Jews and many disciples did. We should not let ourselves be diverted from these words by secondary (and fundamentally insoluble) issues, such as *how* this is supposed to take place, *how* we can believe that what seems to be bread and wine, as it was before, is now the bodily reality of Jesus Christ. Natural reason can give no answer here; therefore we should take another route right from the outset, namely, the route indicated by the New Testament and by the Bible as a whole.

Even in the Old Testament God offers man an inconceivably intimate relationship with him. Just think of the image of conjugal union employed by Hosea, Jeremiah and Ezekiel. God, the All-Holy, wishes to join himself to the continually unfaithful and adulterous Israel, as if to a prostitute. For the word of God contained and proclaimed by the law and the prophets is not some splinter from an unapproachable God: it is God himself, with all his fullness of life, his sublimity and humiliation, his faithfulness that commits him for eternity. He involved himself amazingly closely with Abraham and the patriarchs, then at Sinai with the entire nation, with this unreliable partner. We might almost say he got entangled with Israel for good or ill, although, in doing so, he did not forfeit anything of his sublimity and his freedom to judge. The conjugal union signifies the most intimate communication of one's self, in a way that is creative and generative; new life, and in this case divine life, is brought into being and takes shape in the receptive womb and in cooperation with it.

The Fourth Evangelist sums up the being of Jesus in this formula: God's Word has become flesh. Flesh means the concrete man: toilsome, constantly under threat, consecrated to certain death. It is in this form, which signifies the fulfillment of God's humiliation hitherto and is, in a certain sense, its fruit, that the ultimate union between God and man is to take place. This union is announced in the combination of God's Word and human flesh and blood, but it is intended to stretch out from this beginning to embrace humanity as a whole. At the end of the Bible it is designated the "marriage of the Lamb" and his Bride.

Thus Jesus' whole life, his words, his work and suffering,

are under the banner of his "for us". This is how God offers himself to us, insistently and more concretely than we can ever grasp. For Jesus is always both things at once: the man who, in all that he is and does, makes plain the nature of God, and the man through whom God makes himself plain. When Jesus works miracles he shows not only his own power but God's power as well. When he teaches, he puts forward not only his own human wisdom but, in and through it, God's wisdom. But since the Word became flesh in him, he bears witness to God not only by words and deeds but essentially also by his whole physical and spiritual being. Thus he can offer his whole existence as "the bread of life; he who comes to me shall not hunger, and he who believes in me shall never thirst . . . every one who sees the Son and believes in him shall have eternal life" (Jn 6:35, 40). He goes on, shortly afterward, while, at the Jewish Feast of Tabernacles, the great libation—the pouring out of water from Siloam—is being celebrated: "If any one thirst, let him come to me and drink. He who believes in me, as the Scripture has said, 'Out of his heart shall flow rivers of living water' " (Jn 7:37f.). Just as, in Ezekiel's vision, the river of divine life flows forth from the renewed Temple, so now, from the body of Jesus, which he himself described as the true, new Temple, the waters of the Holy Spirit flow forth, eternally satisfying those who thirst.

Words such as these, however, in reference both to the bread of life and the springs of water, are uttered in the mode of promise, as the Evangelist explicitly says; they can only be fulfilled when the Word's entire Incarnation has been achieved in death, when the side of the dead Savior is pierced and blood and water flow out. Now "it is accomplished". Everything comes together here to form an inseparable whole: Jesus' self-offering in the Upper Room: "Take, eat and drink; this is my Flesh that is given for you, my Blood that is shed for you"; his death on the Cross, which takes place through us and for us; and the Resurrection on the third day, when God makes this surrendered body into a spiritual, eternally living body that can be infinitely shared out; all this is an indivisible whole. It is this same indivisible whole that John means when he says that Jesus, the incarnate Word of God, has come in water, blood and Spirit, and that these three are one. We drink the living wellspring of God's grace from his body, his Flesh and Blood, which is not dead, historical flesh and blood of two thousand years ago but a here-and-now, living Spirit, poured into Christianity so that it can bear witness to the living God.

All this forms a unity, and no stone can be pulled from this wall without causing the whole edifice to collapse. If Jesus Christ is not the incarnate Word of Yahweh but merely, for instance, the last of the prophets or the purely human vice-regent of God, Corpus Christi, the Feast of the Lord's Body, the Feast of the Eucharist, has no meaning whatsoever. If that were the case, we could certainly be edified by his words and deeds, but what good would his Flesh and Blood be to us? The Jews quite naturally wonder what they are being asked to believe: "Is not this Jesus, the son of Joseph, whose father and mother we know? . . . How can this man give us his flesh to eat?" (Jn 6:42, 52). I too would decline if I were offered the flesh of just any son of Joseph—and the only alternative would be some trivial, vague symbolism in which bread and wine would signify something quite different from what they are.

The Bible displays an amazing and shocking realism, both as regards the divine Sonship of Jesus and as regards his Eucharist. Paul pushes this realism to its ultimate conclusion when insisting that the Corinthians examine themselves to see whether they understand what "eating and drinking" mean here. For if they fail to discern the Body and Blood of Christ, they could "eat and drink judgment upon themselves" (1 Cor 11:29), and the Apostle believes that things that have happened in the community go to show that this is in fact the case.

This is a divine kind of realism: in his Corpus Christi gift God is much more real, much more concrete, than we can imagine. It is a pneumatic realism, for God's Holy Spirit, in his nature and his workings and his creativity, is much more real, much more concrete, than our spirit. Thus the two truths can stand side by side, equally valid: "Unless you eat the Flesh of the Son of Man and drink his Blood, you have no life in you", and "It is the Spirit that gives life; the flesh is of no avail." The bodily Lord is also, equally, the spiritual Lord. Only in this way is he the concreteness of the God who is truth.

Spirit and body cannot be separated in the living man. A man's body is permeated, right into its unconscious regions, by a single soul; it is organized with a view to human totality. Man does not have several souls, a few subspiritual souls with a spiritual soul over them. Thus the converse is true, and full of consequences: the body's organization has an influence on the spirit; it enables it to operate and function consciously and freely; this is strikingly clear from many forms of illness. And even if the spirit can move and exert its power far beyond the limited space occupied by its body, it cannot do so without a material substratum, whether we call this an "astral body" or something else. For the most part, individual men communicate with one another without realizing that their *spiritual* communion always takes place on the basis of their mutual communication in the same *matter*.

If we accept that the formula so often used by Paul, "in Christ Jesus", is not a mere pious phrase but, as he himself understands it, expresses the profoundest reality of our Faith, would it be possible to live together merely in the Spirit of Jesus and communicate in this Spirit without at the same time participating together in his body? This is utterly inconceivable if we take the Incarnation of the Word of God seriously. If it were only a question of Jesus' Spirit, the latter would soon fade to a vague "attitude", "approach" or "way of thinking", as happens in all liberal Christianity; and this "attitude", in turn, would quickly become a merely human attitude, with Jesus as an ethical model. No. The true and living Christ is the risen Christ, who, as before, is both body and Spirit. He fills the Church (and through her, the universe) equally powerfully through his corporality and through his Spirit. Only if we take

Corpus Christi seriously can we speak of the Church as the mystical body of Christ and of a "cosmic Christ", of whom the Letter to the Colossians says that "in him the whole fullness of Deity dwells bodily" and that "in him all things were created, in heaven and on earth . . . all things were created through him and for him."

Through the Year

Divine Freedom from Anxiety

"Beware of covetousness!" says Jesus when someone tries to get him to arbitrate in a dispute over an inheritance. "For a man's life does not consist in the abundance of his possessions." Thereupon he tells the Parable of the Rich Man, who, having had a great harvest, sees that his barns are too small to store it. What shall he do? He decides to pull them down and build bigger ones. " 'And I will say to my soul, Soul, you have ample goods laid up for many years; take your ease, eat, drink, be merry.' But God said to him, 'Fool! This night your soul is required of you; and the things you have prepared, whose will they be?' So is he who lays up treasure for himself, and is not rich toward God" (Lk 12:13–21).

In his own way, this man does what everyone is urged to do nowadays, that is, to look ahead, make provision for his old age, arrange for all kinds of pensions and insurances, not least in order not to be a burden on the state and on society. Society has introduced and regulated this whole insurance system so that it and its citizens shall be protected as well as possible against all risks and eventualities. The individual regards this not only as a virtue but also as his duty as a citizen, and the pundits and futurologists urge us to apply this concern to a wider field: we must consider the future of the world's economy and calculate as precisely as possible how long the raw materials will last and with what we must begin to replace them; how man should husband his entire environment; how far, in the long run, particular technological achievements will be of benefit to mankind or will be harmful, and so on. There has never been so much planning for the future as there is today, when nature is no longer (as in earlier times) something inexhaustible, unchangeable and given, but is a reservoir that man has learned to administer and that, in his own interest, he must use with rationality and thrift. At the same time, however, the irrationality of the future was probably never so plainly visible as in this same age of technology. In case our enemies continue to build up their offensive resources, we have filled the world with explosives that may blow sky-high the entire future we have planned for ourselves, not tomorrow, but today. We think we are in control of this powder keg, but who knows who may get his hands on it tomorrow and accidentally light the fuse. We can calculate how many traffic accidents there will be, on average, next year and the year after in New York, but we cannot be certain whether New York will still be there next year or the year after.

God is now even more justified in saying, "Fool!" to the whole of mankind: "This night your life [= soul] is required of you", perhaps the life of the entire human race. Thus all pensions and insurances are superfluous. The more prudent our approach to the future, the more its folly becomes manifest. The cleverer we become, the more stupid we are.

Is there a way to stop this constant spiraling? One thing is certain: the man who sees the increasing threat posed by increasing folly cannot hope to seize hold of the spokes of the wheel and so bring world events to a standstill. The Gospel, however, points us in another direction, one that, from the worldly, economic and political point of view, seems to have nothing to offer and yet in the long run is the only way out of the insane cycle of power, the escalation of the arms race and the vying for prestige.

"Fool!" says God, "everything you have amassed for yourself will be required of you"—much earlier than you thought —"this very night", because you have stored up treasure for yourself and are not "rich toward God".

What does it mean, "rich toward God"? First let us say what it certainly does not mean. It does not mean laying up for oneself spiritual treasure in God. That would be the very covetousness Jesus condemns, albeit transferred to another area. There are Christians who, in their fear of God and his judgment, fashion, as it were, a fireproof cloak for themselves out of good works, in order to be protected against the flames of judgment. They even base their attitude on the Lord's word: "Lay up for yourselves treasure in heaven, where neither moth nor rust consumes and where thieves do not break in and steal" (Mt 6:20). But the only treasure worth anything in heaven is love, and it is written that love "seeketh not her own" (1 Cor 13:5). In other words, love cannot store up anything for itself. It consists, in fact, in the opposite movement, not storing up but giving away. And the more it gives away and becomes poor, the richer it becomes toward God. Why? Because God himself is Love, pure and simple, and his entire wealth consists in self-giving and self-emptying.

Let us reflect on this for a moment. Certainly the Christian God, as the revelation of Jesus Christ shows him to us, is almighty, and so he is infinitely rich. But what form does his infinite wealth take? God the Father, the origin of everything, gives away himself and all that he is and has to his only-begotten Son, who in turn does not store up all this treasure within himself but acknowledges it as the Father's gift and returns it to him; these Two by no means stay enclosed in a kind of mutual egoism but, in mutual selflessness, cause the Holy Spirit to proceed from them, the Spirit of absolute love, the epitome of eternal wealth in this unceasing exchange of gifts. Even though *God's triune nature* remains a profound mystery, we can grasp this: in God, wealth and power are not qualities existing side by side with love and external to it; they are identical with it. God only *has* insofar as he *gives*, and this giving is of his innermost essence. Arianism, the first great heresy that had to be countered by a general Council, held that the primary God, the Father, was first and foremost for himself and only subsequently brought forth a Son. The Church rejected this energetically and once for all. God is never first and foremost for himself: from all eternity he is there for the Other. God only exists as Father in his eternal act of self-surrender to the Son. This is his whole wealth, his whole power. We cannot imagine it, and yet it is so: in God, self-emptying and self-impoverishment coincide with self-being and richness. In man the act of generation is only a contingent expression of his being. In God the paternal act of generating the Son coincides with the Father's Person, the Son's receiving of himself from the Father and owing himself to the Father coincides with *his* Person and the reciprocal self-surrender of Father and Son coincides with the Person of the Spirit.

We get some intimation of this mystery and paradox as we contemplate the *life and work of Jesus*. He lives only for the Father and the Father's purpose, namely, the salvation of men. He does not have some private sphere apart from this; he does not take furlough from the task he has been given. "The foxes have holes, but the Son of man has nowhere to lay his head": this is meant in a spiritual sense at least equally as much as in a material sense. He has nowhere, not even on the Cross, where he hangs, as Mediator, between heaven and earth. Because and insofar as he has given everything away—his flesh and blood given as food and drink for mankind, his Spirit (which he only possesses together with the Father) given to the world—he, the Risen One, the eternally Living One, can be given "all power in heaven and on earth".

Modern thinkers have often distinguished between *having* and *being*, rejecting *having* in favor of *being*. But in Christian terms there must be a further distinction with regard to *being*: I can have nothing and still want to *be* for myself; and I can discard my own self in such a way that what I have or have not is a matter of complete indifference, since nothing belongs to me anyway. Perhaps it is a blessing to have much, for then one has more to give away and be of benefit to others. This applies to both material and spiritual goods.

It is the man who does not dwell on his own being but uses it for God and for the sake of his fellowmen who is "rich" in the gospel sense. Thérèse of Lisieux understood this very well: she often said that she did not want to amass any store of merit in heaven; she wanted to hand it all over to God right from the start, for him to use and distribute as seemed good to him. She wanted to appear before God's judgment throne unencumbered by any personal baggage; to go through heaven's customs, as it were, with an empty suitcase; to float around as light as a feather even while on earth; to give up any notion of her own importance. There is nothing Buddhist-like about this in her case; she does not regard her own "I" as a prison and seek to renounce it in order to enter a personless nirvana; on the contrary, her personal "I", which is loved and affirmed by God, allows itself to be taken over by God entirely and is full of gratitude when it is used, and used up, for God's purposes. Thérèse loved to pull flowers apart for God's glory, not to destroy their beauty but to transform them, as it were, into something fluid, something dedicated to a higher purpose.

Does not this childlike symbol (which has a certain helpless naïveté about it) point to Christ's sublime self-dismemberment? His great farewell discourse in John, which is in fact nothing other than the Eucharist put into words, is very like a dismembering of divine-human love in the way a flower is pulled apart, petal by petal. The more it comes to pieces, the more its form is seen to be a unity; the poorer it becomes, the more its inexhaustible fullness, its divine wealth, becomes apparent.

Every celebration of the Eucharist ought to assimilate us more and more to the Lord's mind and heart as we see them here. This is the only way to change the world and calm the fear of tomorrow and the day after; it is the only way to render our corporal and social works of mercy fruitful in terms of spirit and soul and give them a meaning that transcends all the problems always associated with our social and charitable efforts. The two mites given by the poor widow (see Mk 12:41–44 and Lk 21:1–4) caused Jesus great amazement: to think that such an act was possible—and is continually possible—in this world that is ceaselessly amassing treasure for itself! Without knowing it or wanting to know, she was "rich toward God". No one ever took the Lord's command "Do not be anxious about tomorrow" more literally than she did, for without any reflection she dropped all her meager savings into the offering box, probably without even wondering how she would find a piece of bread the following morning. In all probability she did not feel that what she did involved any risk, even less, that it was a challenge to God to look after her when tomorrow came.

There has always been this lightness of heart in the lives of the saints, enabling them to trust simply to providence. In his autobiography, Ignatius Loyola tells that when, in Barcelona, he had embarked on a ship for Italy he found that he still had a little money in his pocket; so, since he had made it his practice to lay everything in God's hand, he got out of the ship again and gave his few remaining coins to a beggar. There have been and still are great institutes, some of them existing for centuries, like the Piccola Casa della Providenza in Turin and others, that look after great numbers of the poor, the sick and children without any financial capital at all: whenever they need anything, some truck drives up with the necessary goods. To the average Christian such an attitude seems reckless; it seems to tempt God. But I think that Jesus had this very kind of thing in mind when he said, "Therefore do not be anxious about tomorrow, for tomorrow will be anxious for itself. Let the day's own trouble be sufficient for the day." "Your heavenly Father knows that you need all these things" (Mt 6:34, 32). He himself manifested a supreme lack of anxiety, allowed people to invite him for meals—no doubt a frequent occurrence—and had nowhere to call his own home; he let someone look after the money knowing that he would misappropriate it; he paid the Temple tax and had enough to give alms; and he requires this same lack of anxiety of his disciples: "Sell all that you have and distribute to the poor" (Lk 18:22). "Do not be anxious, saying, 'What shall we eat?' or 'What shall we drink?' or 'What shall we wear?' For the gentiles seek all these things" (Mt 6:31–32).

Lord, what miserable disciples we are. Give us, we pray, some of the freedom from anxiety in which you entrusted yourself to your Father, concerned only to do his will and carry out your great mission on earth. We trust that you will also give us whatever we need in order to do your will. Amen.

The Tireless Word

In today's Gospel the disciples return from a missionary journey and tell Jesus all they have done.

> And he said to them, "Come away by yourselves to a lonely place, and rest a while." For many were coming and going, and they had no leisure even to eat. And they went away in the boat to a lonely place by themselves. Now many saw them going and knew them, and they ran there on foot from all the towns, and got there ahead of them. As he landed he saw a great throng, and he had compassion on them, because they were like sheep without a shepherd; and he began to teach them many things (Mk 6:31–34).

There are two opposite movements here: Jesus and his disciples want to take a break; they have worked more than enough and they need rest and seclusion in order to recollect themselves and be refreshed. The other factor is the multitude: not only are people so demanding that the disciples are left no time even to take a meal; they are even overtaken and prevented from having their planned time of quiet. Jesus has no choice but to continue to minister to the crowd; he has to work overtime. Tiredness is of no account in the face of such tireless seeking. Did he come into the world to rest, to make a clear distinction, like a comfortable citizen, between work and recreation? Or was it not rather to work himself to the bone until all his strength is exhausted?

The field of work allotted to him is vast. His task was to search for the lost sheep of the house of Israel, who had no shepherd, and bring them back home to the starting point, that is, to the nation's intimate relationship with its Covenant Lord. This was sealed "in a lonely desert place" where there was nothing else but God and the chosen people he loved, swearing faithfulness to him. "Thus says the Lord, I remember the devotion of your youth, your love as a bride, how you followed me in the wilderness. . . ." Israel was "holy to the Lord, the firstfruits of his harvest" (Jer 2:1–2). But was there ever such a time? Did not the people dance around the Golden Calf even then and engage in wanton behavior, rising up against God and Moses? Is not Jesus' task of reconstituting an ideal Covenant (which never existed) pure utopia? And will this not be evident soon enough, when the so-called shepherds of the nation, the realists and politicians, reject what he is trying to do as illegitimate? The result will be that this utopian, although he gave his all, will end in disgrace and ruin. Or perhaps we should say that his ruin, which was always imminent and came more and more into focus as his life proceeded, was finally and definitively manifested.

Jesus has compassion on this crowd of sheep without real shepherds that runs after him, searching, instinctively drawn to him, in such numbers that he cannot escape them. Did any crowd of men ever look any different? They run this way and that after anyone who professes to show the way, anyone who claims to be a leader or a savior. "And they will say to you, 'Lo, there!' and 'Lo, here!' Do not go, do not follow them" (Lk 17:23). But people will always follow, whether the one they follow is a star athlete, a political hero or a guru.

Never have there been so many movements as there are

now, in our time. Never have there been so many sects, from California to Russia, testifying to a religious unrest among people, but also to an extreme loss of hope and direction. More and more vast "suburbs" are built "out in the country" around the religious core. And the single voice of the Teacher ("he began to teach them many things") splits into a thousand facets, splintering again and again and containing less and less of substance, although every leader of a sect volubly announces that wisdom's very core has been revealed to him. One hears the name of Jesus in most of these sects, now more in the center, now more on the periphery, but it is a name that remains, whereas the names of the other gurus fade away after a few years.

Jesus, however, will not allow himself to rest. The time for resting is already behind him, untouched, unsavored. The endless work he has to do with the shepherdless sheep, work he can never complete, instills a new strength into him: he can go on succoring the people when the countless other popular leaders have dropped behind and dropped out.

This is how the parties are arranged once and for all: on the one hand the immense multitude, leaderless, but driven by an instinct of unsatisfied yearning; and on the other hand the voice of the one Teacher, proclaiming things that are ultimately superhuman and that, from an earthly point of view, sound utopian. Fascinating, of course, but how can what he is talking about be lived and put into practice here and now?

Finally Jesus will send his disciples out among men with the commission to "teach them all that I have commanded you". They must not choose what they will teach or make accommodations; they must not leave out what is superhuman and utopian in Jesus' words. They must place Jesus' teaching before them as an undivided whole, in season or out of season. This is what Paul did, even if, in doing so, he exerted himself to render himself intelligible to the existing horizon of understanding, be it Jewish or gentile. He was very clearly aware that, unless they allowed themselves to be expanded in a

Christian direction, both vessels were too narrow for the gospel, which remains "a stumbling block to Jews and folly to Greeks". Both groups are stretched beyond the breaking point by this totality. Man as such, ordinary, natural, mortal, tired and comfortable man, is challenged beyond endurance by the truth of Jesus. Jesus himself, who needed rest, is stretched beyond the limit by his mission to proclaim the Good News. Paul, too, is stretched beyond the limit "in hunger and thirst, often without food, in cold and exposure. And, apart from other things, there is the daily pressure upon me of my anxiety for all the churches" (2 Cor 11:27–28).

Was it not the same for all who preached the undivided gospel? Look at all the great names, Basil, Chrysostom, Augustine, Thomas Aquinas or someone as different as Peter Claver (to name but a few): all were stretched far beyond the limit. They simply threw themselves into their apostolate (of which their prayer was part and parcel), into the great context that involved them, come what may. Ultimately it was not *they* who were at pains to promote the gospel but the gospel that took care of *them*. Sooner or later they will be brought down in their service of the gospel, but what do they care? They will simply fall into the very ground of the gospel, the Lord's Cross. Charles de Foucauld would have felt like this; so must Mother Teresa feel.

And it is this that draws people to figures such as these. Only in very few cases is it mere enthusiasm for a life of extraordinary dimensions; most people, looking at these figures, sense a secret call: you too should try, at least, to move in that direction. Let us forget these few names, however, and ask the question: What is it that draws us to such people, whoever they may be, good priests, perhaps, or ordinary, convinced laymen? And the answer is surely this: they have transcended themselves and adopted Jesus' concerns, without any techniques such as one learns from psychologists or gurus, simply because Jesus' total mind and approach have convinced them and taken possession of them, body and soul. They do not make a big fuss of having succeeded in forgetting themselves, of having united their little Atman with the great Brahman or of having broken through their egoistic "I" into their divinely filled self. None of that. Their mystery is entirely different. The call that Jesus addresses to them, the task he has in store for them, is so overpoweringly great that all that belongs to their own, private sphere automatically vanishes into it. Thus they do not *act* the part of disciples, let alone perfect disciples, for their mission has acquired absolute preeminence over their entire personality.

It may be that we do not often meet followers and commissioned disciples of Jesus who are thus overwhelmed by his word, by the incarnate Word of God; many complain that, in their entire lives, they have scarcely met one or two people who had this effect on them. "The laborers", says Jesus, "are few." Paul spells it out: "Many are self-seeking and their preaching is impure"; in with the word of God they mix their own word, for example, their know-all criticism or their currying favor with modernity in order to get a better hearing. In the long run, however, people see through such things. Even if the teaching is uttered from a lofty place, they will not listen anymore. For in the words of such "proclamation" they do not discern the original word, the word of Jesus himself.

Our Gospel speaks of Jesus alone teaching "many things" to the multitude who had followed him. The Apostles seem to be tired and to stay tired; once they have arrived at the proposed resting place there is no further mention of them. Jesus, however, who prior to this had been working hardest and no doubt was in greatest need of rest, continues to work unwearyingly. "My Father is working still," he says, "and I am working" (Jn 5:17). He goes on working after his death and Ascension, just as he did during his earthly days. He by no means works only through the words of Holy Scripture, like a poet or philosopher whose influence is continued posthumously through his writings: he works through his ever-living Spirit, transforming men's hearts and the world. He works through his Church, but he also works beyond the confines of the Church, for he is well able to walk through closed doors.

It would be correct to say that, for him, working and resting are one and the same. This is true of God, his Father, whom he represents on earth. He healed a sick man on the Sabbath, and, reproached on that account, he says, "My Father is working still", that is, even on the holy day on which he rested from the work of creation. So Jesus, too, can heal on the Sabbath. So the Christian, too, can be confident: provided he rests in God, in prayer, in meditation, in self-surrender, in readiness to respond to God's call, but also in suffering, incapable of engaging in external works, he is actually working, even without knowing it; he is collaborating with God's tireless word and Spirit. He works through *being*, not necessarily through *doing*, just as the sun works simply through being there.

The Way to the Father Is Not a Roundabout Way

In today's Gospel Jesus has described himself as the bread that comes down from heaven. The Jews are taken aback: Is not this Joseph's son, whose father and mother we know? Jesus replies: "Do not murmur among yourselves. No one can come to me unless the Father who sent me draws him. . . . No one has seen the Father except him who is from God. . . . Truly, truly, I say to you, he who believes has eternal life" (Jn 6:43–47).

Mysterious words, which seem to be very remote from our secular (even our Christian) everyday world. What good are they to us? Why not rather speak about practical questions concerning the Christian struggle against violence and repression? Perhaps, however, such questions only have meaning, only have real bite, against the background that the Evangelist John emphasizes so strongly. So let us try to shed some light on this profound and obscure area; then we shall be better able to find our way about in our everyday lives.

First of all there is the fundamental opposition between knowing and believing. Jesus describes himself as food come down from heaven, from the divine Father of the world; and this food guarantees and communicates heavenly, that is, eternal life. This is not something that can be seen by simply looking at this man standing in the midst of a crowd of people. We can only believe him. This faith has the ground cut from beneath its feet by a "knowledge" that seems very sure of itself: Jesus' parents are known—which shows him to be a completely ordinary man. Jesus contests this knowledge: against Joseph's fatherhood he speaks of quite a different Father: "The Father who sent me" from eternity, from heaven. Once again we have two fathers, as in the words of the twelve-year-old Jesus in the Temple: " 'Son, why have you treated us so? Behold, your father and I have been looking for you anxiously.' And he said to them, 'How is it that you sought me? Did you not know that I must be in my Father's house?' " As his parents well know, and as the Evangelist, in his Prologue, knows very well, he was born "not of blood or of the will of the flesh or of the will of man but of God" (Jn 1:13). He is the Only One, and thus he explicitly says, "No one has seen the Father except him who is from God." This is something that can only be believed; it cannot be established simply empirically. But we can believe it on the basis of Christ's uniqueness, on the basis of his words and works. As Peter puts it a few lines further on: "Lord, to whom shall we go? You have the words of eternal life." This is something we can experience if we allow these words and works to penetrate our hearts. That is what faith is: it is making room for what is unique about Jesus, for what goes beyond the everyday reality. In this way, right faith knows more than mere knowledge.

Now, however, we come to the second passage, which seems so baffling, although it is evidently intended to clarify what has gone before: "No one can come to me except the Father who sent me draws him." What is meant by the Father "drawing" a person? In any case, as to the central issue here, is it not found in most extrabiblical religions too? Man feels an irrepressible yearning for the highest, lasting Good and is so strongly drawn to it that he simply must seek it, even through all finite and transitory goods. He is bound to acknowledge its overwhelming superiority over his own narrow ego, which encloses him as in a prison. The religions are familiar with many ways of breaking out of this prison. "Then the 'I' dies, the dark despot", sings the Persian poet Jellaleddin Rumi. According to the Indian religions it dies when it enters nirvana, bursting like a soap bubble. But it also dies when it discovers, in its deepest layer, something greater and more all-embracing than itself, what the depth psychologists (religious or not) call the Self. Jesus Christ goes beyond all these attempts to attain blissful peace by surrendering the "I": he says that the origin of all beings and all persons, namely, the Father, draws us to him, but not to swallow us up within him: he draws us to him in order to fulfill us in him in a way that transcends our own self. He is the infinite "I": from all eternity he has wanted and chosen us and addressed us by the familiar "thou". At this word, "thou", uttered to each one of us in a quite distinct and personal way, the closed doors of our dungeon burst open. This word "*thou*" comes through to us from him who is the Origin (and nothing can "get behind him", so to speak); it strikes us like a ray of sunlight in the darkness, perhaps even like a flash of lightning that sets us aflame. It is this, bent upon what is most personal and interior to us, that draws us irresistibly beyond the closed sphere of our ego (which makes us refer everything around us to our own center); it draws us out of this dungeon in which, despairing, we seem to see all beings around us just as hopelessly imprisoned as we are. All the religions feel their way along the prison walls for the way out, but they miss it by taking the seeker's great religious achievement to be the relinquishing of his "I". In Christian terms, what is required is not that we relinquish our "I" but that we hand ourselves over to the absolute "Thou" of our Origin, who challenges us and seeks to win our love. But why should he who is the infinite Origin have any desire for us? Does this Origin need us, trivial, insignificant, transitory beings that we are? If this were true, would it not cast a very strange light on the Origin of all being? Perhaps he cannot manage without us?

In attempting to solve this very legitimate question, we come now to the third point. The ray of light, the lightning flash sent to us from the paternal Origin, the word he utters to us, an eternal Word who was with the Father from the beginning and was himself God—this ray, this flash of lightning, this Word has a name: Jesus Christ. This is his earthly name. His eternal name is the Son of the Father, and thus he is the Father's eternal "Thou". For the Father could not be called eternally "Father" unless from all eternity he had this Son as his "Thou", and unless both of them, transcending themselves in embracing the other, were themselves embraced by a Spirit of Love common to them both.

But now, Listeners, something very strange happens: we have spoken of the Father's "Thou", which he addresses to us and by which he draws us to him: this "Thou" can be nothing other than the Son, Jesus Christ. Anyone who knows that he is addressed by the Father's love is standing in the very place of the Son, who is the eternal "Thou utterance" of the Father. Jesus says this in the same discourse: "Everyone who has heard and learned from the Father comes to me." But does this not mean that we arrive at the wrong place, at the Son instead of the Father? Does not the Son somehow screen the Father from view? Is he not a kind of penultimate station, stopping us from arriving at our final goal?

This would indeed be the case if Jesus were only the Father's vice-regent or executive in the world. (This is liberalism's picture of Jesus.) All of a sudden we see how indispensable ancient Christian dogma is: Jesus is a man like us, of course, revealing and interpreting the Father to us in human terms, but at the same time he is God from God, Light from Light, eternal Word from the Father's eternal source, and as such he provides total accessibility to the One who speaks in and through him: "I am the way. No one comes to the Father but by me." But then what is the significance of his humanity, of his suffering and death on the Cross, of his Resurrection, in which he still manifests himself as a man among men? And what then can we say of his Eucharist, in which he gives us his Flesh and Blood to nourish us? What does this have to do with our being drawn to the ultimate Source? Does it not enclose us once and for all in something worldly? Jesus does something quite beyond the grasp of our minds: he identifies the Word uttered from God to us, and that promises us eternal life in God, with his own corporality: "The bread [from heaven] that I shall give for the [eternal] life of the world is my Flesh" (Jn 6:51).

Here, as far as Christian faith is concerned, it is a question of yes or no, being or nonbeing. Yes, this flesh and blood, this earthly reality that makes Jesus our brother, is really the possession of the eternal, divine Word, the Father's "Thou", who is simultaneously eternal *and* uttered to us in this most concrete form. How hideous it would be to have to eat the flesh and blood of a mere man, even if he were God's vice-regent and executive! If we took it seriously it would actually bar the way to our Origin, which is meant to be free and open. The liberal theology of Christ simply cannot take the Eucharist seriously. Only the theology of the New Testament can bring the two ends together by showing that our sin, which barred our way to the Father, has been carried away in Jesus' sacrificial death on the Cross, opening up access to the Father who draws us. As Paul says, he is the author of peace who has torn down the dividing wall and in his flesh, on the Cross, has killed the hostility that kept us remote from God (see Eph 2:15f.). The whole realism of earthly existence is part and parcel of the way opened up in Christ to the Father who calls and draws us.

Now we can also understand why, ultimately, the practical questions that worry today's Christians—the struggle against oppression, torture, hunger and all the inhumanity in the world—can be approached meaningfully only on the basis of this most profound mystery of our religion. We do not have the alternatives of a world-denying, world-fleeing religion seeking God alone, on the one hand, or a completely secular social struggle for justice on the other. Otherwise this struggle would be in danger of being religionless, atheistic, with Christ as a mere liberation theologian. But when Paul speaks of Christ as "our peace", he expressly means the two things at once: Christ reconciles the hostile parties *within the world*, Jews and gentiles, the privileged and the disadvantaged—by reconciling all the warring parties *with God*. The dividing wall is both vertical (between the world and God) and horizontal (between nations and classes). Only when *all* have been reconciled with one another and enjoy a common access to the Father, on the basis of God's word and his addressing them as "thou", will the Christian idea, God's saving plan, have reached its goal.

God's Simplicity

Let us listen to today's Sunday Gospel:

> At that time Jesus declared, "I thank thee, Father, Lord of heaven and earth, that thou hast hidden these things from the wise and understanding and revealed them to babes; yea, Father, for such was thy gracious will. All things have been given to me by my Father; and no one knows the Son except the Father, and no one knows the Father except the Son and any one to whom the Son chooses to reveal him. Come to me, all who labor and

> are heavy laden, and I will give you rest. Take my yoke upon you, and learn from me; for I am gentle and lowly in heart, and you will find rest for your souls. For my yoke is easy, and my burden is light (Mt 11:25–30).

These astonishing words of Jesus, which give so many headaches to the exegetes, the clever and wise, just will not go away. We, the simple, must accept them as they are uttered; for they themselves exhibit a simplicity and clarity that will not admit any artificial "explanation". Hence the jubilant tone of the first sentence: it has pleased the Father to reveal his mysteries particularly to the simple; this leads on to the tremendous claim made in the second sentence that no one but the Son can initiate us into the mysteries of the Father; and this in turn leads to the amazingly open invitation uttered in the third sentence: difficult and problematical people that we are, we can find rest and refreshment with the Son, because the complicated, heavy issues of our lives are transformed, in his simplicity, into light burdens. These three points are quite different, yet all three converge on the crystal-clear soul, mind and heart of Jesus, which are open to us without reserve and show us his relation both to the Father and to us. These two relations constitute his whole interior life, his whole interest and his whole sense of being alive. For the Son, as Jesus here calls himself, is the unique, incomparable Person whose life is exclusively a coming from and a going to the Father; he draws wearied men into this cyclic rhythm in order to free them from their heavy and often totally unnecessary burdens, to save them from internal stagnation. He wants to draw them into the fluid, eternal stream of love that circulates between Father and Son, where the burdens of the temporal dimension hardly seem to weigh anything at all.

This glimpse into the Son's heart reveals to us the complete unity of what to us seems so hard to reconcile. On the one hand we have a staggering self-awareness and equally staggering claims: "No one knows the Father except the Son and any one to whom the Son chooses to reveal him." But on the other hand we have a humility and lowliness that are just as astonishing: "for I am gentle and lowly in heart". How can these two things coexist in the same consciousness? Only as envisaged by the Church's profession of faith: the person who is speaking here is someone who knows of his divine, totally unique sovereignty and plenitude of power; and at the same time, as God, and consequently as man, he is not the origin of himself but the eternal Son, who continually owes his whole being and all that he has to the Source from whence he comes: "The Father is greater than I" (Jn 14:28). This paradoxical union of sublime claims and humility pervades all three assertions. Furthermore, the paradox does not simply confront us as something baffling and awesome: in the third assertion it actually addresses us: we must enter, we must learn from it ("learn from me"), so that we can be rid of our burdens and be the simple people to whom alone God's mysteries are revealed. We *must*, I say; we have no other alternative, because it is only in this center, in the Son, that the sublime and the lowly, God and man meet. For no one can see God as he is unless the Son reveals it to him. Thus these words affect us profoundly. Here the only signpost to eternal life (which we do not want to miss) begins to speak to us and teach us all things. He speaks about our goal, the Father; about ourselves, weary and burdened as we are; and about the way we are to take, which is identical with the signpost: "I am the way, the truth and the life" (Jn 14:6).

Now let us take each of these three points in turn and allow them to sink into us.

The first is a prayer from Jesus to the Father: "I thank thee, Father, Lord of heaven and earth, that thou hast hidden these things from the wise and understanding and revealed them to babes; yea, Father, for such was thy gracious will." The greatest being we can conceive, the creative and governing principle of the entire world, of heaven and earth, reveals his unfathomable mystery, but not to those who invest all their reason in searching for it. True, their rational conclusions will lead them from effect to cause, and so—all being well—back to a First Cause that is the cause of all others. On the analogy of human causation, they may even designate this First Cause the "Father of the universe". But as for this First Cause of whom the "wise and understanding", the philosophers, speak (and the mystics too), is he the same God who, in his good pleasure, determined to reveal himself, his inner nature, his mind, his heart? No, says Jesus. He wished it otherwise. We need to be simple, lest we try to stalk God using the wiles of proud reason; only thus can we experience the Father's heart directly. And it can happen that even one of the clever ones who search for the ultimate ground of being has a simple heart: in that case the Father will also reveal himself to him as he truly is. Why is this? In some way that is beyond our comprehension, the Father himself is simple too; he does not hoard his omniscience but recklessly gives it away, so to speak: "All things have been given to me by my Father", says Jesus. God does not cling to himself; the Father's womb is empty once he has generated the Son, so we must seek the Father in the Son, and only in him. This is expressed by the second, even more astonishing saying: "All things have been given to me by my Father; and no one knows the Son except the Father, and no one knows the Father except the Son and any one to whom the Son chooses to reveal him."

Now things are getting serious indeed. If the Father, in his simplicity, hands over the fullness of the divine mysteries to the Son whom he generates, it follows that henceforth they are to be found in the Son. But does this make them more accessible than in the Father? Does it make them less mysterious, less dependent on the divine will? Apparently not. As the Apostle says (Col 2:3): "All the treasures of wisdom and knowledge" are hidden in the Son, and to that extent "no one knows the Son except the Father". And people are simply amazed that someone who had no higher education claims to know so much: " 'Where did this man get all this? . . . Is not this the carpenter, the son of Mary? . . . And are not his sisters here with us?' And they took offense at him" (Mk 6:2f.). But the second assertion is even more offensive: "And no one knows the Father except the Son." For the Jews at least thought they knew something about the true God, and even the pagans are not totally without some knowledge of God, as Paul affirms at Athens. And now, all of a sudden, all knowledge of the Father is supposed to be concentrated in the Son. It is as if all other instances of religion are secularized by the absolute claim of Jesus: "I alone know the Father." The Father, that is, as he truly is. He is different from Zeus and Jupiter. He is even different, in his hidden face, from Yahweh. For Yahweh had not (as yet) given his entire Godhead to a son of man; he had not emptied himself, had not manifested his simplicity and humility and total self-giving. It is not that the God of the Old Covenant was not the true and living God, but that anyone who *refuses to move further and embrace the Son* as the Father's total self-giving has not really seen God. "He who has the Son has life", says John; "he who has not the Son of God has not life" (1 Jn 5:12). So everything depends on the Son revealing the Father to us as he knows him; we cannot wrest his inner vision of the Father from him; he must make it known to us of his own free will. That is why the second saying concludes: "No one knows the Father except the Son and any one to whom the Son chooses to reveal him." But does he so choose? Yes; that is why he is a man among us. Yes, for it is the Father's will to manifest himself to the world through the Son, to unveil his true, fatherly face through the meek and humble Son. This gives us the transition to the third saying.

"Come to me, all who labor." *All*, he says. This seems to contradict the limitation implied in "any one to whom the Son chooses to reveal him". Does he want to reveal the Father to all those he is now inviting or merely to the few he has called to be his disciples, while the rest, perhaps the overwhelming majority, remain far from him? "All who labor and are heavy laden". This must mean everyone, for where is the person who is *not* heavy laden? The fact is that not everyone admits it; not all realize that they cannot rid themselves of their weariness and bewilderment; they look for a thousand ways of getting rid of the burdens that weigh them down, by distraction, oblivion and even religious techniques and manipulation. In doing so they are the "wise and understanding" who obstruct their own path to the heart of God. They are invited: "Come to me", but they will not join the ranks of those who labor and are heavy laden; they think they are too good for that. They will not take the Son's yoke upon them; they prefer to carry their own yoke, which has the advantage of being their own, even if it is much heavier than the yoke of Jesus. So they are forever running around after all possible ways of salvation. They go after all the latest prophets, who recommend new techniques (often at a high price) for getting rid of their inner burdens and complexes, attaining success in their interior and exterior lives and arriving at religious experiences. They develop contemplative skills and practice group dynamics. For a while this satisfies them, but eventually the old restlessness spurs them on to look for new offers of salvation.

"Learn from me; for I am gentle and lowly in heart, and you will find rest for your souls." The one who speaks these words is not one of the countless quacks promising salvation of whom we read in the Gospel, in connection with the woman with a hemorrhage, "who had suffered much under many physicians, and had spent all that she had, and was no better but rather grew worse" (Mk 5:26). For if what we have said is true, if no one knows the Father except the Son, then the Son alone has the key to God's inner mystery, the mystery in which "you will find rest for your souls". We know what this mystery is, for the Son himself tells us: his gentleness and lowliness. We are to learn them from him, which implies that we actually *can* have them ourselves. Gentleness is not offering any resistance to God; in gentleness we let God's will be done and offer ourselves for his purposes, be they beautiful or hard. Lowliness is a willingness to serve; it feels at home at the lowest place and prefers the good of others to its own. Lowliness instinctively follows the movement of God away from the wise and understanding and toward the simple; it instinctively follows the descending movement of Jesus as he washes his neighbor's feet, makes the others sit at table while he serves them. There is nothing forced in lowliness: the lowly person does not have the feeling that he is really superior and that, in fact, he should be sitting at table being served by others; his attitude is relaxed and natural, as Paul says: "In humility count others better than yourselves" (Phil 2:3). Such a person will find that Jesus' concluding words here come true: "For my yoke is easy, and my burden is light."

Now we can see how the three sayings we have considered belong closely together. We can see why the Father reveals his mystery only to the simple, since this mystery is his own simple, unforced, perfect and total self-giving to the Son. Thus the Son is the only one who completely grasps the Father's eternal paternity; so too he is the only one who can show and teach the Father's nature to those who embrace his filial lowliness. Thus the beginning and the ending are perfectly joined. Nor is this total picture of God only for weaklings, as Nietzsche thought; this God of the simple is really the Lord of heaven and earth, as Jesus addresses him, the Almighty and All-Wise. But his almighty power is not the kind that overpowers and oppresses the weak, and his omniscience is not the kind that despises and abandons the simple. Nothing is more powerful than God's humility, and nothing is wiser and more understanding than his divine simplicity.

The Peace of Christ

The Christian is different from other people in that for him the relationship between "is" and "ought" has been reversed. The natural man is a creature who, because of his needy, unfulfilled nature, must strive to fulfill his potential, to fulfill the wealth of possibilities presented to him, to incorporate what he calls "values" into the area of being. He is in the process of becoming; he stretches out for being.

The Christian, by contrast, is a child of God, sharing in the divine nature, immersed in the breathtaking fullness and superabundance of God through Christ. Unlike the old Adam, he does not need to scratch around in the poor, cursed soil in order to gather together his little bit of wealth and make a tolerably comfortable living; the entire contents of God's treasure house are poured out at his feet. He does not need to pursue a thirsty search for love and hope; they are infused into him in all the fullness and purity with which they spring from God's source. He is rich beyond measure; fullness is his element; it is within him and forms his whole background. His ethical action is nothing other than the *eucharistia*, the gratitude that necessarily follows from this fullness of grace. He can do no other than extoll God's benefits; he can do no other than be radiant, since God has set him afire; he cannot but speak, because God has put the word into his mouth; and he cannot but pour himself out, together with Christ, into the world's emptiness and poverty, because God has filled him with a richness that is beyond this world, a richness that comes from heaven.

In fact, it would be disgraceful if, having been given everything, he were to act as if he were still needy and wretched, still full of demands, still "toiling and striving" (like Goethe's *Faust*). But it would also be a disgrace if he wanted to keep his unimaginable wealth to himself, to stockpile it like a capitalist and not pour it out for others in thankfulness of heart; for the treasure within him is nothing other than the stream of light that flows from the very Godhead. It can only *be* light by giving forth light; it can only *be* the source by welling up and streaming forth; it can only *be* divine love by being given away. God is pure selflessness, the self-giving of Father to Son, of Son to Father, of the Spirit to Father and Son; being filled with God means plunging into this torrent of selflessness of the life of God, that is eternally handing itself over to the Other in a never-ending spiral of giving and receiving.

It is the same with peace. The earthly man, lacking peace, strives for the peace for which he longs and yet can never reach; he envisages it as an ideal, and an ideal it remains here below, a star above the desert, a utopia but also, admittedly, a serious demand to which man must try to respond with all his powers of body and mind. For earthly, restless man, peace is something that lies eternally prior to and above life; there are moments when it seems to be attained, realized, embodied, but, since it is an "ought", a demand, it immediately soars high and floats above the realm of what actually exists. Like a strip of sunlight on the surface of the sea, it sets before us a new, endless path fraught with uncertainty and danger. The Christian, however, comes from peace. It is his basis. He has been given peace just as he has been given faith, love and hope, just as he has been given reconciliation with God and the fruits of the Spirit: "Love, joy, peace, patience, kindness, goodness, faithfulness, gentleness, self-control" (Gal 5:22). He *has* all this, and it would be ungrateful to say that he does not have it. It would be ungrateful to live and act as if it were something he had to elicit by his own efforts. The Christian has peace. He has received it as a gift from God, for God, who is eternal Peace, has made peace with the world through the "Prince of Peace", the "Peacemaker", Christ. Like the shepherds with their flocks, the Christian has heard the proclamation of peace with his own ears: "On earth peace among men with whom he is pleased." But he has not only heard with his ears: this peace has sunk deep into his heart: "The peace of God, which passes all understanding, will keep your hearts and your minds in Christ Jesus" (Phil 4:7). He *has* peace. He has received it from Christ as an express, solemn bequest and testament: "Peace I leave with you; my peace I give to you" (Jn 14:27). What a lie, what a blasphemy it would be for a Christian to say he knows nothing of this testament and the gifts associated with it! If he were to say, for instance: No, he received no such thing; No, he was not aware of it, had never noticed anything of the kind; he had only striven for peace like other men, naturally without ever having attained it; and as for *possessing* it and having it within him, with the best will in the world he could not say *that*. What ingratitude!

Peace is the Christian's element; he flows forth from peace like water from a spring, a ray of light from the sun. He is a messenger of peace. When he enters a house he ought to say, "Peace be with you", not as an empty wish but as a gift he brings with him. He does not need to know (nor can he) how deep the peace is that he brings. For it is the peace "which passes all understanding" (Phil 4:7), which lies deeper than all our conscious unrest, deeper than all the tormenting of our psychological ego: "whenever our hearts condemn us", says John, "God is greater than our hearts, and he knows everything" (1 Jn 3:20). God is greater than our hearts: that is peace. Not as if our heart is restless and it finally succeeds in finding God's rest—by virtue of its eternally restless seeking. No: it is that the eternal peace of God takes over this heart that is full of time's restlessness and plunges it in its great waves; God's peace finds this heart before ever the restless heart has time to seek for God, let alone find him. Everything is the reverse of what the temporal, earthly man thinks: he thinks he must run toward God as fast as his feet will carry him, forgetting that God has long since held him in his arms and rocks him like a little child. He exerts himself, whereas he ought simply to let himself fall. He wants to work, whereas he himself is the object of God's working. With the Jews, he asks the Savior: "What must we do, to be doing the works of God?" But the Lord replies: "This is the work of God, that you believe in him whom he has sent" (Jn 6:27–28). Paul echoes this when he says: "For we are his workmanship, created in Christ Jesus for good works, which God prepared beforehand, that we should walk in them" (Eph 2:10).

We can see now that this is the difference between God's peace and the peace of the world, between the Christian's peace and the peace of the earthly man. Men do not have peace; they search for it, hunt all over for it and cannot reach it. "When people say, 'There is peace and security', then sudden destruction will come upon them as travail comes upon a woman with child, and there will be no escape" (1 Th 5:3). The world promises peace but cannot deliver it. With the Lord it is the other way around: he gives peace but does not promise it: "My peace I give to you; not as the world gives do I give to you" (Jn 14:27). "Do not think that I have come to bring peace on earth; I have not come to bring peace, but a sword" (Mt 10:34). He gives peace, but not as something that can be hoarded; it is a treasure that one only has by giving it away: "He who loses his life for my sake will find it" (Mt 10:39). The Christian comes from peace and must enter a realm of no peace. So ardently is he to burn with his light in the darkness of the world that, as it were, he loses his light to the darkness; he is to shine so brightly in this world that all around him becomes light, whereas he, the one who radiates light without knowing it, stands like a burnt-out candle or an exhausted oil lamp. The one thing this messenger and bringer of peace may not expect in this life is peace. He must not expect God's peace for himself, as a possession to be enjoyed by himself, or the world's peace; for wherever he finds himself, with this peace of his, there will be the hissing produced by the meeting of water and fire: "I have come to set a man against his father, and a daughter against her mother, and a daughter-in-law against her mother-in-law; and a man's foes will be those of his own household" (Mt 10:35–36). "Brother will deliver up brother to death, and the father his child, and children will rise up against parents and have them put to death; and you will be hated by all for my name's sake" (Mt 10:21–22). "It is enough for the disciple to be like his teacher, and the servant like his master" (Mt 10:25).

So it almost seems as if the Christian has no peace of any

kind: he has seen through the illusory, superficial peace of the world, the smiling *fata morgana* of ultimate earthly security (for the world *is* evil and there is no security against God and his judgment), and as for the new peace that Christ brings, it cannot establish itself but only foments wars and strife among men. The Christian originates in a peace that is greater than he can understand; in turn this baffling peace, through the Church's apostolate, is aiming to produce conditions in the world that are greater, higher, more mysterious than the world can grasp; in fact, since the world resists anything it does not understand, it can only react to this peace with hostility.

Once, in the Old Covenant, God gave the gift of a rational, civil peace in the land of Israel—under King Solomon. Then every man sat under his fig tree and ate his bread and his grapes. This was the *shalom* of which men still dream. But this peace, like everything that happened to the Jews (1 Cor 10:11), was only by way of being an illustration. God himself made sure, even under the Old Covenant, that his people did not forget that it was only symbolic. It was a very fragile peace, threatened and indeed withdrawn time and again by every sin and infringement of the Covenant on Israel's part. Just open the Old Testament, which is saturated with war and blood, and you will see how intermittent this peace was. Primarily it was a symbol and an illustration of God's promise, the promise of an eschatological peace, announced by the prophets in God's name. Well and good: this peace has come in Christ. But the end of the ages has not yet come. Christ has not yet returned. So we live between the times, dying daily to the old man and the old eon, daily waiting in faith, hope and love for the new eon. We come from the peace of Christ that has been given to us and go forth into war and contradiction; we go through this war and contradiction and proceed toward the coming, definitive peace of Christ. And the peace from which we come is the same peace for which we are bound; we live within the vast umbrella of peace, which is so great, so firm, so secure, that it has room within it for the cross, war and death. "As it is written, 'For thy sake we are being killed all the day long; we are regarded as sheep to be slaughtered.' No, in all these things we are more than conquerors through him who loved us" (Rom 8:36–37). "He came to his own home, and his own people received him not" (Jn 1:11). Thus it may well be that anyone who goes out into the world bearing the new peace of Christ—and this world also happens to be the realm of his fellow Christians, the Church—will meet with a sword and will himself act as a sword. The peace of Christ in the kingdom of Christ may well initially adopt a warlike shape. For even in the Church we remain men who strive for security; we attempt to reinterpret the peace of Christ in terms of a security that is *contrary to* Christ, with the result that, when the saints come to us with God's true, pristine peace, we do not act very differently from the Jews and pagans outside, and the house of God resounds with the noise of battle. Paul is persecuted by the fanatical Jewish Christians; John is driven out by the ambitious Diotrephes; Teresa's confessors pronounce her to be possessed; John of the Cross is thrown into a stinking dungeon by his brethren and scourged daily; John Eudes and Grignon de Montfort are persecuted by their bishops and proscribed; Ignatius is thrown into the Inquisition's cells; Thérèse of Lisieux is tormented by her superior; Joan of Arc is condemned by a clerical court to be burned as a witch. What saint did not have a similar fate? Which of them did not share the most bitter cup drunk by his Lord and Master? "He came to his own home, and his own people received him not." Not strangers, but his own people! What saint, canonized by the Church, was not first *fashioned* into a saint by this same Church?! Part of this fashioning is the Church's maternal love in which she offers her child the bread of grace; but equally, part of it is the almost inhuman severity that applies punishment where punishment is least deserved, since Christ himself, the Sinless One, atoned for us all. Let him who is without sin in this matter cast the first stone! As for the man who dares, on this account, to separate himself from the Church to whom he owes everything, let him rise up against her! In doing so he will be failing to understand the most profound mystery that exists between the Bride and the Bridegroom; for in this mystery the Bridegroom, bleeding from the wound inflicted on him by the faithless Bride, goes on to initiate the Bride into his blood mystery: "A sword will pierce your own soul also"—my Mother and my Bride!—a sword for which you will be indebted to me, for which you will thank me, because *I* give it to you as a sharing in the wound inflicted on *me*. This wound was given to me by sin, by men, by you, Synagogue and Church, by God the Father, who gave me up as the redemption price for all "because he so loved the world".

So we rest in "the peace of Christ which passes all understanding" and are borne up by it, even when we try to resist; we are embraced by it even when we try to escape; and it holds us and will not let us go even when, in our blindness and desperation, we lash out against it. The *vinculum pacis*, the gracious chains of peace, hold us fast and compel us to rejoice in them, as Paul and Silas rejoiced in their chains at the midnight hour. "Suddenly there was a great earthquake, so that the foundations of the prison were shaken; and immediately all the doors were opened and everyone's fetters were unfastened" (Acts 16:25–26). What seemed to be chains was in fact freedom.

Assumption of the Blessed Virgin Mary

Bodily Faith

How strange it all seems to us! We know nothing of the way the cosmos, of which our earth is a part, is related to a heaven that occupies no localized position. Is not God everywhere? Does he need a special throne room as well, somewhere beyond the stars? We wonder why it is important to attribute such an improbable privilege to the Mother of Jesus, to assert that her body does not belong to the dust from which it was made, like everyone else's, but—as the old legends depict it—is supposed to have disappeared from its grave, to the amazement of the assembled disciples, leaving roses blooming on the sarcophagus.

Let us press the point: we may be believing Christians, but we hardly know anything about the relationship between death and resurrection. It is a brutal fact that we have before us a dead body, and it must go into the earth or into the fire. Another fact, an uplifting one, is that the Christian lives in the hope of being kept safe in God's hands after his death; but how, in concrete terms, can we envisage this? From time to time, throughout the Church's history, people have felt that man—at least the holy man, the man who has lived for God, body and soul—will be brought, whole and entire, into an intimate closeness to God. See, for instance, Giotto's wonderful painting of the bodily assumption of John, the "beloved disciple". Then there is that mysterious passage in Matthew 27 concerning the "bodies of the saints who had fallen asleep", whose graves open on Good Friday and who appear together with Jesus after his Resurrection; the majority of theologians consider it probable that they too were "assumed into heaven". But what a dark, opaque realm we are getting into! Would not the Church do better to concentrate on the brightly lit center of the Faith and leave this peripheral twilight zone to look after itself?

The question is, however, does not this ancient Christian feast, Mary's Assumption, belong to the center of the Faith after all? And this applies to the other great Marian feasts too: her conception, her reception of God's seed (March 25), her motherhood (January 1) and, so that she may be capable of this, her preservation from every stain of sin (December 8). If we are to see this, we must rid ourselves of any prejudice and repugnance we may have toward the "cult of Mary" and try to understand what is really at stake.

Let us try to approach the question from the point of view of the Bible. God's Covenants in the Old Testament with Abraham, with the patriarchs and with the people of Israel are the basis of all hope for salvation within world history. God binds himself in an ever-new and ever-closer way to the humanity he has created. Man, originally fashioned out of the clay of the earth but endowed with the breath of God's own freedom, has always existed in a twofold relationship, to what is below him and what is above him. God binds himself to man with the aim of forming something indivisible and unique in collaboration with him; namely, he intends to implant his eternal, divine Word in this mortal flesh and so enable this flesh to participate in his own life. Ancient Israel lives in hope and faith, looking toward this point, this messianic point in history. Israel knows well enough—and is made to feel it more and more—how little it responds to God's plan and expectation, how little it acts as an apt receptacle for the word of God, this word that is always hovering above its head, whether as a promise or as a threat. All the same there grows among the people a movement of penitent humility on the part of "Yahweh's poor", hollowing out a vacant space to serve as a receptive womb for the fruitfulness that will come from above. Sarah, the mother of Samson, Hannah, Elizabeth—all these barren women who are given children by God's grace alone are anticipatory images of what we know as the Incarnation, in Mary, of the Word and Son of God: this is the destination and consummation of the Old Testament development.

Mary, a young girl in an insignificant provincial town, becomes a representative personality. She stands for all the elements that, albeit imperfectly, yearned for the descent of the Word of God among men. Exegetes assure us that the Woman of the Apocalypse, clothed with the sun and with the moon under her feet, encircled by twelve stars and crying out in childbirth, is the epitome of the earthly community of salvation, which, in pains, awaits the Messiah and will actually give birth to him. This bodily birth, however, will naturally take place through a concrete person, a person in whom the ready obedience and hope of the ancient faith has taken pure and perfect shape but who also sums up and embodies all this world's longing and expectation. Moreover, the Woman of the Apocalypse, whose child is "caught up to God", is given a place (in the face of the opposition of the enemy, the dragon) in the earthly desert; the vision goes on to speak of "the rest of her offspring", those who "bear testimony to Jesus" and whose task is to fight against the demonic powers. This makes it quite clear that the ancient community of salvation, from which the Messiah has come forth, has been transformed into a new community of salvation, the Church. Mary stands as the tangible, personal embodiment of all the energies of salvation history; she stands in an integrating, intermediate position between Israel and the Church; she is, in person, the bodily fruitfulness of the entire people of God.

But now we must go on to understand that the central event of the "Incarnation of the Word of God" could only take place when, at some point or other, the faith, hope and love of the people of God had become so unconditional that there was no longer anything in the receptive womb that would resist the implanting of the divine seed. "Behold, I am the handmaid of the Lord"—here we see a readiness, a receptivity that is totally unreserved: body, soul and spirit are utterly open, "openings" to God. Here the essential thing is that the body is involved; that the Handmaid's consent echoes right through her, down to the lowliest and most unconscious fibers of her being; her whole self, in its materiality, from its lowest level upward, makes itself a womb for the Wholly Other, for God's self-utterance (and hence his "substance"). Never before had this substance taken up its abode within the straitened dimensions of a mortal body.

(The Gospels are our guarantees that this really took place. This man alone, who came from Mary's womb, "made God known" [Jn 1:18]. He alone has enabled us to see God through his transparent humanity and has shown us how almighty and how humble, how lofty and how lowly, how just and how loving God is. In his existence—right up to and including the Cross and the Resurrection—he has taken all the irreconcilable images of God that are scattered about in man's mind and brought them into a unity, a stupendous unity that has fascinated and baffled the world for two thousand years because it will not fit into any of its categories.)

The wonder of this man, however, should not make us overlook the uniqueness of the womb in which a divine-human unity took shape. The intimate relationship between a mother's whole being and her child is much more profound than former centuries thought. From the mother within whom it grows, the child receives physical, psychic and spiritual being, inseparably interwoven. In Mary's case, her Son receives from her all that is man's response, in faith, love and hope, to the Covenant God. So, from the very outset, this receptive womb must be completely oriented to furnishing the Son of God with everything the Covenant requires, so that he, the Son, can become a bodily unity embodying the Covenant.

Jewish thought constituted a preparation for the Incarnation insofar as (unlike Greek thought) it always saw man as a unity of body and soul; it never pursued a one-sidedly spiritualized ascetical ideal or envisaged an immortality of the soul apart from the body. This mode of thought, which is not only biblical but does justice to the nature of man as he is, facilitates our approach to this most mysterious union between God and man that took place in the womb of the Virgin Mary. This human womb was exclusively prepared to allow God's seed to develop in it without any hindrance; it was like a subterranean mine whence the Son of God could draw all he needed to equip himself fully as a God-bearing man.

What, therefore, is the Church celebrating today? That a simple human body, inseparably united to its soul, is capable of being the perfect response to God's challenge and of uttering the unreserved "Yes" to his request. It is a single body—for everything in Christianity is always personal, concrete, particular—but at the same time it is a body that recapitulates all the faith and hope of Israel and of all men on earth. Consequently, when it is taken up into ultimate salvation, it contains the firm promise of salvation for all flesh that yearns for redemption. For all our bodies long to participate in our ultimate salvation by God: we do not want to appear before God as naked souls, "not that we would be unclothed, but that we would be further clothed, so that what is mortal may be swallowed up by life" (2 Cor 5:4); and God, who caused bodies to die, "subjecting creation to futility", has subjected it "in hope" that it "will be set free from its bondage to decay and obtain the glorious liberty of the children of God" (Rom 8:20f.). So we are celebrating a feast of hope; but, like all the New Testament feasts, it is celebrated on the basis of a fulfillment that has already taken place; that is, not only has the Son of God been resurrected bodily—which, in view of his life and death, is quite natural—but also has the body that made him man, the earthly realm that proved ready to receive God and that remains inseparable from Christ's body. Today we see that this earth was capable of carrying and bringing to birth the infinite fruit that had been implanted in her. Today we celebrate the ultimate affirmation and confirmation of the earth.

Contemplating the center of the mystery we are celebrating, we would do well to refrain from speculating about questions that are insoluble; for these speculations lead to abstract regions with no way out. By contrast, if we look at Mary, the towering central point between Israel and the Church, our gaze rests on something utterly concrete; we see our Sister who succeeded in doing for us what, in virtue of her example, we must attempt to emulate, namely, to allow God's Word to dwell in us bodily. Furthermore, he will never leave the house that has once given him shelter. Whatever Jesus received from Mary —not only a body, but also the whole power, the whole tradition of the earthly response to God's word—he incorporates into his divine-human nature, the indissoluble nuptial relationship between God and his world. The Son's most profound attitude is that of owing himself to the Father, in a word, Eucharist. All his love for the eternal Father is gratitude that, in its overflowing, brings back to the Father everything the latter has created, now redeemed and transformed. And all his love for his earthly Mother is manifested in giving and showing her what, in God's plan, she always was: the first creature envisaged in connection with God's becoming man, worthy to be the first to experience perfect transfiguration in God. She is the model for all men kept safe under her bright mantle.

Heaven and Earth

Surely none of the Bible's fundamental affirmations has so thoroughly come adrift, as far as we are concerned, as the very first one: "In the beginning God created heaven and earth." As if dazzled, we stare at the ancient Babylonian picture of the world, in which the "fixed" heaven encompasses the earth like a sphere; or we adduce a mass of other material culled from the history of religions to show that this dualism between two halves of the world, the heavenly and the earthly, which generally implies a corresponding dualism between the inhabitants of heaven and those of earth, is found throughout the whole world. But perhaps, after all, this is not the strict counterproof that people usually think it to be? Perhaps it corresponds to a religious instinct in mankind that is continually creating mythical and fantastic forms of expression, things that, while we can safely dispense with them, basically are intimations of something right and true?

If we confine ourselves to the Bible, we find that this first statement it makes persists through all subsequent developments. It changes and acquires depth but is never abandoned, so much so that the tension between earth and heaven is indispensable for the New Testament—the Book of Revelation concluding with the promise and symbolic depiction of a new heaven and a new earth.

According to Genesis, heaven is just as much "created" as earth. It cannot be simply equated with God, for he *was* before the creation came into being. And when heaven is represented as the privileged "place" and environment of God, whereas the earth is man's "place"—"The heavens are the Lord's heavens, but the earth he has given to the sons of men" (Ps 115:16)—the Old Testament is well aware that God is high above all heavens and that the earth belongs to him just as much as heaven does. Thus the tension found in the whole Bible can neither be traced back to ancient cosmology (and hence demythologized) nor equated with the tension between God and his creature. It is rather that the created world has this fundamental realm of tension and of action, this atmosphere; within it it can live and, as a result of its action, develop. What the Bible has in mind is a living relationship in which what comes from heaven renders the earth fruitful, and the earth, in receiving from heaven, reaches its own, most specific potential and achievement. This view is already found in the Old Testament: "For as the rain and the snow come down from heaven and return not thither but water the earth, making it bring forth and sprout, giving seed to the sower and bread to the eater, so shall my word be that goes forth from my mouth; it shall not return to me empty, but it shall accomplish that which I purpose and prosper in the thing for which I sent it" (Is 55:10–11). Here the "mythical" element (rain and snow, symbols of salvation among peoples of the desert and the steppes) has faded right into the background: the central point is that man lives and becomes fruitful by the word or "breath" of God (Gen 2:7; Ps 104:29f.), and that it is for the sake of this fruitfulness that God's word is sown as seed in the earthly field, implanted into human flesh. This event may be expressed in Jesus' simple Parable of the Sower ("the seed is the word of God"), of the Leaven and of the Grain of Wheat That Dies, or in the rich imagery of the wedding banquet and the marriage of the Lamb, but in each case the same thing is meant. The aim of the "word" and the "Spirit of God" that come from "above" is to penetrate to the innermost core of the "flesh" that man is in order to bring this fleshly reality to that ultimate fruitfulness for which it is designed, and which it cannot achieve on its own, no more than a woman can conceive a child without a man's instrumentality.

This latter image is the profoundest, although it must not be pressed too far. For the man's fruitfulness is likewise dependent on the woman, whereas the sending forth of the divine Word and Spirit into the earthly world in no way indicates any need or necessity on God's part but springs only from his overflowing goodness. God is not a heaven that needs earth in order to fulfill itself, for "in the beginning God created heaven and earth".

According to the Bible, the ultimate meaning of human life lies in hearing, understanding and carrying out the divine word; all other, purely worldly significance and activity are "folly" when compared with this ultimate meaning. For Abraham this word can be a "promise" to be believed; for Moses and the people it can be an "instruction" (*torah*) to be carried out; for the disciples of Jesus this word is the living Man from Nazareth, the "Word of God made flesh", who calls men to follow him. In each case it is a question of receiving the word of God in the context of a living existence: the word must penetrate into all the fibers of the "flesh", to the innermost "heart". Knowledge of music and a feeling for music will not by themselves make a pianist; there must be constant practice. The New Testament frequently uses the image of the athlete.

Mere deeds ("orthopraxy") are not enough, however, for the word of God to become embodied: it was precisely the opponents of Jesus, the Pharisees, who prided themselves on the correctness of their conduct, but their hearts had not grasped the tenor of the word that comes down from God. The heart, man's center, where soul and body are one, must decide to become a womb for God's seed. Here the heart, the most secret and yet most vulnerable, the most central and yet most exposed part of man, has the power to open or close itself. Very much more is involved than the mere correct "understanding" of the word with the reason ("orthodoxy"); that involves no pain, whereas the naked heart, offering itself to the Word, will not go unscathed: "A sword will pierce your heart", the sword of the word of God, which is "living and active, sharper than any two-edged sword" (Heb 4:12).

Now the question arises, how can the Word of God become flesh right down to the last detail? We see this Word, in Jesus of Nazareth, faced with a crowd of disciples who have hardly any understanding and who, at present, are incapable of following him wholeheartedly; he is the man who carries out perfectly the Father's perfect will—"on earth as it is in heaven"; how did this Jesus come into being? The answer can only be found in that "Yes" that Mary gave the angel: "Behold, I am the handmaid of the Lord; let it be done to me according to your word." It is God himself who, so that his Word may become flesh, prepares a human, earthly vehicle with a receptivity and readiness that go right to her innermost core. There is not a trace of resistance within her; from her the Word will draw sustenance for his Incarnation. And he will use every last part of her, for his Incarnation, his embodying, is to be total. Furthermore, since the Word becomes flesh in order to become acquainted with man in his remoteness from God, to experience this remoteness and take the burden of it upon himself, so unburdening his brethren of their guilt, there is bound to be pain when the Mother offers her maternal heart for the Son's purposes. Not only the Mother's body but also her innermost soul and heart will have to be "stretched" in order to prepare that flesh that will "take away the sin of the world". Her innermost substance must "simply believe"; otherwise God's seed would not have found the "fertile ground" in which it can yield fruit a hundredfold.

Once again this follows from the primal tension between heaven and earth. What heaven sends cannot attain perfection without the cooperation of the earth, the *matrix-materia-mater*, which in turn cannot utter a full, unreserved and vulnerable "Yes" by its own power but only through the power of the Holy Spirit of God.

Thus, in the Incarnation itself, we have a model of the relationship—and it can only be represented as a perfected relationship—between Christ and his Church. Unless we see the Church of Christ coming into being in that little room in Nazareth, we shall not understand anything about her; that is, we shall confuse her with the Synagogue, which always lagged behind the demands of the Word of God, refusing to let his full Incarnation take place. The Church would never, subsequently, have become the "Bride without spot or blemish" if she had not been this Bride from the very outset, through the Incarnation grace given to Mary. Thus the Church is always (has always been) that earth, that soil, that is open to heaven, broken up so that she can breathe, more profoundly open (and hence more wounded) than other human hearts, which always have some closed-off area. But in this openness, this being dispossessed for the sake of others, we find the reason why this unique Mother must be both Virgin—totally at God's disposal—and Mother—the fruitful heart's tilth. She is "Church" right from the start because she is dispossessed: she is the Church's most interior, most purified reality, a reality that always remains fundamental, however many all-too-human and questionable layers are built on top, superstructures that always stand in need of reformation.

What we speak of as the "communion of saints", that is, the interrelatedness and osmosis of human destiny, has its origin in Christ, the bearer of all guilt; but a profound element in Christ is the self-renouncing "Yes" of the Handmaid of the Lord, a "Yes" that creates a space accessible to all, where all may dwell and "plunder" its goods.

Christ, the Son of God, came to bring us, inhabitants of earth, into an entirely new relationship with the "heavenly Father". Not only does he lift the estrangement that had developed between heaven and earth as a result of sin (when the New Testament speaks of "the world" in a pejorative sense it means the earth insofar as it is closed off, shut in upon itself); he also intends to bring a previously undreamed-of intimacy in the relationship between earth and heaven. By his perfect carrying out of the Father's will "on earth as it is in heaven", the "kingdom of heaven" has got a foothold, in principle, on earth; at the same time Jesus' earthly flesh, resurrected by God, has been equipped with heavenly qualities and been given rights of citizenship in heaven. Thus one of earth's dimensions, previously only a yearning, has attained fulfillment. Of course this dimension cannot be defined by science or depth psychology; God's word will not allow itself to be assessed as a natural element in man's physical or psychic constitution. The word is a sovereign revelation from above, and only the faith that says

"Yes" can discern its reality and share in it. The heaven where the Risen Lord dwells cannot be localized relative to earth: on the one hand he dwells among us as the eucharistic Lord "to the end of the world"; on the other hand we are promised that he will return visibly at this world's end. The new dimension the earth has acquired through the Resurrection belongs simultaneously to heavenly and earthly spheres; Christ, God and man, indwells both.

He does so as "the firstborn from the dead" (Col 1:18), as "the firstfruits of those who have fallen asleep" (1 Cor 15:20), in order to open up to us the path leading to this intimacy between earth and heaven. For we would not be men without our bodies, in which we have developed our spiritual dimension and caused it to bring forth fruit; and it is through our bodies that we open to and communicate with one another. No one can say exactly how and "when" this transition takes place for the individual, or "when" the "end of the world" happens for him. For Christ it took place on Easter Day. Strangely enough, Matthew gives a (meticulously detailed and thorough) description of how Jesus did not rise from the dead alone but together with many of the "saints who had fallen asleep", whose graves had already opened on Good Friday (Mt 27:51–53). Just as he did not wish to become man on his own but with the consent of Mary, just as he did not wish to hang on the Cross alone but in solidarity with two notorious sinners, so too he does not want to found this new mode of existence on his own but together with an indefinite multitude of chosen ones whom he takes with him into the new dimension.

Karl Rahner rightly observes at this point:

> It would not do justice to the normative significance of Scripture to set aside this testimony on Matthew's part as a "mythological" interpolation or to argue away the text's eschatological meaning with sophistries, suggesting that the Resurrection was a temporary event or one involving some kind of "phenomenal body". The fact is that, right up to today, by far the majority

of the Fathers and theologians have always held fast to what, in exegetical terms, is the only possible eschatological interpretation.

This is the context in which we must see the Church's ancient belief, which was subsequently given dogmatic formulation, the belief in Mary's bodily Assumption into heaven. Resurrection takes place perpendicular to the linear time of world history. Apart from Mary, who, on the basis of her "Yes", was "mature" and ready for this consummation, we do not know who will be translated into this final state "before" the world's chronological end. Mary's consent could be deepened, in a human way, through the phases of her earthly life, particularly through ever more painful suffering, but this only revealed the already existing, though hidden, dimensions of that consent. Nor is this anything extraordinary, in Christian terms: it is quite possible for something that perfectly *is* to *develop* over time. Christ himself, who was always totally obedient to the Father, "with loud cries and tears . . . learned obedience through what he suffered" (Heb 5:7), plumbing the unfathomable abyss of obedience.

Mary, whose consent was embodied more and more deeply throughout her life, right up to the sword that pierced her under the Cross, was uniquely mature and ready to step into the new dimension of the world along with her Son and to enter its ultimate form. It is quite immaterial whether others had risen "before" her, for none of them had uttered the "Yes" that was so crucial for the salvation of the world, and all had "been acquainted with decay" and had paid the wages of sin and of solidarity among sinners. But just as Mary's "Yes" was from the outset a function of the christological event, establishing a new solidarity in Christ over against this solidarity in sin, so her death could only be a function of Christ's redeeming death, in which he took "Adam's" death upon himself and reinterpreted it.

We have already said of Christ that we cannot tell whether

his eucharistic presence dwells more on earth or in heaven. It would be quite foolish to imagine him moving from his heavenly "place" to some "earthly" place. Wherever he becomes present, genuinely, newly, in the here and now, whenever a community celebrates the Eucharist, it is not as if this "coming" involves any "going away again". Christ can both *be* there *and* continually come in a way that is always new. And if there seems to be a distance (at least a spiritual distance) between earth and heaven, the converse is not true: the earthly people who have passed over into the heavenly dimension have not thereby left the earth behind them. The virtue of *parrhesia* so extolled by Paul, the joyful boldness and confidence of believers toward God, give us immediate access to heaven, to Christ, to God, at every moment of time. It is permanently true that we "have come to Mount Zion and to the city of the living God" (Heb 12:22), to the "Jerusalem above . . . our mother" (Gal 4:26), for "our commonwealth is in heaven" (Phil 3:20). This applies eminently to the baptized who share in the Eucharist.

At the heart of the Church, however, stands Mary, and what applies to her Son's Eucharist applies analogously to her: it is not that she is either in heaven or on earth, but she is earth lifted up into heaven and heaven turned to face earth. Nor is there anything strained here; it is all perfectly natural, for this is how the creature's ultimate state was envisaged.

If we add up everything the Gospels tell us about Mary, it makes an astonishing total. The Bible tells us more things about Mary than about any other woman, things that are so varied and ever new. If we make connecting lines between the various episodes, as we are absolutely right to do, the perspectives that open to us are practically boundless. At the same time Mary always remains the handmaid, standing in the background, only stepping forward where she is needed. In Cana, for instance, she has to come forward to let us see something of her administrative function, and at the Cross she is indispensable. Then we have the picture of the assembled

Church prior to Pentecost, with Mary at the center—and then nothing. Nothing else is needed. The fact that the Mother prays *at* the heart of the Church and *as* the heart of the Church, and disappears, as it were, praying, into the Church, there to continue her real existence—this is the plainest possible statement of her truth.

What we must avoid is importing into this picture our own ideas of distance between heaven and earth. The same goes for the distinction we make between the heavenly ("triumphant") and earthly ("militant") Church. Both these aspects of the Church interpenetrate totally. We live in the communion of saints, whether these saints have already been sanctified so that they cannot sin or are poor sanctified saints like ourselves, still subject to temptation and sinfulness. Whether we want to or no (but we ought to want to!), we already participate in the "festal gathering and assembly of the firstborn who are enrolled in heaven" (Heb 12:23), and we should not be surprised if, when we "enter heaven" after death, we find that we have already been there without noticing it.

All Saints

God's Holiness in Us

Let us reflect for a while on the feast that the Catholic Church is celebrating today. What has "All Saints" to say to us today? Even describing someone as a "saint" seems terribly anachronistic to us, like an echo from a world long past; indeed, many people now only use the word in a tone of mockery. It means less to us than, for instance, "a good man", someone who has dedicated himself totally to the common good or to justice, someone to whom people in trouble can go, someone who understands and steps in to help. Is such a person a saint?

Let us begin quite simply with the word *saint* or *holy*. In the ancient religions, including that of the Old Testament, it refers to a thing, an animal or a person consecrated to the deity. This thing or being was chosen by the community to be taken over by God and to be at his disposal, or an individual may have personally decided to so consecrate himself. Thus, in this primitive sense, an animal placed on the altar of sacrifice and consumed by fire is "holy". The Levite also, however, chosen for Temple service, is "holy". And the whole people of Israel, chosen by God from among the nations to be a people for himself, is a "holy" people, consecrated to God. Why? Because holiness is the prerogative of God, and everything that enters into his sphere is made to participate in his divinity. As far as a person is concerned this means that, if he is called upon by God in this way, he must also adopt the appropriate attitude and disposition: "Be holy", says God to his chosen people, "for I am holy." To give Israel an idea of how a man is to behave when drawn into God's circle, it is given two tables with the Ten Commandments, later to be summed up in the great Commandment, namely, to love God above all else and with all one's strength. At this point Jesus introduces a twofold deepening and clarification of the concept. In the first place he reveals a new vitality in the nature of the God who concluded a Covenant with Israel: God not only looks for love in response to his gracious condescension to man; he himself is absolute Love, since he has given up his beloved Son for his Covenant partners—and now all men are such. Now "holiness" means being admitted into this sphere of absolute love; it means consciously entering into it and becoming assimilated to the disposition and attitude of this God of love. In the second place, however, the act of self-giving on the part of the "holy" God is the Incarnation of his Son, who wills to take upon himself the guilt of all men vis-à-vis God; henceforth the guilt of mankind, the sin of the world, can and must be found concentrated in Jesus Christ; henceforth the presence and the forgiving love of God can and must be recognizable behind the person of every fellowman: "What you have done to the least of my brothers, you have done to me"—which is why Jesus, in his preaching, joins the two greatest Commandments into an inseparable two-in-one: "Love God above all else . . . and your neighbor as yourself."

If we are really speaking about holiness—and not only about the good man, the humanitarian ideal, which men are quite capable of envisaging for themselves—if the word *holiness* is to have a real content, it must lie in the twofold Commandment of Jesus, precisely as he intends, formulates and lives it. So now, being handed over to God's sphere and laid on his altar means being inflamed by the fire of the love of God, who has gone to his death for love of us, and being assimilated, in the love of neighbor, to God's disposition and attitude, his commitment to the world. This sequence is important if we are to grasp the fundamental meaning: God's love for us is primary;

it is the standard by which everything is measured, the flame that ignites our love in response. The other is the consequence: since God's love for us embraces the whole of mankind, our love for him will also join in that movement; we too will share in his work of salvation for the world. Since the word *holiness* is now, once and for all, inseparable from the biblical understanding of God, we have no right to separate the love of neighbor from the love of God or (I will not say "to raise it to the level of a criterion") to make it out to be the whole content of holiness. This is true in spite of the words already mentioned on the part of the Judge of the World: "What you have done to the least of my brothers, you have done to me", and in spite of the Parable of the Good Samaritan, who simply performs an act of neighborly love and is exhibited as a model by Jesus. One only needs to read this parable in depth to see that Jesus is here portraying primarily God's activity on mankind's behalf, his own activity as God's Son for the sake of the sick and half-dead. We only have to compare these words of judgment with the conclusion of the Sermon on the Mount, and we shall understand what they really mean: "Not every one who says to me, 'Lord, Lord', shall enter the kingdom of heaven, but he who does the will of my Father who is in heaven" (Mt 7:21). Here too Jesus is speaking expressly as the world's Judge. But the criterion of neighborly love is applied as a test of the genuineness of our love of God. What decides the issue is not words and professions of piety but action that is assimilated to the action of God himself.

Now it becomes clear why All Saints is a distinctively Catholic feast. To call a man "saint" and "holy" presupposes that he can—somehow or other—respond to God in virtue of divine grace. He will always be aware of being infinitely far behind the demand, and the more saintly he is, the more this awareness will burn within him. (Only a philistine could imagine that his response to God is generally satisfactory.) "So you also, when you have done all that is commanded you, say, 'We are unworthy servants' " (Lk 17:10). Because man must speak like this, because he experiences his unworthiness more and more deeply the more he responds to God, most non-Catholic Christians prefer not to apply the words *saint* and *holy* to men at all, reserving them for God alone. This is very understandable, and it is a view we can respect. Yet it does not correspond entirely to the biblical way of thinking and speaking. In the Old Covenant, as we have seen, things and persons consecrated to God really do bear the epithet "holy"; and when the Old Covenant is fulfilled in the New, Christians are continually challenged to be "holy", "blameless" or "unspotted"; and they do this, as Paul requires, by adopting in themselves the disposition of God and of Jesus Christ. It is everywhere assumed that this is objectively possible; and this, rather than the subjective feeling of one's own unworthiness, is ultimately what counts.

At this point, however, two further and quite disparate questions arise. The first asks the Catholic Church: Why should individuals be picked out from the crowd and elevated into a special category of "saints", which somehow isolates them from other Christians? The second question concerns our contemporary sensibilities: Can Christian holiness be realized today in the clearly distinctive way that was possible in former times? Does the saint still have a profile and a face today? How can he be recognized?

Let us take some time to answer the first question and then proceed to assess the meaning of today's feast; in conclusion we shall take up the second question.

The idea that someone can be more or less an example to others is by no means exclusively Catholic or even biblical. Such people exist in all cultures and religions. Buddha and Socrates are exemplary men. On the squares of our towns we find representations of people who have earned the gratitude of the community for their contribution to the common good in one way or another; the names of some of them have entered into our language, while others are soon forgotten and scarcely anyone looks up at their statues. But we cannot make a direct connection between this way of recognizing the achievements of great men and the existence of great saints. For in the latter case there is a further element: God's choosing. " 'Arise, anoint him; for this is he.' Then Samuel took the horn of oil, and anointed him in the midst of his brothers; and the Spirit of the Lord came mightily upon David from that day forward" (1 Sam 15:13). So it is with all the great chosen ones of the Bible. I know you, says Jesus to someone brought before him, a simple fisherman, "You are Simon, son of John", but now you will be something else: "You will be called Cephas, that is, the Rock." In the Bible it is God who chooses people in both the Old and New Covenants. He chooses great and small, known and unknown, pious and sinners. God's choice is grace, and grace is twofold: it is a particular task and the ability to embrace it and carry it out. Qualified Christian holiness begins with man's free "Yes" to his election and his faithfulness in carrying out his commission. It would be quite wrong to say that this "Yes" is equally weak and feeble in all who are thus called; on the contrary: some give a full "Yes", others a clear "No"; others say, "Perhaps"; one says, "Not now, but later", or, "Yes in part". Those who utter a wholehearted "Yes" will sometimes stumble or hesitate or fail to live up to their first ideal, but grace will help them up again. They will stick to their path, and very often it is the case that God's task takes over and relentlessly drags their poor, protesting person ever onward. Thus God has gained the upper hand in them over themselves. It is not they who possess a mission, but their mission possesses them. This mission can be anything: a mission of prayer, of suffering, of active involvement for the poor and oppressed, a mission to a small circle of people who need support and the comfort of a light, a public mission or a hidden mission, a successful mission or one doomed to failure: the only important thing is that man stays faithful to it.

Now we are at the center of the mystery of Christian holiness, and also at the center of the mystery of today's feast. The man in whom the mission has won precedence over his private personality has become dispossessed, expropriated in favor of it, for the sake of God and his fellowmen. He is a ploughed field in which God's word can and will bear fruit. The original meaning of holiness was this: being transferred to God's sphere. Anyone who has been dispossessed in this way is no longer subject purely to the laws of human cause and effect but—because God can do with him what he will—to the laws of divine fruitfulness. Just think of the metaphor of the vine: "I am the vine; you are the branches . . . apart from me you can do nothing. . . . He who abides in me bears much fruit" (Jn 15:5f.). The principle of fruitfulness of a mission imparted by God is no longer primarily a human principle but a divine one. The fruit will be, we are told, "thirtyfold, sixtyfold, a hundredfold". Not in the man himself, of course, but in the gigantic vineyard of the Lord, which is not only the Church but the world too. The Church is rather the place where God chooses his instruments and sends them out on their mission; the world is the field in which the word of God is sown. So a saint does not know what fruit he may be producing: it is God who picks and distributes the fruit, mostly without the man's knowledge. In fact, it is best if man has no notion that he is yielding fruit at all. He may feel like a tree that has been completely stripped, simply because God keeps picking his fruit as he needs it. "The harvest is great; the laborers are few"—this is true for the whole of the Church's history. Particular individuals may work with such dedication that God produces more fruit with them than with fifty mediocre and lazy laborers. Numbers are irrelevant in the kingdom of God. We might almost say that the opposite is the case: one really dedicated person is a foundation stone on which God can build entire houses, entire towns in his kingdom. Practically the whole of Western theology was built on Paul and Augustine; myriads of members of religious orders have lived on the basis provided by Benedict, Francis and Ignatius, bringing forth fruit for centuries in the kingdom of God through their prayer, work and witness.

The person who has been dispossessed by his mission becomes a universal, anonymous principle of fruitfulness. This anonymity is at the root of the "communion of saints". Anyone who allows himself to be dispossessed by God and his mission is a foundation stone of community, a place whence others can draw sustenance and find materials with which to build themselves up. Essentially, every saint is holy, not for himself but for God and his fellowmen. A saint who cultivates his own sainthood is a contradiction in terms. He would not be aglow with God's fire, which is always a purifying love, but with his own fire, which ultimately can only come from hell. In the communion of saints the spheres of the loving parties interpenetrate: each lives from the others and shares his own with them. Together they form the Lord's vine. No one thinks of enriching himself through sharing with the others; no one calculates how much he is giving the others. They all think solely of the Lord's great task in which they share, the kingdom of God that is to be established and made habitable among men. But each one, by being absorbed by his task, which is one part, one charism, within the Church's great mission in the world, acquires his distinctive and personal face. There is nothing in the whole world as personal and personalizing as a God-given mission. To see this, one only needs to look at the faces of the saints, their real faces, not the plaster faces stuck onto them like masks by pious industry, making them look all the same. How unique is the face of a Paul, an Irenaeus, a Hildegard or Elizabeth of Thuringia, a Don Bosco or John Vianney or little Thérèse of Lisieux! Each one is a whole world. Figures such as these show us the truth of the Gospel saying "he who loses his life will gain it". In giving his saints a mission, God imparts a very personal face to each of them; or, as the Book of Revelation puts it, each one is given a new name known only to God and the person thus endowed with grace; this name is subsequently made known to everyone when the particular mission is properly carried out. For God is always the Unique One, and all he gives to his creatures bears this stamp: it manifests and embodies his uniqueness.

Of course the saints certainly cannot be made into a special category of men and kept separate from the spectators by a fence, like animals in a zoo. In the kingdom of God there are no mere spectators; each person has some task or other. And there is a fluid spectrum from the great, attested missions that the Church sets before us as models to be imitated and the little everyday tasks that most of us have. At "All Saints" we are by no means celebrating primarily the great and impressive model missions but also the missions of all who are called to holiness of whatever kind and have reached it in whatever way. These include all Christians of goodwill who ultimately are not seeking their own private happiness and salvation but are endeavoring to serve God and their fellowmen. Nor is it crucial whether these real or so-called saints are dead or still alive, for there are no separating walls between heaven and earth. This is something the Catholic has always been aware of: he has always known that, living on the earth, he has direct access to the communion of saints in heaven, that he can call upon them for their help and intercession and that, to those in heaven, anything is possible on earth. In the Book of Revelation there are scenes that could be taking place in heaven or on earth or in both places at once—we cannot tell. When it speaks of those who follow the Lamb to Mount Zion and bear the name of his Father on their foreheads, it can mean equally people in heaven and people on earth. It does not matter whether they exist before or after their bodily death, provided they stand within their mission and thus follow the Lamb of God, who is the origin of all personal missions. Neither the Bible nor the early and medieval Church erected barriers between this world and the world beyond such as we modern men erect; the Church goes right through both realms; the communion of saints embraces both, including the transition zone, namely, that purification that takes us from earthly to heavenly existence; we are compelled to assume the existence of this zone, which emphasizes the continuity between the two worlds.

But is it Christian to celebrate in honor of mere men? Does not Christian celebration always refer to God alone? Indeed, and the Feast of All Saints is no exception. What we are celebrating is the grace of God, *charis*, which assumes the character of missions or charisms in order to take effect in individuals. It is grace alone that unfolds its power in man as he opens himself to it; it alone can succeed in gaining the upper hand in our hearts over our inborn self-seeking; it alone can deprivatize our narrow minds and make us more responsive to God's suffering and the suffering of the world than to our own suffering. Of believers we are told that "God's love has been poured into our hearts by the Holy Spirit". It is only by love being thus poured into created hearts that the God who wishes to reveal himself can achieve his purpose and his goal.

The Old Testament spoke in similar terms of God's wisdom permeating the whole of his creation; it was always the same, unique wisdom, belonging to God alone, which is multiplied, as it were, through the multiplicity of creatures and—as Paul says—is split into many colors. Even at that early stage there was no mere ossified opposition, with a monolithically simple God on the one side and an earthly world with its myriad colors on the other: even then there was the inner richness of the living God, open to the world's multiplicity, not only vaulted over it like a seven-hued rainbow but inwardly penetrating it—"unique, manifold, subtle, active, incisive . . . for Wisdom is quicker to move than any motion; she is so pure, she pervades and permeates all things" (Wis 7:22, 24). And this is demonstrated far more in the New Testament, where—going to the very limit—God is "rendered fluid" and poured into men's hearts, thanks to the self-giving of Jesus Christ on the Cross and in his Eucharist. Here are holy Flesh and holy Blood, set before us to eat and drink: we are to receive them and take them into ourselves, make them part of ourselves, if we want to have eternal life within us. Who, in the face of this, can still want to draw fixed boundaries between what God is in himself and what he wants to be in us? Who can still want to draw clear distinctions between the holiness God has in himself as the eternally Uncreated (totally unlike us), and the holiness he wants to have in us insofar as he, the Wholly Other, wishes simultaneously to be with us, on our side, among us and in us, making us his children and household, fellow heirs with his eternal Son? If God's concern is to overstep the boundaries between the uncreated and the created, should we try jealously to maintain them? If God desires to be all in all, which Scripture says is the ultimate goal of creation, how could we wish to hinder him by confining him, as it were, to his own holiness and declaring the created world to be nondivine, profane, secularized and self-sufficient?

This brings us to the second question. Nowadays, in this fundamentally secularized world, can "holiness" still have the same meaning it once had among people who took a particular delight in sacral ideas and images? Has the ideal of holiness still any attraction for us, or must there not be a fundamental change, at least, in the image of holiness if it is to remain plausible? And what would such a changed holiness look like?

I must admit that I cannot really see the sense of these suggestions. If we take the plaster masks from the faces of the saints, they seem to me to be just as much alive, just as credible as they have always been. The fundamental Christian ideal has not changed, nor can it, for nothing greater can ever be envisaged than the synthesis it aims for: namely, to believe in God as Love that goes to the ultimate, and to set out, on the basis of this love on God's part, to transform the world according to Love's pattern. There can be no question: this synthesis is the prerogative of Christianity. The religion of the East, which exercises such fascination nowadays, can only realize one-half of this ideal, that is, opting for the Absolute in preference to all transitory things and seeking union with this Absolute through techniques of meditation and consciousness expansion. What good is that to the secular world? For its part, communism only implements the other half, calling for the individual to make the utmost sacrifice for the sake of transforming society while disbelieving in God's operative power and imagining that everything can be achieved by man's unaided strength. And it is precisely these two halves of the total ideal—which must come together if man and humanity are really to attain salvation—that Christianity joins together in its ideal of holiness. For Christ is God and man. Following him means loving the Father together with him and being sent, along with him, into the Father's vineyard, the world, to share in the work of redemption. Moreover, arising from this work, it means being dependent on God as the giver of all effective and sanctifying graces. This synthesis is such an unexpected stroke of good fortune, such a stroke of luck, that Christianity can never exchange it for the mess of pottage of a new ideal of humanity. Seeing the two halves of the ideal fitting into each other in a way they cannot do anywhere else, Christianity has an ever-present proof of its own truth. Here she has visible and tangible proof that it would be a lesser ideal to seek God alone, even with all one's strength, if it involved forgetting the world; and that it would also be a lesser ideal to dedicate oneself, even one's entire energies, to the amelioration of world conditions, if it meant denying God or despising him as powerless.

The ideal of Christian holiness is a maximal ideal and hence can never be superseded. How it can be taken up and followed nowadays is quite a different question. But no doubt it will continue to be practiced in the multiplicity of charisms that God gives to his Church. Why should a vocation of suffering, for instance, following in the obedience of the Cross, be obsolete or less relevant nowadays? And very closely related is the vocation of genuine contemplation, as practiced by the Carmelites, for instance, where contemplation means immersing one's whole existence in the mystery of Christ, being dispossessed of one's entire life so that it may be available and at God's disposal. It may be that there are not as many of these vocations as the Middle Ages thought; perhaps the number of contemplative religious houses will decrease. But that does not mean that they are dispensable, as Thérèse of Lisieux never tired of telling us. All active missions, those of priests and those of laymen, are designed to draw their sustenance from the prayer and sacrifice of the contemplatives, and so it will remain.

Nowadays the saints may possibly have a more hidden existence than heretofore. Contemporary church architecture wants to do away with the pictorial; the saints are forgotten; their feast days are confusingly moved about; their communion and mediation remain unused. There are still canonizations, but they hardly evoke any wide resonance. Thus the saints go underground, at least for a time. They are not interested in being venerated anyway. If their disappearance meant that God would be loved better and more deeply, they would be the first to approve. It remains doubtful, however, whether we see God any more brightly in the absence of their light; I think we do not. We shall have to set the light of the saints on the lamp stand once again if we are not to stumble around in a night of our own making. For it is by the light of the saints, which is nothing other than God's light in the world, that we see *the* Light.

Communion of Saints

From time immemorial the Catholic Church has been acquainted with the custom, spontaneously created by the people and subsequently clothed in a juridical form, of "canonizing" certain especially radiant Christian lives. In this way she sets them forth as a "canon", a pattern and model of Christian living. Many and various questions can be posed with regard to this process, but initially we shall hold them at bay while we make one preliminary assertion: namely, that, in the first place, the "canon" of Christian living was seen by ordinary people in the light radiating from saintly lives. It was this spontaneous acclaim that raised them to eminence; in principle, Church authorities simply gave official recognition to this spontaneous act, albeit after the required critical examination of the case.

Just what is raised to the status of a model, however, what is called "holiness" in this special sense, is *love*; for love, quite simply, is the norm of all holiness. This love, according to Christ's word, is the love that must characterize those who are his in the world; in certain lives it attains that special, luminous warmth and radiance which makes those around them stop in their tracks, aware of being touched by something that simply goes beyond their notions of fellow feeling, humanity and neighborliness.

This first point, namely, that it is a question of love, that love which is held up as exemplary in the saints, is infinitely consoling to all who have to live in the thick of the human hurly-burly. For clearly, if it is *love* that is canonized, what is presented for our admiration and imitation is not the extraordinary side of the lives of many saints, which makes them particularly visible in the world, but that strength of heart that alone can work genuine miracles. And these miracles are not necessarily or even primarily visible; they belong to that hidden, holy realm in man's heart and in the heart of mankind whence—as experience shows—every creative and beneficent initiative comes. It is exclusively in this realm of the heart, hidden or somehow made manifest, that mankind's real progress takes place; this is where the great decisions of history are made, the destructive forces are defeated and the constructive forces are set loose, giving us grounds for something like hope. Only this realm of the heart can determine the sphere of validity of works of culture as well as of the secular, rational technology that produces machines and is produced by them; it is this realm of the heart that weighs and assesses them: "*Mene, Mene, Tekel, Parsin. Mene*, God has numbered the days of your kingdom and brought it to an end; *Tekel*, you have been weighed in the balances and found wanting; *Peres*, your kingdom is divided and given to the Medes and Persians" (Dan 5:25–28).

True, the holy realm of the heart where love—as event—takes place is the still, hidden chamber, seemingly remote from the noise and bustle of the world; but it would not *be* this all-irradiating sun if, in its hiddenness, the heart did not first have the courage and find the strength to be true to itself, if love did not achieve the improbable, that is, enable the heart to soar to its true stature, transcend itself and overcome its own self. For only in this act of self-transcending love can two things happen at once: the founding of the person and the founding of community. By opting to love (and hence abandoning its closed stance), the heart allows holiness, and holy community too, to take root within it. This opening up of the private sphere, this surrender of merely personal interest, which even puts one's own assurance of being saved and "holy" second to that "whole", "wholesome" and "holy" reality that actually *takes place*, as event, when the heart transcends itself: this opening up *is* the basis of the "communion of saints". From this, directly, flows all the mysterious alchemy associated with this concept (in all its straightforward simplicity and at the same time its unfathomable profundity).

What kind of reality are we speaking about here? Is it something specifically Christian? Or something common to all men? Is it something that makes the Church to be what she is—not of this world—or something that is behind all friendship, conjugal love, family, tribe and nation? Can we say that the Church is the communion of saints, of the holy? Would this make the so-called natural community a communion of the unholy? Does this mean that there are two different energies of the heart? Can the heart take the leap of self-transcendence twice, simultaneously resolving to seek the "I" and the "thou"?

The answer to this question lies buried under a great deal of ideological debris, yet, once the latter is cleared away, it is not difficult. Clearly, in Lacordaire's well-known formulation, there are not two kinds of love. How then can the Christian perspective differ from the universal human perspective? Why is what we call *caritas* not simply equivalent to what the Greeks called *eros* and *sympatheia*? Let us reflect first, therefore, on Christian love; second, on *sympatheia*; and third, on the union of the two.

1. The program of love that Jesus unfolds from the Sermon on the Mount onward exhibits an overpowering simplicity and intelligibility. There are things that "even the pagans do", such as loving one's friends. There are things that the pagans do not do, things that, *if* Christians do them, mark them out from the rest of mankind: namely, they go beyond the limits *sympatheia* sets for itself and find strength to love their neighbor, the person who is nearest to them, be he a stranger, uninvolved or a determined enemy.

Christ points out that this neighbor, whoever he may be, is a brother, since all men have a common Father in heaven. He is always our brother, and when things get serious, for example, if he falls among thieves and lies half-dead in the street, and equally if he suddenly appears to make demands of us and hale us before the courts or greets us with insults—in such cases he is most particularly our brother. At times like this we realize that our hearts tend to close in on themselves and seize on all possible excuses for avoiding the demand of self-transcending love. Faced with love's clear challenge, we become aware of the heart's inertia and lack of power; and if we are honest, we see that what we call *sympatheia*, family affection, the love of friends and sociability, is permeated with nonlove, egocentricity, self-seeking desires and the love of all kinds of comfort, and that this *sympatheia* is largely based on tacit compromises with collective egoism and tacit nonaggression pacts. We just do not have a sphere of intact natural love that is excelled and exceeded by Christian love; it is rather that, faced with the demands of genuine love, our so-called natural love is continually being unmasked to reveal a fallen heart that takes no real delight in love.

The heart's lameness cannot be overcome, however, by anything other than love. It cannot be overcome by ambition, for instance, or the desire to be loved or to be a hero or to have power over men, but only by love itself. And how can we acquire it if we do not have it? Here we begin to discern the role of Christian faith. By faith we admit our own inability to love and ask for strength of heart from him who can give it: "Lord, I believe; help my unbelief!" And the "Lord" here is the God of love who reveals himself in the man Jesus as the One whose love is real. He reveals himself as the One who himself possesses this heart's energy and therefore (since it is directed toward the brother, toward all brothers) can communicate it. "By my God I can leap over a wall", says the Psalm (Ps 18:29). The Christian does not merely say, "What I cannot do, you can do in my place, and I will accept what you have done as being done for me"; rather, he says: "What I cannot do on my own, I can do in and through you, since you first did it for me and now, therefore, you do it in me and with me."

Thus those who make Christian love a reality build the foundation for the genuine communion of saints. But because no one but Jesus has been able to perform this all-inclusive act of embracing even the most repulsive sinner, the most demonic perpetrator of hate, it is Jesus who is the founder of the communion of saints. Everyone who strives to follow this way of life is nourished by Jesus' infinite power of love. The communion of saints has its origin where love really transcends, giving the "thou" the preeminence over the "I"; and it does so in the power of God's love, which always has preeminence over our "I". In fact, it underpins our "I" by showing that it comes from God's pure self-outpouring into the world, in the ecstasy of love that we call the act of creation. Thus Denys the Areopagite truly described it. So when a finite "I", responding to God in discipleship, decides to open itself to love, it opens itself thereby to the love of God that is its ground, the infinite Spirit that blows through it and fills its sails. If it really loves, it knows perfectly well that what swells within it is not its own power; rather, in humility of heart, it knows that it is God who gives his love, and that this love comes from far, far away and is to cover an immense distance, further than the heart can imagine. And it knows that the heart permeated by love also comes from very far away and has further to travel than it can realize or even wants to realize. "The wind blows where it wills, and you hear the sound of it, but you do not know whence it comes or whither it goes; so it is with everyone who is born of the Spirit" (Jn 3:8).

2. If we look back, from this vantage point, at what we are accustomed to call "natural love", we find that the usual division of love into two kinds also becomes questionable. How could natural love differ from Christian love? Only by in principle setting limits for itself: I love my own child but not someone else's; I love my own family but not anyone else's; I only regard some people as my brothers, not the rest. . . . But, when it comes down to it, would not such a love negate itself? Does not the clear refusal to allow love to cross all boundaries constitute an attack on the very nature of love? It is possible to school a child's receptive heart to this kind of view, presenting it as something normal, customary, as the governing ethos; people can elevate the human heart's poverty of love into a universally valid norm, tolerating it and giving it the sanction of a convention, allowing the term *love* to cover much that is nothing but greedy desire; indeed, people can even suggest that it is predominantly egocentric desire. It may hide under the mask of "love", but in reality it is its opposite.

In the most pure and patent relationships, however, such as those between mother and child, father and child, friend and friend, this restriction is in principle brushed aside. Even analogies from the mere realm of nature, like the instinct of mother animals that can lead them to sacrifice themselves for their brood, are superseded when it comes to men, for in human love the mother is not simply borne aloft temporarily on a tide of vital functions: the transitory relationship is deepened into a permanent spiritual constitution. In other words, our common nature as men, which makes us all brothers since it makes us all children of the heavenly Father, is potentially oriented toward the communion of the saints, that is, of those who love. Thus the idea that someone could seriously be concerned for his own eternal salvation without being equally concerned for the eternal salvation of his brother and neighbor (and who is *not* my neighbor?)—this is not only an un-Christian idea: it is also an inhuman idea. It is true that this idea has persisted down the centuries on the basis of a misreading of the Christian teaching on conscience, arising from another idea, namely, that some men are chosen and others are not. In Christian terms, however, the one who is chosen is chosen for the sake of those who (initially) are not chosen; he is someone who is sent to them. In other words, by God's grace, he has been selected and equipped for love; he is to proclaim love by carrying it out; he is to make the communion of saints known by allowing it to take root and grow in him.

Wherever it takes place among men, and under whatever disguise, it is when the heart renounces itself and gives pride of place to the "thou", bearing the other's burden and ready ultimately, if it comes to it, to put the other person first, that the communion of saints is realized. From the simple "Yes" to love in the heart of a schoolchild who accepts without complaint some unjust punishment on the part of a teacher, in order to spare the real culprit, to the seemingly dramatic and yet quite sober assertion of Paul, namely, that he would wish to be cursed and banished from Christ instead of his brother Jews, there is no demarcation or border, no stopping. It is impossible to see where the ordinary steps over into the extraordinary, the normal into the heroic.

That is why, in the Bible, perfect love is not a counsel but a command; moreover, it comes across more and more clearly and challengingly as the one and only command, which, in the sight of God, gives meaning to all other precepts. Without love they would all be nothing but police regulations designed to prevent the coexisting predators from devouring each other at will. On the contrary, it is clear how profound and radiant an influence is exerted by genuine love on the development of all the individual norms of personal and national ethics, affecting even the outermost regions of nature in its material aspect and its automatic processes. One example of this is the way wild, instinctual man was infused with Christian mores in the medieval cult of *Minne*, courtly love, in the Renaissance ideal of the *cortegiano* and the Baroque concept of the *honnête homme*. While such cultural forms are always in danger of coming adrift from the heart's love matrix and sinking to the level of a superficial social game of politeness, yet, where they are permeated by love, something tremendous results: in such cases, loving self-denial becomes the form not only of Christian and ecclesial holiness but also of civilization itself, of an order in society that is worthy of man. It signifies a terrible attack on man by man himself, therefore, when he consigns the forms of politeness, the external embodiments adopted by love, to the scrap heap, deeming them to be mere formality and hence in conflict with honesty and sincerity of heart. This is barbarism, and it evinces a total misunderstanding of the nature of love.

It is true, of course—and the Gospels take great delight in emphasizing the fact—that love and convention can so diverge as to be totally opposed to one another. God's heart rejoices over the prostitutes who turn from false love to true love, whereas it must mourn for the Pharisees, in whom the spark of love has been extinguished. The apparent confusion that the woman who was a sinner introduces into the Pharisee's correctly arranged meal, with her ointment, her tears and her loosed hair, testifies to a deeper culture of the heart than the host's loveless dinner-formality does. Nothing is more dangerous, more fatal to the realm and community of hearts than sacred forms claiming to be sacred in themselves, not backed up by love. This applies to Church authority, to the Church's juridical aspect, just as much as to a nation's government with all its organs and functions. For, in both spheres, once there are areas that are no longer animated by the human heart and motivated ultimately by love—and this applies even to areas like economics, which on the face of it seem to be so impersonal—they are dead limbs on the organism, and their foul rottenness is bound to bring death, horribly, to the members that are still living. How much more is this true of the regulations enacted in the legal code, in politics and even in education! Their particular juridical nature does not mean that they may cut themselves loose from the sustaining power of human love, as if they belonged to some allegedly objective and autonomous dimension. And how much more it applies to the Church, where the sphere of official ministry is always and only a function of love and is justified solely by its vital relationship with love! Separated from love, it immediately becomes a rock of offense, blocking the way to the realm of the heart: "Woe to you, scribes and Pharisees, hypocrites! because you shut the kingdom of heaven against men; for you neither enter yourselves, nor allow those who would enter to go in . . . you have neglected the weightier matters of the law, justice and mercy and faith" (Mt 23:13, 23). This terrible possibility—objectifying the "holy" and alienating it from the heart, making what ought to be the kingdom of God into a weapon in the hand of this "brood of vipers", continually "whitewashed" and renovated "tombs" that outwardly are impressive and splendid "but within they are full of dead men's bones and all uncleanness"—this possibility, which causes love to harden in the hearts of many, is doubtless one of the monstrous horrors referred to in the Book of Revelation.

Every feature of the Church of Christ must be love. For we can dwell in the Church only of our own free will because we want to love, to drink at love's fount, to sit at the table where the Lamb's love is eaten and drunk, to kneel at the spot where the Prodigal Son falls into his Father's arms. We only do this because we want to take responsibility in an un-Christian world, empowered by the Holy Spirit, who, from the depths of the communion of saints, accredits us as members of this communion. The Church has only understood herself and her world mission properly if she makes the communion of saints a visible reality, so that this is seen immediately, and not through a confusing no-man's-land of forms, laws and authorities, which have to be gone through before one finally enters the blooming flower garden. The Church must be the place where people catch a glimpse of something of the mysterious realm of love, of the communion of saints. According to Jesus' plan and design, what is to be seen in the Church is genuine, active love, *his* love united with the love of those who are his, and nothing else.

3. This brings the third point into focus: the unity of love wherever it is found, in the Church or in what we call the world. No mortal eye can mark the boundaries of the communion of saints. For no one knows how far love is able to radiate, how much it can sustain and act on behalf of others. All sinners are borne up and revalued in the power of love of Jesus Christ's heart, whether they know it or not, whether they accept it or not. This establishes a center of community, an ecclesial a priori that, while it is not as yet the concrete love relationship between men themselves and between men and God, creates the space, through a love that is superabundant and overflowing, in which this can become a reality. Within this field of force everyone can draw strength and power to join in the exercise of love. Who can say where the passive reality of being loved—love having banished the coldness of this passivity at the crucial spot—passes over into the active reality that transforms the loved person into a lover? Who can say when a man stops resisting the cross because he has come to see that his whole resistance has been overtaken by the facts themselves?

Shortly before his death, Bernanos uttered some profound words, words that come from the very heart of the communion of saints:

> There is a danger of seeing God's love as a benevolent, condescending love. God desires his creature with a desire that would crush us to dust if we had even an inkling of it. That is

> why he implants this desire deep in the gentle and loving heart of Jesus Christ. Jesus did not come as a victor but as someone pleading for sanctuary. He is in me like a refugee under my care, and I am to entreat his Father for him. We really want what he wants; we may not know it, but we really want our sufferings, our pain, our loneliness, although we may think that we only want happiness. We imagine we are afraid of death and are running away from it, whereas in fact we want this death, just as he wanted his own death. . . . We want everything he wants, but we are not aware of wanting it; we do not know ourselves; sin causes us to live on the surface, and it is only in dying that we return into ourselves, to find him waiting for us. . . . If we resist him, it is only at the price of tearing our whole inner being, squandering our own selves monstrously. For our will is united with his ever since the foundation of the world. Together with us he created the world. How calming is this thought: that, even if we offend him, we never completely stop yearning for what he yearns for, in the innermost sanctuary of our soul.

Thus Bernanos divines the ultimate laws of the communion of saints. There is nothing physical about our being drawn into God's loving will in Christ, no natural necessity, but our whole spiritual being is plunged into his free Spirit of love. This is where the communion of spirits takes place, the communion of destinies, of graces given and fates incurred; it is not a case of mechanically balancing good and ill fortune and producing some fatal compromise: what happens is that, in Christ's loving will, all the negative things are dissolved in the pain of crucified love, and all the good things are poured out infinitely over everyone, shared out among everyone. The tiniest act of genuine, self-denying love comes from God's eternity and so must continue to transmit its effect through all eternity.

Love wants to help to bear the burden of the world. The destiny that comes to us in world history, rolling over us, overwhelming and overpowering us, is met and mastered by the power of the praying and sustaining heart, even when this heart is trampled down by worldly powers: victory comes to it even as it bursts asunder. The heart we see on the Cross is similarly crushed, violated and insulted to the uttermost; but it does not run headlong against the iron justice of a Kafkaesque God: God's love for the world was contained in this crushed heart, and it has flowed out of this winepress into all the world. This folly on God's part, says the Apostle, is wiser than the wisdom of men. Does it not encourage us to pursue every folly of love, whereby we offer our own "nothing" in order to lift "everything" from its hinges? Thus we offer our poor little prayers, for Israel, for Moscow, for the capitalistic countries. "They all contributed out of their abundance, but she out of her poverty put in all the living that she had" (Lk 21:4).

It is only God, and he in whose heart the Father implanted all his love and to whom he entrusted his entire Spirit, who can sustain the world and its contradictions to the end and beyond. All the same, finite man has received an infinite dowry from the crucified Heart, enabling him to share in thus bearing the world. It is expressed in the words of the Mother and Virgin: "Behold, I am the Lord's handmaid; let him do to me according to his word"—his "Word of the Cross", his crucified Word. Man is simply unable to perform this whole task, but he *can* produce a readiness for the whole without setting limits and making objections. And when the Spirit overshadows the Maid, and when the Spirit gasps in the Maid's heart and cries out with her in childbirth, we perceive that man's readiness to accept all suffering is greater and more divine than all his "achievements" and abilities and neat solutions. God's relation to the world is not only masculine, as *Deus faber*, but womb-like and feminine, achieving the redemption of the entire universe through pain.

> We know that the whole creation has been groaning in travail together until now; and not only the creation, but we ourselves, who have the firstfruits of the Spirit, groan inwardly. . . . For we do not know how to pray as we ought, but the Spirit himself intercedes for us with sighs too deep for words. And he who searches the hearts of men knows what is the mind of the Spirit,

> because the Spirit intercedes for the saints according to the will of God (Rom 8:22–23, 26–27).

This groaning longing for God on the part of all creation is at the heart of what we call the communion of saints. It is a communion that goes beyond all the laws fixed by the world, all the world's "givens", and that lives by what is given by God alone. It is a communion of unspeakable hope. So it is a communion of open hearts, concerned only about their common object, no longer preoccupied with the boundaries of "I" and "thou". Since this "dividing wall" has been pulled down and the bastions, once demolished, will never be reerected, henceforth God's salvation and his ultimate and conclusive love can be encountered only in the *We*.

Christ the King

Where Is the Kingdom?

Today's Gospel has the little scene in which Jesus watches a poor widow in the Temple putting a tiny coin into the box; in amazement he exclaims, "Truly, I say to you, this poor widow has put in more than all those who are contributing to the treasury. For they all contributed out of their abundance; but she out of her poverty has put in everything she had, her whole living" (Mk 12:43–44). This little scene must have struck the Evangelists Mark and Luke as something very special, for both of them place it right at the end of Jesus' public ministry. After it come the prophecies concerning the end of Jerusalem and of the world, which introduce the Passion narrative.

We can look at the widow's gesture in various ways: we can be moved by it, or, if we are psychologists, we can ask whether she might have acted from some superstitious motive —in order to have a bit of "pull" with the Almighty. Jesus sees it quite differently. He sees something that, evidently, occasions profound astonishment in him: he sees that such things as this are possible. Here is a person who, when giving an offering, gives not from a position of plenty, like the rich who dispense large sums; she gives of the very necessities of her life. "She put in everything she had, her whole living." In material terms this "everything" was practically nothing, but a "practically nothing" that was her very all.

Here it is as if, as Jesus' earthly days draw to a close, he is given assurance that his preaching of the kingdom of God has not been totally in vain. During his lifetime the disciples had grasped little or nothing of it. And now here there suddenly appears a person who, whether she ever heard Jesus preaching or not (nor does it matter), has grasped the very core of what it is all about. In his preaching of the kingdom of God he spoke of quite ordinary things: a bit of leaven; a few grains of wheat happening to fall on good soil; a mustard seed that when it is sown, is the smallest of all seeds. One day it will grow taller than all other shrubs, but that time is much later; only if the seed falls into the earth and dies will it bring forth much fruit. What is precious lies concealed in small, hidden, everyday things, things often overlooked. It is the person who plows someone else's field in the sweat of his brow who comes unexpectedly upon the hidden treasure. Unexpectedly, for he did not go plowing in order to find this treasure. The words of these parables communicate a kind of shock: namely, that the greatest thing is found to lie in the smallest, the most unexpected thing in what is everyday. But there is nothing fairy tale about this: the unexpected encounter with the immensity of the discovered treasure, the delight and the grace it brings, the pearl of great price on which one stumbles by accident, demands that the discoverer break out from his everyday routine and adapt to the proportions of this unexpected gift. Thus he will sell all he has to buy the field that contains the treasure; he will surrender all his possessions for the sake of the matchless pearl. The unconventional gift calls for a response and a gratitude that are equally unconventional. This is the only way actually to *receive* such a present; otherwise one is engaging in egoistic theft and deception, buying someone else's field and concealing from its owner the fact that it contains something of great value. This is what Jesus was aiming at in the parables of the kingdom: hidden beneath the apparently insignificant and ordinary lies something precious and utterly extraordinary, something given totally freely and in no way due to us. In the face of this grace, this miracle, we must immediately adopt the appropriate attitude. We must no longer calculate and haggle but sell all we have, give it all away for absolutely nothing.

We do not give everything away in order to make a great profit. Doing so would mean that we had still not understood anything of the miracle of grace. We give it all away for nothing, because what we give away we received for nothing in the first place. We need only to look at another of Jesus' parables to see what is meant by this "for nothing": the Parable of the Unmerciful Servant (Mt 18:26f.). He has been confronted with the miracle of grace: his unpayable debt has been canceled, for nothing, for no discernible reason. He is right to rejoice at this, of course, but only if he immediately adopts the very same attitude himself. For the real gift that he has been given is not the canceling of the debt but the "for nothing", the unfathomable mind of his merciful master. *That* was the pearl of great price he had found, and he should have made it his own and thus pardoned his fellow servant, who owed him but a little. This parable links up with all the images that show us God's great, prodigal squandering of love: thus he invites us to huge banquets, to which we should respond with the same magnanimity and absence of calculation, instead of making plausible excuses and so rendering ourselves unworthy of God and his kingdom.

"You received without pay, give without pay" (Mt 10:8), says Jesus to his disciples, applying to their preaching the central concern of his own proclamation of the kingdom. God is always pure, uncalculating grace, love that gives itself for no ulterior motive; that is why it is impossible to make a "deal" with God. It is impossible to treat God as a market product, as capital, to be used by man in his negotiations, nor can God be regarded as a partner with whom man can do business. That was the basic assumption behind the attitude of those pious and zealous Pharisees who were so summarily dismissed by Jesus; that was why he rebuffed them, not on account of their pious deeds. Pharisees like these may have been among the people Jesus watched in the Temple, putting large sums into the alms boxes.

This brings us back to the poor widow. In her Jesus sees his own preaching of the kingdom bearing fruit. There can be no doubt that, at the end of his earthly life, the word he had sowed in the world seemed to him to have borne very little fruit. How much trouble he had taken with people, and how little success he had had! Disappointingly little success. He had never been concerned about external success; in fact, he had always turned away from it as something misleading. He did not want the crowd to acclaim him as their king, nor did he want the disciples to proclaim him as the Messiah. His mission was different: to awaken in people's hearts a sense of the boundless love for sinners that lies in the heavenly Father's heart; to strike a spark of this divine flame even in the niggardly hearts of men. "I have come to cast fire on the earth." Fire does not rest until it has consumed everything within its reach. This fire is at work in the widow's heart. She does not even need to know that it is there. "She out of her poverty has put in everything she had, her whole living." She does not calculate or apportion what she has. She simply gives, forgetful of herself. She has gone beyond the boundaries that human reasonableness regards as essential, in material as in spiritual things. There is something of God's infinity about her, something of that unconcern about tomorrow that Jesus commended in the Sermon on the Mount. She has the freedom of the birds of heaven and the lilies of the field.

Many people nowadays are bored with modern culture and are searching for this freedom. They manifest their disgust at this culture by deliberately neglecting their physical appearance, their clothes, and by the way they interact with others. One can understand them. But one can also ask whether this is the freedom that Jesus meant, the freedom of the kingdom. And sometimes it can be—for instance, when the hard-won freedom has resulted in selfless, limitless self-giving—and this is never achieved without severe self-discipline. If we are to understand the kingdom, we must not only free ourselves from the desire for earthly possessions but must also avoid adopting an attitude of indifference and contempt toward them, of "not giving a damn". Christian selflessness, as intended by Jesus, has love for its center. The widow deprives herself of something very necessary so that she can show gratitude to God—for she was giving for the Temple. She does not give for some humanitarian purpose, for the poor, for Third World development; she just gives, purely and simply, and she does not give *something*, she gives all she is and has, herself.

Jesus' entire proclamation of the kingdom is directed to this point. For God does not give us just something: he gives us himself, his heart, his word, his mind. And what he requires from us, in response, is not just something but the entire investment of our selves, our binding word, our heart. And just as God changed the world's situation by stepping in on its behalf and accepting the suffering of the Cross and the profound concealment it entailed, turning everything upside down by transforming its cul-de-sac into a thoroughfare, a hope, so it is by investing his whole heart (and ultimately in no other way) that man can really help to change the world, starting with that hidden place where the grain of wheat dies in order to bear much fruit. "Thy kingdom come", we pray at Jesus' command. It comes through God and from God, and yet it does not come without our cooperation. But we cannot bring it about by erecting an earthly structure, a kind of Tower of Babel, an edifice of culture and progress that will reach to heaven; we can only cooperate with God, adopting God's approach, in a movement that comes down from above, implanting the Spirit of total self-giving in the hard, dry, egoistic soil of this world's field. Nor is this done in the grand manner, with a dramatic gesture, so that the world can look on in wonder, but in the same unspectacular way that the widow put her halfpenny in the box. As far as she is concerned it is nothing out of the ordinary, and no one sees it but Jesus alone.

Her hidden action fulfills the meaning of Jesus' prayer that he puts on our lips and in our hearts. It does not begin "My Father" but "Our Father", yours and mine; since he is our Father, all of us possess all his gifts in common. Thus it was not good for the younger son to be given his share of the inheritance prematurely; in the end he realized that he would have done better to continue sharing his father's undivided inheritance; then he would not have had to experience want.

Then come the three great petitions, each of which asks basically for the same thing: that God's name be sanctified on earth as in heaven; that his kingdom take effect not only in heaven but also on earth; that his will be done on earth as in heaven. These three, name, kingdom and will, are all the same: they are the inner, hidden nature of God, his mind and heart. Thus God's heart is to begin to beat in the midst of this heartless world.

And how great is the contrast! The world is heartless, on the whole, because we are so limited; everyone thinks first of all of his own bit of life, his own self-preservation and well-being. *Après nous le déluge!* We are not only small: we are petty. The natural restriction of our consciousness shrinks even further to the artificial, deliberate narrowness of our egoism. And then there is God's heart! Here the breadth, the panorama, is so great that we cannot imagine it. The divine Father is Father from all eternity. That means that his generation of the Son is always prior; from before all time the Father has given all that he has to his Son; he has never possessed anything by himself that he had not already, from all eternity, given away. In fact, this giving away constitutes his most distinctive, divine wealth. God is the richest of all because he is the poorest of all. Whatever he has, he has not for himself, but always for someone else. The Father for the Son, the Son for the Father and Father and Son for the Holy Spirit common to both. Again, the Spirit has nothing for himself; all he has, he has for Father and Son. Nor is this a mutual (twofold or threefold) egoism, for in God each Person really thinks only of the Other and is only concerned to enrich him. God's entire wealth consists in this giving of self and receiving of the "Thou".

The poor widow who gave away all she had is very close to this God. Perhaps we can say that God put all he had into the world's alms box when he gave us this man, this unspectacular, hidden man named Jesus of Nazareth, scarcely to be found in world history. In this "almost nothing" he has given us more than he gave us in the rich and vast universe, because in giving his Son he "put in everything he had, his whole living", so that we could live from his eternal life, even at the cost of his death.

When Will the Kingdom Come?

In today's Gospel we read these words:

> Learn a lesson from the fig tree. When its tender shoots appear and are breaking into leaf, you know that summer is near. In the same way, when you see all this happening, you may know that the end is near, at the very door. I tell you this: the present generation will live to see it all. Heaven and earth will pass away; my words will never pass away. But about that day or that hour no one knows, not even the angels in heaven, not even the Son; only the Father (Mk 13:28–32).

How mysterious it all sounds, particularly when we consider that the words "when you see all this happening" refer to the coming of "the Son of Man in great power and glory". We are plunged into the heart of an event that is inescapably rolling forward; we are told that we—"this generation"—will experience it; and finally we are told that no one knows this hour, not even the Son who speaks all these words. The kingdom of God is coming, and it will arrive very soon, with the power and splendor of the divine, yet its advent is not something we can grasp, calculate or objectify. The most we can do is read the signs, as the Parable of the Barren Fig Tree teaches us. What are we to do with such words from the mouth of Jesus? How can we come to grips with them or situate ourselves within them?

The first thing is clear: no one knows the hour; no more than anyone knows the hour of his death. The hour possesses us, not we the hour. All calculations as to the hour are mistaken. People have always tried, for nearly two thousand years, to calculate when the end of the world would come, and they have always been wrong. "Not even the Son!" Jesus lived day by day, hour by hour, in an attitude of self-surrender to the Father. He knew that the hour of suffering would come, as well as the hour of Resurrection that lies perpendicular to it; he even knew that it was very close; he yearned for it, yearned to perform this decisive work of his—reconciling the world to God—or rather to suffer it, to be baptized with this baptism of fire; but in no way did he desire to know when this hour would strike. The Father would give the signal. This is the exemplary attitude that every Christian should adopt. It is only Christian if we lay ourselves, childlike and trusting, in the Father's arms, without the anxious tension created by wanting to decide things, observe things and direct things ourselves. For ultimately this is rebellion against divine providence. This applies to Christians of every period, including ours, which is a time of increasing social and political confusion, a time that looks toward a future that may well bring apocalyptic events. We shall not be able to be spectators in the face of these events, for they will drag us unceremoniously into their forward march. By nature we are afraid of the uncertainty of things, things that threaten us. But we are to place this entirely natural fear—and I think that Jesus too experienced this fear as he faced his approaching suffering—in a simple, childlike manner in the Father's hands.

This passage teaches us a second thing. Jesus knows that

"the end is at the very door"; he knows that "this generation" will experience it. If we are to understand this, we must remember that, from Jesus' point of view, the world will come to an end with his Passion and death. He has borne the entire sin of the world, of all past, present and future generations. "The prince of this world is judged"—"I have overcome the world." For him, this old world, which will still carry on for millennia, is obsolete. The sign that it is at an end, for him and with him, is his Resurrection from the dead. Thus the new, eternal world begins. This is the plain truth, and it applies not only to Jesus Christ personally but also to us together with him. God's great power and glory have already manifested themselves on the Cross, when the Lamb of God was laden with the world's guilt and the sign of the Son of Man was raised up forever in the clouds, between earth and heaven. That itself was the end of the world, because in it God set aright all the world's disorder, accomplished his purpose for the world, settled his account with it. Not for nothing do the evangelists portray the event of the Cross in eschatological, apocalyptic colors: the sun is darkened from the sixth to the ninth hours; the earth trembles; the graves open—this is the scenery of the Last Judgment. No purely earthly hour will ever surpass this hour when God settled accounts; rather, the continuing unfolding of secular history, drawing us along with it, can only unfold toward this hour. The judgment that lies before us is the judgment that took place once and for all on the Cross; it is before the Crucified that we shall have to appear and make our case, before the great power and glory and majesty of the Cross. And none of us will be able to justify himself: all will be justified solely by *him*, by *his* intercession, by *his* intervention on our behalf.

This is already our situation today. For we are told that "heaven and earth will pass away, but my words will never pass away." We already know about the difference between this passing world and the word that lasts forever. We experience fleeting things in all their transitoriness and inconsistency; their very form shows that they have no permanence, and even today we can count them as things that are past. We could even write off heaven and earth, had they not been granted the possibility of survival in the word of God, which does not pass away. Things are the reverse of what they seem: it is not that heaven and earth form a kind of eternal framework within which, among innumerable other mortals, the figure of Jesus Christ suddenly turns up and just as suddenly disappears; on the contrary, Jesus Christ is the definitive utterance of God. He is his eternal and abiding Word, and as such *he* is the all-embracing framework; only within this ultimate, immovable sphere do heaven and earth come and go, to return in a transformed shape. This Word of God descends into time and then, in Resurrection, arises out of time, and by doing so expresses the meaning of all time. Only within this Word do heaven and earth and the whole of world history acquire a genuine meaning. In the absence of this Word, heaven and earth are stray comets coming from nowhere and going nowhere, lacking all sense and purpose. It is a source of astonishment that people who reject the all-embracing meaning to be found in Christ or do not even know it still think they can find a meaning in existence. In pre-Christian times it was possible to do this to some extent, since all peoples believed in some divinity or other; but how could this be possible in the post-Christian era? For there is no going back to the more childlike world models of ancient civilizations. Heaven and earth are empty, the moon is a heap of stones, man is alone in this barren waste and all will pass away.

And now we come to the third point: "Learn a lesson from the fig tree." In this strange situation between the Resurrection, which has already taken place, and the Judgment, which still lies ahead of us, there are certain indications, road signs, milestones, recognition marks. "You know that summer is near." Let us put it in concrete images: the whole atmosphere of human history tells us that the fingers of the world clock are moving forward. We sense that it is later than we thought, later than we would have liked. Much beauty, and much that was inchoate, already lies behind us, gone forever, and we can have a rough idea of the path that lies ahead of us in world history—namely, the path of technology, of concentrations of power, of the use of violence—even simply in order to survive. Mankind will with difficulty learn to avoid doing things it can do, for it is made up of too many heads. And since, outside the path of Jesus Christ, history's paths will seem to be increasingly meaningless (whatever man tries to do), there will be more and more explosions of this sense of meaninglessness—unless people can really be changed into that flock of lambs that cannot see further than the next blade of grass, like the "last men" portrayed by Nietzsche. A lot of busy planning is going on already in this regard. Nowadays, however, we do not plan in the grandiose, Promethean style of the nineteenth century, which believed in unlimited development and ever new discoveries that would rise higher and higher before the marveling eyes of humanity. How naïve this notion of progress seems to us today! Now we plan feverishly simply in order to survive for a little longer—lest half of mankind should soon die of hunger, lest we should all suffocate in an air that is no longer breathable and become poisoned by stinking seas and infected rivers. And, equally feverishly, we plan reciprocal annihilation with ever more frightful weapons. People will not gape for much longer at new airplane speed records, new conquests of distances, new interplanetary flights; and the more these things are presented as ultramodern and "of tomorrow's world", the more people tire of them in advance. Many young people have already found it out: for them, happiness cannot lie in the future but instead, if at all, in the past, in the simple life such as our forefathers led. There is no great certainty here either, particularly as the way back seems thoroughly to be blocked, impassable without the use of violence—and perhaps of drugs, too, enchanting us away from all that is meant by "today".

People yearn for something else but dare not utter the word

nostalgia without a wry, distancing smile, as if it were a mere whim, a caprice. Ultimately, after putting up a certain amount of resistance, people give in and are locked in the prison of the contemporary world, which has no genuine tomorrow, no genuine yesterday, and has the distinct smell of the end of time about it. The great options are clearly set forth; it is quite out of the question that new solutions will emerge. We are looking at a naked horizon. The confusing din of world journalism, enshrouding everything in its chatter, can do nothing to change this. True, it would suggest that there is a pluralism of opinions, standpoints and proposed solutions seeming to be much richer than in the times when, in Europe at least, it was possible to speak of Christian culture. Everything seems possible. But if we look at the whole picture there is very little that is still possible. What we are looking for here is not so much the future that can be steered by technology but the available meanings that can be given to the whole process. There are very few such possibilities. We can take flight from the meaninglessness of the present and put all our efforts into the future, working for a more just distribution of goods; but will this make people happier? Or, like the Oriental religious man, we can try to escape from the senseless, endless turning of the world's wheel; but what kind of meaning does this leave the world? All that remains is the third possibility, the way of Jesus Christ, which, while it does not explain the origin of suffering in the world—no one can do that—shows us that God has declared his solidarity with our suffering and has given it a positive valence, totally reversing its significance, in his Son's Cross and Resurrection. These, then, in the stark relief that characterizes the end time, are the possible decisions with which mankind is faced. The scenery is already being taken away, and the actors are standing, freezing, on the stripped stage. They are playing the final drama of world history—and it is immaterial how long it lasts.

Perhaps we now understand this parable a little better: "When its tender shoots appear and are breaking into leaf, you know that the summer is near. In the same way, when you see all this happening, you may know that the end is near, at the very door." We cannot calculate when the end will come. At any time, now or later, we may hear it knocking at the door. All we need is to be ready.

The King and His Kingdom

"Pilate said to Jesus, 'Are you the King of the Jews?' Jesus answered, 'Do you say this of your own accord, or did others say it to you about me?' Pilate answered: 'Am I a Jew? Your own nation and the chief priests have handed you over to me; what have you done?' " (Jn 18:33–35).

A strange, inconclusive dialogue. Questions are met with counterquestions. The governor's question can only be asked from within the perspective of Roman politics and administration. Jesus could have answered with a straight "No": he raised no claim to authority in this area. But how could Pilate have arrived at such a question in the first place unless there were, in the background, a third factor, God's chosen people, for whom the phrase "King of the Jews" had an entirely different religious and messianic import? "Did others say it to you about me?" Is there something of their view, their problems and their questions in your question to me? For if both of you, Jew and gentile, together ask this question, it acquires a new and far greater scope. Then the whole world is asking who I am and what is my authority.

Pilate gives a strange answer. Indirectly he admits that he is not asking of his own accord: "Your own nation and the chief priests have handed you over to me", evidently on account of the word *king*, which has a messianic ring as far as Jews are concerned and is meant to sound political to the gentiles. But Pilate says, "Am I a Jew?" He rejects any kind of solidarity with the Jews. He is not interested in the associations the word *king* has for them. He is Rome's representative. Thus he falls into the trap laid by the Jews and operates on the basis of the secular-political implications of Jesus' kingship. And after all, was that not what interested the Jews too? Anti-Roman politics? Israel's liberation struggle? What else did they want from the promised Messiah? And why had they handed Jesus over to the Roman governor? Because Jesus' whole approach was not secular, not political, not messianic enough for them. The people had long wanted to proclaim him king when he distributed bread to the multitude. Only a few days earlier, at his entry into Jerusalem, the people had greeted him with hosannas. But to the leaders of the nation he was a maverick idealist, merely an obstacle to their realistic political goals; he came bringing ethical demands that were of no use, for he put forward no political theology of any kind. What good to them were his miracles of healing, which placed him in the line of the old prophets? Basically they needed no prophets now, only resolute, ambitious men of orthopraxy. Of course, Jesus had deeds to his credit, but as far as Israel's pundits were concerned, they were not the right ones. On the basis of his deeds they insinuated to Pilate that he was a troublemaker, stirring up the people. "What have you done?" Pilate asked him.

> Jesus answered, "My kingship is not of this world; if my kingship were of this world, my servants would fight, that I might not be handed over to the Jews; but my kingship is not from the world." Pilate said to him, "So you are a king?" Jesus answered, "You say that I am a king. For this I was born, and for this I have come into the world, to bear witness to the truth. Everyone who is of the truth hears my voice."

When asked, "What have you done?" Jesus replies, "My kingship is not of this world." He leaves much unsaid. He does not say that he has done nothing, nothing *in* this world. For he came into this world for the express purpose of doing something, something *in* it. His deeds are performed in this world. And they are intended *for* this world. The world is to see and apprehend the testimony he gives in it. We need to realize the whole tension that lies between, on the one hand, the words "not of this world" and, on the other hand, the expression "for this I was born, and for this I have come into the world". He is not someone who happens to find himself in the world and, oppressed by its narrow confines, strives to extricate himself from it. He is not someone who flees the world. He is not a Buddhist. For him, the world is not the starting point of his yearning transcendence toward some higher life; on the contrary: "For this I have come into the world." The world is the destination of a movement, a journey. He comes from outside and from above in order to show the world something, in order to proclaim something of which it is unaware, something that is not simply a confirmation of its longing for escape. He came because he had something to do on this earth, something the Jews would gladly have exploited for political ends, something Pilate is at pains to understand and evaluate in political terms, but something that, as Jesus says, "is not of this world".

He illustrates this by referring to the fact that his servants did not fight to prevent his being arrested by the Jews. In fact his arrest did include a pusillanimous scene of political theology, namely, Peter's sword stroke, which ridiculously managed only to shear off an ear and was immediately disavowed by Jesus. For this political theology on Peter's part put him willy-nilly in solidarity with the pseudoreligious views of those Jews who wanted no other Messiah but a political one.

No. "My kingship is not of this world." And yet, Jesus has come to this world. He came to his Father's kingdom, the kingdom of God, whose King he is. He says this just once, here, as he appears before the court and faces death. His enthronement as King will be complete on the Cross, when the famous inscription is placed over his head in the three languages of the world of that time. So that everyone will understand. And now the assertion is categorical: "King of the Jews", not—as the Jews would have liked—"he called himself the King of the Jews". No. *Truly* King of the Jews. "For this I have come into the world, to bear witness to the truth." Thus, royally, he bears witness.

How strangely he speaks. What has this being a king to do with bearing witness to the truth? The two are identical. And they coincide with the assertion that "my kingship is not of this world". Why? Because the truth is that "God so loved the world that he gave his only-begotten Son", finally and decisively, on the Cross, when he took the world's guilt upon himself and, as the Lamb, the scapegoat, bore it away. It is in carrying this guilt that he bears witness to the truth. The truth of divine love. It is the only credible testimony to this love. The world is an ocean of suffering and injustice—how can God say that he loves it?! The whole idea is laughable! But on the Cross there is no laughing; God shows that he and his love are serious: he hands over his Son. And the Son shows that he and his testimony are serious: he cries out as he undergoes that forsakenness by God that belongs to sinners. This is the most extreme, most high-profile solution imaginable, and God has carried it through. That is why, on the Cross, the world that is opposed to God and mocks God is vanquished. "Be of good cheer, I have overcome the world." And so he says, "Yes, I am a King." Not a king within the vanquished world but a King who sits on a throne exalted high above it. Exalted by the Cross. And naturally the vanquished world belongs to this kingdom, although the kingdom is not of this world.

Jesus does not permit the world he has conquered for God on the Cross to continue to exist as it was. He implants God's rule in it. In men's hearts. Divine love has become "at home" on the earth through him. In the hearts of the poor, of children, of the merciful, the gentle, the persecuted, in pure hearts. In canonized saints and many other saints. They do exist. Together they constitute a kingdom, and now and then we actually see or feel some small piece of this kingdom. Everyone knows that they are not interested in world conquest; they cannot even organize themselves to form a significant power in the world's terms. They have no plan to change the world so that, in subsequent generations, the greatest possible number of people may experience the greatest possible happiness. Their plan concerns the present: now, today, here, in the immediate surroundings, something of the love of God is to become reality. Some suffering is to be soothed, something of the bliss of self-giving is to be experienced. For God's love is selfless, and it can only take effect in the world when the world has accepted something of the spirit of selflessness, of giving for no reward.

One might think that this message from God comes from so far away and from such a height that man is incapable of grasping it. Christianity seems to be a teaching that is not for this world. Not realistic enough. But Jesus ends with these words: "For this I have come into the world, to bear witness to the truth. Everyone who is of the truth hears my voice." Everyone. Not only the person who has studied theology, not even the person who has learned his catechism or has merely listened to a sermon. Everyone. This King has a way of making himself understood to everyone. Perhaps it is that, on the basis of the Cross, every human suffering has acquired a new hue, a special quality that comes from the Cross and lends wings to his voice. It is true, however, that only those who are of the truth will hear it. Anyone who, somehow or other, perhaps unconsciously, bears within him something of the mystery of divine love knows that ultimately only loving can give a meaning to existence. Everyone can hear this voice. Christians have no monopoly here; they only have a special task, namely, to carry out into the world, quite explicitly and deliberately, the testimony they have heard and experienced in their own lives. They need not be surprised to find, in many places in this world, already existing traces of the truth they are openly proclaiming. Often these traces are so clear that they put Christians to shame. For the world in its totality already belongs to the kingdom of God, which is not of this world. The passing world in which we live is part of that vaster, abiding kingdom in which God lives, who is all in all.

Advent

The Future Has Already Come

The whole question is this: What is the goal of man's efforts? For he cannot act without a plan and a goal. By his actions he brings previously nonexistent things into being, but the result depends on the power of the idea animating him, for it is this idea that thus asserts itself in reality. It is through man that it is brought about. All the same, he is not simply its inventor, for he looks up to it as something above him; he sets course by it; it irradiates him with its light, is sublime above him and independent of him; he is only its servant, making room for its true reality in this transitory world.

The Greeks thought in this way, for instance, when they created their magnificent sculptures. Their minds and hands were guided by the pattern of a divine man; they had encountered this model, not "invented" it. According to Plato, man was originally with God; he is capable of clearing away the debris smothering his mind to reveal the radiance of his origin. Then, for the first time, he will be able to see things as they are and act properly as a result. All religion, all mankind's philosophy, sees man thus suspended between beginning and end, between his source and his ultimate return to the ocean of life. He is equipped with a picture that, embracing his origin and final goal and all that lies between them, transcends the given realities of the present. Thus man the agent is provided with a *meaning*, a direction, an inclination, a current drawing him forward; only on this basis can he both act and be. The present is neither alpha nor omega; but if there is an alpha, there must be an omega, whatever objections the theory of evolution may present.

But let us leave alone the paths of Greece, and of Asia too. They may have sufficed to permit the individual to escape from time and return to the lost divine home; or to give him, in the work of art, an intimation of unconditional truth; or even, as with Epictetus and Marcus Aurelius, to offer the individual man a model of an all-embracing world order, a divine Logos. But they cannot provide mankind, which is both individual and social, person and community, with an overall justification of its activities, its creativity as it marches through time. Indian asceticism is not enough here, for it excludes relationships with both the "thou" and the national and human communities. Art is not enough, for it is essentially contemplative. Nor is even Stoic ethics enough, for if all is Logos, the distinction between what ought and what ought not to be remains unclarified, and there is no difference between present and future. No model is sufficient unless it takes man seriously in all his inadequacy, in his weakness, sickness, mortality, futility, guilt and evil; in his turning away from God, his Origin, and in his essentially crippled nature when it comes to realizing the good, that is, when it comes to love.

Christianity alone has given mankind a total blueprint. In the act of Jesus Christ, the Origin himself has entered into time; God has reconciled himself with his recalcitrant creature; one man, in death and abandonment by God, has expiated for sin; one man has loved all other men unto the end that has no end, winning for all, through his living and dying, both access to the Father and the seal of the Holy Spirit of God. But if this act, in itself, contains and dispenses all the fullness of grace, it necessarily puts itself "before" each man, presents itself as a model: what has been done, if it is to become the meaning of existence, is what *is* to be done; what has taken place is what *is* to take place; the past is what must come about in an ever-new way; history is Spirit.

The foregoing assertion sounds abstract and unintelligible:

let us unwrap it. When a Christian acts—and he is always engaged in action—his standard is always God's action in Christ. Not some mere abstract law of nature or of Sinai but the living God's concrete act, which, in Christ, is Spirit and life. This act is *before* the Christian: he can only go toward it; he must make room for it to become reality in every situation with which he is confronted and that constitutes his future. It depends on him whether or not it will be embodied, incarnated, now. Such incarnation takes place when the Christian sees in his neighbor, existentially encountered, someone whom Christ has redeemed, someone who, through Christ, is in principle freed from guilt and thralldom to sin, someone whom the Father loves as his child and to whom the Holy Spirit has been given (or at least promised). He does not see him primarily in the terms of human experience and psychology (depth psychology or any other psychology). What the Greek succeeded in doing in his hymns and statues, that is, to see God in man, the Christian must be able to do with regard to his fellowman, however un-Godlike he may be, however unlike Christ. That is precisely what is required if he is to call himself a Christian. And that is precisely what, humanly speaking, seems impossible to him, even intolerable; he feels that it blows his human norms to pieces, and so he is always ready to rebel against it. And in fact it lies quite literally beyond what is possible to man; that is why he needs the grace of God and the Spirit of Jesus Christ. Just as it is only through God's grace that the "thou" is the true "thou" to whom I relate, so too it is only through God's grace that I am the true "I", capable of relating, in a fully Christian sense, to a "thou". "Apart from me you can do nothing." Christian action, and hence Christian being, is an ever-new stepping forth beyond the secular, available, understandable "thou" and "I" and a moving toward a supra-human prototype beyond "I" and "thou". Only in this context are "I" and "thou" real and intelligible.

We may boldly affirm that the whole of Christian dogmatics contains nothing other than what is implied in this Christian encounter between "I" and "thou". For what takes place in this encounter is not the satisfying of the subject's religious needs (from which, incidentally, no dogmatics can be deduced, as the Modernists falsely thought). No. Here the subject is continually transcending himself in the obedience of faith: here he makes the supreme effort to see, experience, and treat the reality that *comes to meet him* as it has *become* through Christ's decisive deed. To see myself as Christ sees me, to see my neighbor as Christ sees him—this act of faith, genuinely performed, already implies the death of the old man of which Paul speaks; it implies the daily taking up of one's cross that Christ commands, and it is the proof of discipleship, which must lie in deeds, not in mere words or in mere professions of faith. The man who even attempts this—and he will never manage more than an attempt—he, and he alone, will learn what is the dogmatic content of the Faith of Christians. He will learn that Christ is completely man but only by being completely God (for Christ's humanism begins precisely where all human humanism comes to an end). He will learn that he himself is never Christ but a branch of his vine, a member of his body. He will learn that he can never say that he embodies the Spirit of Christ but that there is such a thing as the Church, the *communio sanctorum*, which does possess this Spirit, and that he is integrated, steeped in failure as he is, into her integrity. Finally—to pass over many other things—he will experience in a very exact way that all this reality that bears and sustains him, with its aspect of institution and its rootedness in the past, is at the same time always future, always coming to meet him. "Thy kingdom come."

But we must say more: in every situation that the Christian has to face, there is a baffling hiatus. I, a mere man, can never fully deal with the situation; but in Christ, who lives in me and in whom I live, it has already been dealt with. Furthermore, what we have said about the specifically Christian situation can be applied to everything that takes place within the ambit of transitory time. No moment, be it ever so sublime, is totally fulfilled; in fact, whenever it *does* seem fulfilled, it is always because it is full of promise, pointing beyond itself to what is above all time, to what is eternal. For the most part, however, things slip away unexplored, undone, unexhausted, unlived; beings touch and feel each other but without recognition, without penetrating one another. And what is more frightening, lovers fall apart again; they cannot maintain their love; habit and familiarity cause life to turn to stone. Time proves the most genuine avowals of faithfulness to be false. All that is transitory is shipwrecked on the sandbanks of reality, whither the waves of time draw it, to be smashed to pieces. At this level there can be no talk of evolution. In a hundred thousand years mankind will not be a finger's breadth nearer the prototype, Christ, than it is today. In fact, the idea of a convergence of the kingdom of the world and the kingdom of God toward some world "omega point" would destroy Christianity at its foundations; all Christian faith experience flatly refutes such a convergence.

The synthesis is of another kind. It draws nearer to us with every little Christian step we take. It comes closer to us precisely when, acting in faith, we walk toward it. That is what is meant by the puzzling assertion that believers can hasten Christ's coming. Even the Jews were acquainted with this mystery with regard to the advent of the Messiah (and today genuine Judaism still looks for God's coming). The only horizon the Christian can have for his life within the bounds of time is this: the unveiling of the reality of Christ. The meaning of existence and history can be found only in this final thought and plan of God. That is why, for the world and for every individual in it, Christ is God's alpha and omega. In Christian understanding, therefore, all work undertaken within the world —even apart from the existential encounter with one's neighbor in our common Redeemer—can be nothing other than the renewed (and constantly failing) attempt to give bodily form, in terms of the world's substance, to the idea of Christ. We act in hope, in longing, and thus we sense the Spirit of Christ stirring within us: "Blessed are those who hunger and thirst for righteousness." But this world horizon does not totally enclose the world: it is the open door to God. Only here is God revealed ("made open") as he is: Father of the world and of the Son, Abyss of Love, Mystery that is always greater and more unfathomable, Blessedness beyond all speech and understanding.

Christ's return in judgment is thus the precise expression for the final implementation of what has already and always been taking place within history, namely, the application of a standard, which definitively establishes the right by definitively rejecting everything that does not correspond to it. "To judge" here means "to apply the straightedge", "to direct" and "to erect" man, lift him up to the real and ever-present idea. This can and must imply a dismantling of the worldly elements in the world of nature and the human spirit, right down to the foundations; what is preliminary must be refashioned into what is definitive; what is temporal must be rendered super- and supratemporal. Let us really appreciate this point: there has to be a transformation of the temporal. It is embraced by the alpha and omega; it is defined, delimited, measured and parceled. In no way does it run on indefinitely according to its own whim. And precisely *because* it is temporal, it cannot understand its own limits, nor can it envisage them or catch up with them through ratiocination either by old-style apocalyptic calculation or by new-style prognoses à la Teilhard or à la Bloch. Consequently the problem of the imminent versus the remote expectation of Christ has no theological significance at all. Whether it is near at hand or far off, the horizon toward which the world is moving (or developing, if you will) is no less relevant to the present moment; it is visible in the smallest Christian or secular act as what is imminent, threatening, about to take place. How is it visible? In the gap, the difference between the situation and its fulfillment in Christ. For the absolute standard applied by Christ has already been made visible by him. There is nothing vague or nebulous about it;

on the contrary, all secular and contemporary ideas are vague and nebulous when compared with its steel-hard clarity, twilighted and blurred compared with his noonday brightness. In this noonday light, as John says, *the world is* (and always has been) *judged*.

All things will return to us bathed in this light; only in this light, therefore, do we see that they have eternal faces. (One need only take a look at contemporary literature to realize that, apart from this light, things are simply not worthwhile.) No other standard applies anymore; this is the terrible thing Christ has wrought by his first coming. The measure applied by Christ is so evident that everyone who will not accept it is compelled to renounce all the other plausible measurements and become, in some shape or form, a nihilist. The only hope the world still has lies in the *parousia* of Jesus Christ.

As we have said, all things will return to us bathed in this light, and only in this light do we see that they have eternal faces. And only if their faces bear these features is it worthwhile pursuing them in love and action. We are not like Faust with his appetite for infinity: we cannot forcibly enter into things and so learn that we have already gone beyond their finitude and transitoriness. Such action only produces more Gretchen tragedies. What we must do, in all earnestness, is to examine things with regard to their eternal content and eternal promise or, even better, allow ourselves to be addressed and fashioned by the eternal promise that is embodied in them. Then we shall love them as they are in reality, as the eternal Father sees and loves them, as creatures and situations that have been redeemed in his Son. How else could they possibly manifest traits of eternity? Since the Son became man all other possibilities have been eliminated. Myth has vanished; the "eternal recurrence" of all things would only render our thirst eternal, and hence a hell. The "transmigration of souls" and similar ideas do not take the historical moment fully seriously. And as for the attempt to elicit the whole of eternity from the temporal moment, as we have said, it is the Faustian spasm that tries to stop the flow of time and thus strangles the freedom of further movement.

All the same, a certain uneasiness remains. The picture of Christ coming again, bringing the truth of history to the light of day, applying his measuring rod to all the things and situations in the world and in the grace of the Cross (now openly manifest) bridging the eternally gaping abyss between promise and fulfillment—this picture could seem ultimately somewhat limiting. Man and the world strive toward the infinite God, and the more we become aware of freedom's realm, the more openly we desire it. Is it possible, then, for an image of God that is ultimately finite, albeit "in great power and glory", to give a conclusive answer to all the world's striving? An image in place of imageless truth, a delimited outline instead of the pure opening into a realm that is limitless? At this point we must remember that it is not the Judgment, with its measuring rod, that is ultimate; what is ultimate is the opening of the door into eternal life: "Come, O blessed of my Father, inherit the kingdom prepared for you from the foundation of the world"—and even earlier, as Paul tells us: "God chose us in him before the foundation of the world." All that constitutes the world, all that has shape and form and outline, is really only a parable. Not in the sense that it must vanish in smoke and mist to make room for the Infinite, for all room and all places belong to God, and he grants his creatures an eternal place with him. But the finite is not petrified: it is a fluid motion, coming from God and returning to him. "I came from the Father and have come into the world; again, I am leaving the world and going to the Father." Our following of Christ is also drawn into his Ascension, his return to God's heart. The Image, Christ, opens and points beyond himself to his Origin; he is utterly and totally *the* exposition of the Primal Ground; he is our invitation and initiation into the mystery of God's heart.

In the Son's *parousia* there takes place the *parousia* of the Father, which is communicated to us by the Holy Spirit; we are endowed with this Spirit in advance, so that we may live in the bridal, thirsting longing for God's coming, as the Bible's final words tell us: "The Spirit and the Bride say, 'Come'. And let him who hears say, 'Come'. And let him who is thirsty come, let him take the water of life without price" (Rev 22:17). The waterless paths through the world's desert seem unimaginably vast, ever stretching to the horizon, but the millions of years that precede us are not even part of human time; in fact, before we know it, our end has come and we step across to the beyond. The world is constantly rising vertically to its end; it passes over, experiences ascension and leaves the mere mathematical appearance behind. Man alone has historical time, and not he, but Another, is master of it. *In manibus tuis tempora mea* ("my times are in thy hand") (Ps 31:15)—they exist nowhere else.

Waiting for God

Advent means "arrival". Who is coming? And if Advent concerns us, if we are waiting for someone, who are we waiting for? For the Christian—the only person who is really waiting for the Coming One—Advent is like a great gate through which he passes to enter some shrine. This gate is flanked by two figures guarding it; if we are Christians, they ask us why and with what intentions we are seeking admission. The two figures are very dissimilar, yet they are always found on old pictures, on the right and left of the Expected One (who is in fact the One Who Has Come). One stands tall and straight, haggard, an angel clothed in camel's hair, who wants to be nothing but a Voice resounding through the wilderness of the world, the desert of time: "Prepare the way of the

Lord." The other figure is shrouded and wrapped in her own thoughts; only her body tells of the One she is expecting; her soft words reecho: "Behold, I am the handmaid of the Lord." Both know who they are waiting for; for the moment they alone know with such precision and urgency who it is: they are waiting for no one less than God. Not for a leader or some hero, not for better times, not for some vague utopia, not "for Godot", but really for God. For Emmanuel, God-with-us. Moreover, they are waiting in the certainty that he is actually at the door; they know for sure that, now that John the Baptist and the Virgin Mary have prepared the way for the coming of the Expected One, nothing can hold him back; the event is already under way and no one can stop the avalanche.

What a difference between the two figures guarding the gate of the Christmas shrine! But both are indispensable; both are examples to us. Of the one, Jesus says in today's Gospel, "What did you go out into the wilderness to behold? . . . A prophet? Yes, I tell you, and more than a prophet" (Mt 11:7, 9). And the other says of herself, in joyful humility, "He has regarded the low estate of his handmaiden. For behold, henceforth all generations will call me blessed" (Lk 1:48). And "blessed", Jesus confirms, "are those who hear the word of God and keep it" (Lk 11:28). Larger than life as they are, both figures are only transitions to the *Adveniens*, the Coming One.

The first is simply waiting for God. There is no room for any prophet between him and God's Advent. God is coming to create order, to judge and to save. To provoke radical decisions: "Even now the axe is laid to the root of the trees." The fire is already set for the tree that does not produce good fruit. God's "winnowing fork is in his hand, and he will clear his threshing floor and gather his wheat into the granary, but the chaff he will burn with unquenchable fire" (Mt 3:10 ff.). The one who speaks thus is determined to carry out his mission to the very last; he is not afraid to address the great men of his nation as a "brood of vipers" and to speak of the king's infamy to his own face. He has no fear of being imprisoned and beheaded, for he is merely a Voice penetrating everything, even stopped ears.

The second figure is also waiting for God. She knows what the angel told her: "The child to be born of you will be called holy, the Son of God, Son of the Most High, and of his kingdom there will be no end" (Lk 1:31ff.). And she knows what the Holy Spirit of God—he and no other—has done to her. Unlike the Baptist, who is waiting for someone unimaginable to appear with fire, with an axe and a winnowing fork, she is waiting for a little child; but, for this anxious Mother, is not the idea of a human child who is God much harder to imagine? For this child will really come "to cast fire on the earth", to be baptized with a terrible "baptism". And as for the Mother, will not a sword pierce her own heart also?

Both wait for the Coming One with a yearning that fills their whole being and at the same time with such profound and violent emotion that they do not know how they will be able to face up to the gigantic event that is about to take place, through them, on the world's stage. "After me comes he who is mightier than I," says the Baptist, "the thong of whose sandals I am not worthy to stoop down and untie" (Mk 1:7). "After me comes a man who ranks before me, for he was before me" (Jn 1:30). "He must increase, but I must decrease" (Jn 3:30). He sets an example for all Christians, all apostles, priests, all who proclaim Christ: none of them may proclaim themselves, chatter about their own religious experience: they are to be only the voice of him who is "increasing", who is always greater.

Advent is the end of the Old Covenant, which genuinely looked for God's coming. But who, in fact, did come? One who is "gentle and lowly in heart", and "nor will any one hear his voice in the streets; he will not break a bruised reed or quench a smoldering wick" (Mt 11:29; 12:19f.); so John, in prison, wonders and becomes unsure, seeing nothing of fire and axe and winnowing fork: "Are you he who is to come, or shall we look for another?" (Mt 11:3). But Jesus sets his mind at rest: look and see whether the prophecies have not been fulfilled. Have not the proud been toppled from their seats by me; have not the poor been lifted up from the dust; have not those who see become blind and the blind regained their sight? Is not the world order changing through the presence of God in my ministry?

As long as Jesus lives, however, this is only a preliminary answer. The ultimate answer, which he knows in advance and foresees, will be his death on the Cross, and then the fire and the axe and the winnowing fork, and the sword in his Mother's heart, will really do their work. Then there will take place the vast, tremendous event for which the Baptist and the Mother have waited, which causes the gentile captain to exclaim, "Truly this man was the Son of God!" (Mk 15:39).

Paul and the primitive Church will devote themselves to profound pondering on Jesus' puzzling destiny. He lives a life both of lowliness and of majesty; he dies a death echoing with the cry of abandonment by God only to reappear, transfigured, on the third day: this destiny—inseparably cruel and glorious, is certainly that of a physical man, the Son of Mary, but it is decidedly more. It is also the destiny of the God who has come in this bodily nature, sealing with his blood the new and eternal Covenant with man. This is Paul's interpretation, and it is the Faith of the Church, preserved in the writings of the New Testament.

So the point of departure and the destination point match one another. At the beginning there is the time of waiting for God, in all the seriousness that entails. At the end there is the profession of faith that the One who has come, who was born of the Virgin Mary, suffered under Pontius Pilate, was crucified, died and was buried, has risen from the dead and ascended into heaven, and who will come again to judge the living and the dead—that he must be no less a Person than the interpreter of God; furthermore he himself must be the Word, God's self-interpretation. Thus the circle that runs from the Baptist to Paul is complete, and no one who calls himself a Christian can break it. So too, no theologian who intends to interpret what is attested by faith, by the Church and by Scripture will ever be able to dissolve the unity of Jesus Christ's human and divine being.

Let us add that world history after Christ can never be the same. In the year nil, at the beginning of our calendar, the absolute change of direction occurred. A certain naïveté, once possible, has been lost forever. Jesus said, "He who does not gather with me scatters" (Lk 11:23). The modern technological world may have tremendous problems that seem utterly remote from the Gospel, but ultimately it comes down to the attitude adopted by Jesus in his living and dying: the attitude of perfect, selfless love, service to the very last and the fruitfulness that comes from it. This is the innermost meaning and core of all mankind's questions, including those of politics, economics and other fields. And the attitude shown by Jesus is the attitude of God himself to the world. Thus anyone who follows Jesus is walking in God's footsteps, in the footsteps of absolute truth and goodness. Many people may do this without knowing Jesus, but since he has come to us, his fragrance has spread invisibly through world history, and many a one follows this fragrance without knowing it. "God is able from these stones to raise up children to Abraham", says John the Baptist.

We are in the season of Advent, and it sends a shiver of fear through us, warning us of the approach of something that is final and ultimate; it is as inevitable as that an expectant mother must give birth, as certain as that a voice in the wilderness presupposes someone crying out. So we must look and listen; we must pay attention; we must turn and attend to this voice. Turn and repent of your sins, says the Baptist again and again. What does this mean? It means we must search for that turning point in our innermost self, the place where we turn from the "I" to the "thou" and to God, from sterile living for ourselves to fruitful living for others by following God, Emmanuel: God-with-us and God-for-us. Then, together with the Virgin who is with Child, we too can bring a real, tangible child into the world, a child who will be fruitful in the world and in world history; and not just any child, but the same Child that Mary bore: "For whoever does the will of my Father in heaven is my brother, and sister and mother" (Mt 12:50). That will be the real miracle of Christmas. For it is not merely that at some time or other, two thousand years ago, a rather special Child was born in Judaea. As Scheffler wrote in his *Cherubinischer Wandersmann* (1657): "Christ may be born in Bethlehem a thousand times, but if he is not born in you, you will be lost for all eternity just the same." And again: "If only your heart could become a crib, God would become a child again on this earth." Such ideas seem extreme and farfetched to us. But we only have to recall the words of Jesus when he says that unless a man is born from above, from God, he cannot enter into the kingdom of God (Jn 3:3); and that he, Jesus, has given us power to be children of God, born of God, above and beyond all earthly begetting and birth that result from the will of the flesh and the will of man (Jn 1:12f.). If it is true that we are born not solely of mortal parents but also from an immortal womb, it will also be true that, as John says, "God's seed" remains in us (1 Jn 3:9); so we too will be capable of a suprahuman generation and birth that can make us, as Jesus says, his "mothers". We can plant God's life in this world and make it grow; we can make God's kingdom come and cause his will to be done on earth as it is in heaven; we can cause his Name to be glorified in this godless and blasphemous world, despite all aggressive atheism. If we live out our lively faith in the God who wants to become man on earth, we are already "pregnant" with him, empowered to carry him until he is born—and that will be a Christmas. And I would like to add this: just as in the woman's case the birth happens of its own accord, so our bearing of God need not worry us at all: if we live by faith we shall surely bring forth our fruit. It is like the man in the parable: "The kingdom of God is as if a man should scatter seed upon the ground, and should sleep and rise night and day, and the seed should sprout and grow, he knows not how" (Mk 4:27ff.). Our whole lifetime is Advent: bearing fruit in patience, not being curious, not wanting to see with our own eyes the results of our life of faith. For, as in the case of the Woman of the Apocalypse who cries out in childbirth, the child we bring to birth will be "caught up to God" (Rev 12:5). On earth we keep Advent; Christmas is in heaven, with God, who will receive the fruit of our travail and distribute it to earth again, using it according to his good pleasure to build up his coming kingdom.

There is something strange about the Christian festivals: for us Christians they are all simultaneous; they stand still while the Church's year moves on. It is always Advent until our life's end on the earth, always Christmas in the hiddenness of heaven, always Good Friday, always Easter and Ascension, always Pentecost, when, in the end, the Holy Spirit comes upon the Church as he came at the beginning upon the Virgin of Nazareth. All is present in everything. So let us hold on patiently in the darkness, in the blessed fullness of our Advent.

"Foreigners' Sunday"

You Too Were a Stranger in Egypt

The Sunday Gospel for today tells a parable of the kingdom of heaven. Ten virgins are waiting up for the arrival of the bridegroom. Half of them have brought oil for their lamps with them; half of them have not. When the one they are waiting for—that is, the kingdom of heaven—is delayed, they all nod off to sleep. Suddenly, in the middle of the world's night, a shout is heard: he is coming! Now, at the last moment, the neglectful girls want to borrow oil from the others, but it is too late: they should go and buy some. And while they are away looking for oil, the bridegroom comes and the door of the banquet chamber is shut. When the others eventually arrive and ask to be let in, they hear the answer from within, "I do not know you." And Jesus draws the conclusion: "Watch therefore, for you know neither the day nor the hour" (Mt 25:13).

There are an astonishing number of images in the Gospels for this mysterious kingdom of God. Nothing is more certain than that it is really coming: it is like the seed growing, the leaven working in the dough, the fish collecting in the net, the king who has already prepared the banquet for his son's wedding, the lord who is traveling abroad and distributes his money among his servants so that they shall use it and bring interest on it. The kingdom is not something that begins only at the end of world history; as Jesus says, it is already hiddenly present among us, though we cannot put our finger on it and say, "Here it is!" or "There it is!" That is why we have to wait for it to come openly and publicly.

The strange thing is this: it is precisely those who are properly *waiting* for it who already *have* a share in it in advance. And who is the one who waits properly? The person whose innermost heart is set on the kingdom. He does not doubt that God is coming to him; he *believes* that one day he will meet God face to face. His faith is *hope* too, for in this meeting the deeply hidden meaning of our existence will be made plain. Consequently he looks forward with *love* to this meeting with God.

This is precisely what is meant in our parable by the oil in the lamps: it means believing, looking forward in hope and love to God's coming; for then my life, with all its toils and hardships, will receive its meaning and justification within the context of this promised wedding feast. Then we may sleep in peace, like the wise virgins in the parable, or as Jesus slept in the boat in the midst of the storm. Quite a different sleep from that of the five virgins who fell asleep with weariness and lassitude; they told themselves, "There will still be time later; we will wait and see what the future brings; live for the present. A bird in the hand . . ."

As we have said, those who properly wait for God already have a share, by way of anticipation, in him and his kingdom. The oil of faith, hope and love is the same oil that, later on, will nourish the flame in the festal chamber. Faith, hope and love are what the Bridegroom knows, what he desires, for it is his own mind and heart; nor will there be any other disposition in God's heaven but this.

Then all the other things that seem big and important on earth will be played out: science, technology, power. But the other three, as the Apostle assures us, will abide forever, and the greatest of them is love. For only the man who loves God really believes in him and hopes in him. In the kingdom of God love will be the attitude governing everything; even among men, genuine love produces mutual faith and trust and hopes for a return of love. This is the way God approaches us: he loves us, has faith in us, that is, he trusts us and hopes that we will love him in return and so find in him the eternal meaning of our lives.

But now comes the second aspect in our parable: a distinction is drawn; a separation is made. We find it everywhere in the Gospel of Christ. It goes right through the entire Old and New Testaments. We cannot argue judgment away by saying that, after all, God is good, God is love, he will always have mercy on us and take us into his kingdom; or that everything will turn out all right whatever the clergy may say about hell.

Jesus is ruthlessly hard: "I have not come to bring peace, but a sword." "Not every one who says to me, 'Lord, Lord', shall enter the kingdom of heaven, but he who does the will of my Father who is in heaven." On that Day, therefore, he will have to say to many a one, "I never knew you; depart from me", just as the foolish virgins in the parable were told, "I do not know you."

How are we to understand these harsh words? First, we must see them in the context of what we have already said: the attitude of right living and waiting for God is identical to the attitude of the eternal God himself, who waits to meet us. When Jesus says to some people, "I do not know you", it means "I do not recognize myself in you", "I do not recognize God's mind and heart in you." The center of your lives is foreign and opposed to me, to my Father and to the kingdom of God; you are living like egoists, seeking power, position, pleasure and security on earth—and perhaps in heaven too (for you call me "Lord! Lord!" as if you already had me in your pockets); everything revolves around your darling "I", even God. But I have clearly told you: "He who clings to what is his will lose it, but he who lets go of it for my sake will find it."

Dear Listeners, the only proper way of listening to these words of Jesus is to apply them to oneself. Where these words are concerned there is no neutral vantage point from which to divide people into sheep and goats. What do I know about the innermost heart of anyone else, however bad, externally, his conduct may seem, and whatever deeds he may have committed? Paul warns us: "Do not pronounce judgment before the time, before the Lord comes, who will bring to light the things now hidden in darkness and will disclose the purposes of the heart" (1 Cor 4:5). And the Apostle adds a further crucial point: "I do not even judge myself. . . . It is the Lord who judges me." In other words, I cannot say with certainty whether I have brought the right oil with me, the true faith, the true hope, the proper, selfless love, the attitude of God and his kingdom. I cannot put myself in a prominent position in church, like the Pharisee, and pride myself on my love; I can only stand at the back and, with the tax collector, beat my breast: "God be merciful to me, a sinner."

When, one day, the tremendous lightning ray of God's eternal love pierces my heart, will it find there anything even remotely related to it? I do not know. I can only hope. I can only pray that it may be so, just as I must pray that no one, no one will be found to be without some little drop of oil, without a tiny spark of genuine love. To hope this is not presumption but trust in the power of the divine love. There *is* the possibility that the Judge may have to separate some of us from the others, but we are right to hope (for we cannot know this) that this possibility will not become a reality.

It is particularly apt that today, according to the wishes of the Swiss Bishops' Conference, we are celebrating "Foreigners' Sunday" under the motto "Christ accepts us all."

He accepts us all, whatever nation we belong to. "You are all brethren", Jesus said explicitly to his disciples. The primitive Church passed what may have been its hardest test, theoretically and practically, when it proclaimed, fought for and implemented the equality of Jews and gentiles, rich and poor, masters and servants or, in modern terms, employers and employees. In all ages men have continually erected these kinds of barriers, but Christ's Church does not recognize them, because Christ himself has torn them down once and for all. Not by uniting all the people within one fatherland; the Church is not international: she is Catholic, that is, she is the same throughout all nations and fatherlands. For a Christian there is hardly a greater joy than to encounter one's own Faith in a foreign country, to share in the same worship and above all to be met with the same Christian attitude that one would like to have oneself. Perhaps you have had this wonderful experience when traveling or as a tourist; let us pass it on to the foreigners who live and work among us in our land.

There is something else I would like to say. If we show friendship only to our own countrymen and treat foreigners badly, our friendship itself, from a Christian point of view, is very suspect. It can be suspected of being mere fellow feeling at the natural level, what Jesus meant when he said in the Sermon on the Mount, "Do not even the gentiles do the same?" It was an issue in the Old Testament as well, when foreigners came from Moab and elsewhere to work among the people of Israel. The law prescribed not only that Israel should pay them a just wage but also that they should be treated kindly, and the remarkable reason given was this: "Remember that you were once strangers toiling in the land of Egypt, and that I delivered you." If you are a nation today, says God to Israel, you owe it to me alone.

Jesus knows the weakness of the Jews as a people, as he knows the weaknesses of all nations. Several times in his discourses, therefore, when he wants to illustrate true Christian love, he picks not Jews but particularly hated foreigners who manifest the true attitude and approach. Pious and unseeing, the Jews walk past the man lying wounded in the gutter; it is the Samaritan who becomes his neighbor by looking after him in the spirit of Christ. The only one of the ten cured lepers to return to thank Jesus is a Samaritan. The great penitent woman in St. John's Gospel is a Samaritan.

How especially beautiful it is when foreigners give us a genuine sign of selfless Christian love, almost more so than when one of our fellow-countrymen does this. Many of us, no doubt, have een amazed and deeply moved by the unforgettable experience, in Italian and Spanish villages and elsewhere, of a hospitality that is practically unknown in our own land. We ourselves are not particularly famous for it. "Which of these three, do you think, proved neighbor to the man who fell among the robbers?"

According to both the parable and our own experience, there *are* people who clearly show evidence of having sufficient oil in their lamps. We should try to radiate at least a little of this evidence.

Let us close with a prayer to God: O God, give us your Holy Spirit, for he is the oil of eternal love, eternal faith and eternal hope. Of ourselves we possess none of this. We depend on you; you alone can grant us the grace of anointing with the Spirit, the same Spirit you gave to your Messiah, the One anointed with holy oil, the Christ. May the meaning of our lives be a waiting for you, even when night comes. Amen.

Immaculate Conception

Abolishing the Boundaries

In today's Marian feast the Church celebrates a very essential aspect of the salvation of which we have all been made sharers but an aspect that is not readily grasped at first sight.

What, then, is meant by the expression "immaculately conceived" or "conceived without the stain of original sin"? In a nutshell it means that the human being in whom God's Son was made man received this gift from heaven with a readiness, openness and availability that were boundless and restricted by nothing at all. Her consent did not contain the least reservation or condition, no "Yes, but . . .", no "Yes, if . . .", no "Yes under certain circumstances . . .", no "Yes, for the present . . ." We could call it the Feast of the Immaculate "Yes" to God.

And what is "original sin"? It is the moral deficiency of every man who comes into the world as a member of the human race. Every man has some personal knowledge of what this means; he knows that he is not as he should and could be. He may do his duty more or less, but there it is: more or *less*. He loves his fellowmen more or less, but precisely when he tries to love them more he feels that he loves them less, that he ought to love them far more selflessly. Somehow or other his achievements fail to come up to the mark. For the most part he consoles himself by saying, "To err is human; no more can be asked of anyone. In any case I do what I can." But even while saying this he is aware that he could do more. The personal deficiency that, at his most secret level, everyone senses, is also a social deficiency, one he shares with all others. The child grows into it, acquires it from his environment but also from within himself. The youngster may rebel against it and want to be different from those around him, but in striving for freedom and the heights he overreaches himself; so he falls below his ideal and slowly learns to accept his limits, to be "only a human being after all".

Young people nowadays like to talk about completely changing the world's prevailing conditions. Those who are totally naïve think this can be done by changing the social structures. The less naïve are aware that, while it is possible to change these structures, using violence—or they may even change of their own accord—man is an animal of the herd and remains an egoist. Precisely where the structures relieve him of the need for personal effort, he produces even less than before, as famous examples show, and where the ability to achieve is whipped up by social pressure, ambition and the traffic in gossip grow too, and society is turned into a total system of informers. Let us take a look at Israel prior to the time of Jesus. It too, probably more than any other nation, knew the longing for a total change in world conditions. It longed for a kingdom where all things would at last be in tune. But Israel also knew that it could not bring this kingdom about by its own power. God would have to do it. God, as Isaiah said, would have to rend the heavens and come down, just as the rain falls from above onto the earth, awakening the dry ground to the seed and the possibilities latent within it, so that the earth should become green, putting forth shoots and bearing fruit, producing bread for the sower and fruit for the planter. People of piety and faith in Israel knew this. We are the dry ground; we shall never do right of ourselves. God must come, like rain and dew, giving us the power to do it, through and with him.

This longing on the part of Israel contains a further fundamental insight. Here, among us, everything is hopelessly mixed up and confused: right and wrong, good and evil, what is of God and what is godless, not only within a single community but also in each individual heart. Perhaps the Jews saw the latter aspect less clearly than the former, but their hymns also contain passages in which God is entreated to rid the heart of its unknown, unconscious sins and to test the heart to see whether, and how far, it trusts in God alone. However, the other idea was more powerful, namely, that God should come to carry out a judgment that would bring salvation, choosing the good from among the wicked and rejecting the latter, so that in the end a real world order would come into existence in the messianic kingdom. This would be a spotless kingdom, free of all social solidarity in guilt, a kingdom on earth as in heaven. Thus, in the prophet Daniel, God's regent, the Son of Man, comes on the clouds of heaven to institute judgment, and he reigns on earth together with his saints, that is, with those whose lives are perfect and righteous, who live in expectation of God's coming and are totally dedicated to God's will.

Here, in fact, we have all the elements necessary for a historical understanding of today's feast. In it, Israel's expectation of the world's total transformation by God is fulfilled, and yet—as is always the case in the transition from the Old to the New Covenant—it is outstripped and turned upside down. The salvation that comes from God is totally different, precisely because it comes from God, from what any man might imagine. Where does the difference lie? Man, even the man who is religious and righteous, sets limits, unconsciously, automatically, because that is his originally sinful nature. "Yes, but . . ." "Yes, provided that God acts as I expect a true God must." But God is limitless, and he aims to abolish the boundaries set or demanded by men. When he comes, it is not to draw a boundary between the pious and the godless or between Jew and gentile but, as Paul says, to "break down the dividing wall". Of course, God *is* a just Judge; but his judgment itself will be salvation, and not as men imagine, that is, salvation for only one group, but universal salvation—although his salvation will not be a mere harmless amnesty but a real judgment. For he is and remains the Lord of his creatures, and the final verdict as to whether they are in the right or in the wrong, destined for weal or woe, lies with him. At this point everything becomes highly mysterious: God comes—as Israel expected—as both Judge and Savior, not by separating and establishing boundaries, however, but—and this is something Israel did not expect—by judging as Savior and by saving as Judge. Faith tells us how he achieved this: as the Lamb of God who loaded the world's sin upon himself, the sin of the entire race and the sin of each individual, the sin of Jews and gentiles, of the pious and the godless.

Now, suddenly, we see the meaning of this feast. This God who pulls down the barriers erected by men does not want to keep his own total lack of barriers to himself: he wants to bring this absolute positivity into the world and communicate it, like rain and dew falling on the soil, to the earthly realm itself. Somewhere on earth there must ring out, in response to his word, not a half answer but a whole one, not a vague answer but an exact one. It must ring out precisely where he comes to the earth. He must be accepted and adopted by the earth; otherwise his coming would be irrelevant to it. If he is to bear what is ours he must be one of us; he cannot bear it from outside, only from inside. And so he must be let in, not only physically, as, for instance, a woman conceives from a man who has violated her, but "with all your heart, with all your soul, with all your mind and with all your strength". By the power of heaven, the earth must accept the arrival of grace so that it can really come to earth and carry out its work of liberation. On its own the earth would be unable to do this. We have seen this from the Old Testament: the earth longs for the righteousness that comes about through separation. The word of consent, however, that is necessary if heaven is to be accepted by earth, is a "Yes" beyond all separation, all divisions and distinctions; it is a "Yes" that knows no conditions and boundaries. Such a word of consent can only be given to earth from heaven's treasure house of love.

And there is something else. The Child who will be given the name Jesus is to grow in the womb of this Mother and be brought up by her after he is born. Even physiologically, the relationship between mother and child is much more intimate than that between father and child; it is more than physiological: it is spiritual, that is, of the totality of human nature. A mother does not only give her flesh and blood to the child but also something of her soul and spirit. And this continues after the child is born, as the child is nourished and brought up. Jesus has to learn from his Mother how a man devotes himself totally to God and utters a limitless "Yes" to him. He learns this from her not only by what she says but also in the only way children really learn anything: by example. This does not mean that his Mother has to be superhuman; the only important thing is that she is a perfectly clear mirror for the Child, reflecting God's total readiness to say "Yes" to the world. All that is necessary for this is a perfect humility, something completely human that is hardly noticed and recognized when it is there, but the absence of which is painfully obvious. This Mother never disappoints. She can be trusted as totally as the Father in heaven. Just as Jesus erects no barriers of distrust between himself and God, he sets up none between himself and his Mother; and in this way he learns in human terms that the restrictions of man under original sin, erecting ultimate barriers between men, really can fall down. He needs this human experience in order to be able to fulfill his Father's great commission of destroying the world's sin, this barrier against God; he must load it onto his shoulders as Samson one night unhinged the gigantic city gates of Gaza and carried them off.

In this way, therefore, God creates a human heart that is open to him, so that he can enter into it with his limitlessness and involve it in his work of salvation, a heart that will never stop at some point and say "thus far and no further". A heart such as this can be asked to do anything; it can be stretched beyond its limits and laden beyond measure, and still, in virtue of the consent it has given, it will go on, right up to the Cross, to the night of forsakenness and futility; it will persevere in the same humility, the same courage, being of service in this work of salvation although, on the Cross and on Holy Saturday, neither Mother nor Son will be able to see its meaning anymore. In the dark night the limits of sin are lifted and the boundary stones are shifted, so that next morning no one can tell where he is: the last shall be first.

"The Light came to his own . . . , and his own did not receive him." This applies to us all, original sinners and setters of boundaries that we are, who at some particular point refuse to follow the Light. Yet the passage goes on: "But to all who received him he gave power to become children of God." In the first place this means those who have really and unreservedly accepted the Light—"Behold I am the handmaid of the Lord; let it be done to me according to your word"—always according to *your* word, into which my will is once and for all taken up and submerged. Then it applies to all those who follow their example as well as they can, who really *would like* to say "Yes" and who trust in the Son's grace and the intercession of the Mother.

Defenseless and Fruitful

Today Catholics are celebrating the feast of that unique woman whom, for two thousand years, the Eastern Church has called the "Panagia", the "All-Holy". The shadow of the guilt that entangles us all, which falls upon and darkens all other human lives, has never fallen upon her. Why is Mary an exception to this universal human predicament? Because she was to conceive, bear and bring up the Child whose divine mission would be to take away the sin of the world, as Scripture says; and the close mother-child relationship would not allow any shadow of inordinate desire, of egoism and egoistic introversion of any kind, to fall upon him from her. That is why Mary's straightforward reply to the angel of the Annunciation, "Behold, I am the handmaid of the Lord; be it unto me according to your word", has such tremendous significance; for, while it sounds so natural, ordinary and unemphatic, on it depends the coming to Israel of the promised Messiah, the coming to the entire world of the long hoped-for Redeemer and Savior.

In this brief reflection we shall try to imagine what Mary's life may have been like, a life lived in the midst of a humanity entangled in and habituated to sin.

First of all, the sin that was visible and tangible all around her must have seemed infinitely foreign to her. Sin, somehow, is something she cannot understand at all, initially. *Her* world is the world of Israel's faith, of the Lord's Commandments, of the prayers of the psalmist, a world in which the great deeds of Yahweh are commemorated in thanksgiving and eucharist and on the basis of which people hope for the fulfillment of God's promise, loving him and his Covenant with all their heart and all their strength. No doubt she has read much about sin, grave sin, in the Bible, and in her everyday surroundings she has had plenty of opportunity of seeing what it is. But it is something outside her own sphere of life, beyond her borders.

And yet, men are not hermetically sealed monads; their worlds interpenetrate and interact. So Mary experiences the effects of others' sin in herself, and, since she does not selfishly retreat into herself, she is bound to suffer as a result. Faultless as she is, she cannot think of revenge and striking back. She is defenseless. She embodies the attitude her Son will call for as he sets forth the burden of his preaching: "You have heard that it was said, 'An eye for an eye and a tooth for a tooth.' But I say to you, Do not resist one who is evil. But if any one strikes you on the right cheek, turn to him the other also" (Mt 5:38–39). This saying has provoked much puzzlement, and people have laughed at it: they say it is impracticable in both social and private life. After all, man is an animal, and, if he is attacked, he must defend himself in order to survive. Why do animals have claws, beaks and fangs, why does the spider spin its web, if not in order to exist? Nietzsche speaks of man as the animal that is "not yet established", but this much *is* established: men have always taken up arms, whether in defensive wars or wars of aggression. If, confronted with today's mankind, we ask what kind of an animal man is, one answer is beyond all doubt: he has the power to annihilate his enemy not once, but many times over. All the innumerable small wars that are constantly burning or breaking out are getting nearer and nearer to the fuse that, once lit, will change the whole picture into a chaos of death.

Power, in the abstract, is not evil. It is something inherent in the vitality of a living being, part of its ability to assert a claim to *Lebensraum*; it is associated even more with the person's legitimate freedom to develop creatively in his environment. But what is power, in concrete terms? In the animal kingdom everywhere there is the domination of one class by another; life is a matter of flight, hunting and falling victim. Nature's continuance, natural selection, depends upon it. In the human kingdom, however, power enters and totally permeates the sphere of freedom and hence of ethics, of good and evil. Because of his freedom, man has power to do good and power to do evil. In everyday life it even seems that he cannot get along without both of them. The exercise of power for power's sake, in order to assert himself, seems something normal to him; it seems necessary for the development of his personality, and hence it seems something legitimate and good. This applies to all spheres of life: in social interaction; in sexuality; in economics, where eliminating an opponent is a generally acknowledged rule of the game; not to mention the realm of politics. And if we step over into the area of the Church, we find today, clearer than ever, two types of power, both claiming to represent the Christian Faith and both totally opposed to each other in positively mortal hatred. On the one side there are the so-called conservatives, or, more emphatically, the traditionalists, who look for salvation in holding onto the inherited religious forms. They are most definitely not the kind of people to offer the other cheek when they have been struck—unless they do so in a martyr's pose, which shows once again that they regard "holding on" as the most important Christian attitude. They ossify and turn into stone; they retreat into their citadels. In their hands, tradition, which in itself is something fluid—the message of Christ and his Cross handed on from generation to generation—becomes a weapon. They hand on nothing to others; they acknowledge no future; they look back and play the part of Epimetheus.

In opposition to them there are the progressives who, in a Promethean manner, turn theology into politics. They plan the Church's future according to their own designs, without listening to the message of the Cross. They want to gain control of what is in fact pure grace that comes down from above; they want to manipulate it horizontally by means of psychology and sociology. They fail to see that "progress", in the context of the life, death and Resurrection of Christ, is a contradiction, explicitly condemned by the Apostle John in his Second Letter: "If anybody does not keep within the teaching of Christ but goes beyond it [*ho proagon*], he cannot have God with him" (2 Jn 9).

These are two power positions, two pseudo-Christian ideologies inspired by the lust for power, and they are united in refusing the same thing, namely, what is genuinely Christian. They will not surrender themselves; they will not let go; they will not allow themselves to be defenseless vis-à-vis God, open to Christ's teaching and work and Person. Being defenseless does not mean being passive—an attitude never enjoined on us by the Gospel. "Let your light so shine before men, that they may see your good works and give glory to your Father who is in heaven" (Mt 5:16). Thus God is glorified when a person finally acts not for the sake of power but out of love and pure self-giving. And this is a possibility for both those on the "right" and those on the "left". Those on the right could show active openness in accepting Christ's message, which has come down to us from the saints of all ages, in acting on it, responding to it and handing it on to others. Those on the left could work out and implement a theology of mankind's liberation that would have a far wider scope than the political, social and economic areas; such a theology would certainly encompass these areas, but it would also relativize them and so be able to envisage the true freedom of the whole man.

All this may be very hard for us, implicated in guilt as we are; whenever we start wielding power, Jakob Burckhardt seems to be right in saying that power is corrupt. But this is the very place to reflect on the one person who succeeded in using her power, a woman who had totally surrendered herself and hence was the most active and the most powerful: she was so powerful that she brought God into the world. Many people dream of doing the same, but they only produce the very opposite effect because they do not give themselves totally; they fail to be a believing and loving vessel so that God may fulfill his wish: to become man, to become humanity and world.

All the failure of individuals in their relationships with one another; the failure of nations, with their reckless ambition and their desire to annihilate each other; all the failure of Christians in their divisions, setting up in opposition to one another in each individual church and parish; all this failure is enveloped by the cloak of the Immaculate One, as we often see depicted so graphically in old pictures.

Of course she is not grace, for grace is God and comes from God, and Mary is a mere creature. But she is the only creature who presented no resistance to grace, the only person who did not monopolize the grace she had been given; she was not a sinner, using grace, using grace up for herself; she does what grace wants, namely, hands it on, gives it away, pours it out for others. The more receptive a person is to grace, the more active and productive grace becomes in him and he in grace.

Thus the Immaculate One is not a motionless image, a petrified icon, seated in lofty seclusion above teeming humanity. Rather, she is someone who has a pervading influence on this whole picture, fashioning it according to the mind of her Son, who wishes to become ever more profoundly man.

At the start of our reflection we portrayed her as living defenseless in the guilty world and hence essentially suffering because of the world, through it and for it. New swords were continually piercing her during her life on earth, and under the Cross she finally learned from her Son what the world's sin is. Here her heart is so opened and spiritually pierced that it cannot close again. "Woman, behold your son" (Jn 19:26). She has essentially become the Mother of Christians and of all men. And since she wants nothing for herself but everything for God and for her Son, her maternal concern is to teach everyone to have the mind of Christ, the spirit of perfect self-giving, which is ultimately the most powerful thing in the world, more powerful than all powers and authorities, for they are all subordinate to it.

So we may close with Elizabeth's words to Mary:

> "Blessed are you among women, and blessed is the fruit of your womb! . . . And blessed is she who believed that there would be a fulfillment of what was spoken to her by the Lord." And Mary said, "My soul magnifies the Lord, and my spirit rejoices in God my Savior, for he has regarded the low estate of his handmaiden. For behold, henceforth all generations will call me blessed" (Lk 1:42, 45–48).

Christmas

Setting Out into the Dark with God

And the angel said to them,

> "Be not afraid; for behold, I bring you Good News of a great joy that will come to all the people; for to you is born this day in the city of David a Savior, who is Christ the Lord. And this will be a sign for you: you will find a babe wrapped in swaddling clothes and lying in a manger" (Lk 2:10–12).

On Christmas night the shepherds are addressed by an angel who shines upon them with the blinding glory of God, and they are very much afraid. The tremendous, unearthly radiance shows that the angel is a messenger of heaven and clothes him with an incontrovertible authority. With this authority he commands them not to be afraid but to embrace the great joy he is announcing to them. And while the angel is speaking thus to these poor frightened people, he is joined by a vast number of others, who unite in a "Gloria" praising God in heaven's heights and announcing the peace of God's goodwill to men on earth. Then, we read, "the angels went away from them into heaven." In all probability the singing was very beautiful and the shepherds were glad to listen; doubtless they were sorry when the concert was over and the performers disappeared behind heaven's curtain. Probably, however, they were secretly a little relieved when the unwonted light of divine glory and the unwonted sound of heavenly music came to an end, and they found themselves once more in their familiar earthly darkness. They probably felt like shabby beggars who had suddenly been set in a king's audience chamber among courtiers dressed in magnificent robes and were glad to slip away unnoticed and take to their heels.

But the strange thing is that the intimidating glory of the heavenly realm, which has now vanished, has left behind a human glow of joy in their souls, a light of joyous expectation, reinforcing the heavenward-pointing angel's word and causing them to set out for Bethlehem. Now they can turn their backs on the whole epiphany of the heavenly glory—for it was only a starting point, an initial spark, a stimulus leading to what was really intended; all that remains of it is the tiny seed of the word that has been implanted in their hearts and that now starts to grow in the form of expectation, curiosity and hope: "Let us go over to Bethlehem and see this thing that has happened, which the Lord has made known to us." They want to see the word that has *taken place*. Not the angel's word with its heavenly radiance: that has already become unimportant. They want to see the *content* of the angel's word, that is, the Child, wrapped in swaddling clothes and lying in a manger. They want to see the word that has "happened", the word that has taken place, the word that is not only something uttered but something done, something that can not only be heard but also seen.

Thus the word that the shepherds want to see is not the angel's word. This was only the proclamation (the kerygma, as people say nowadays); it was only a pointer. The angels, with their heavenly authority, disappear: they belong to the heavenly realm; all that remains is a pointer to a word that has been *done*. By God, of course. Just as it is God who made it known to them through the angels.

So they set off, heaven behind them, and the earthly sign before them. But, Lord, what a sign! Not even *the* Child, but *a* child. Some child or other. No special child. Not a child radiating a light of glory, as the religious painters depicted, but on the contrary: a child that looks as unglorious as possible. Wrapped in swaddling clothes. So that it cannot move. It lies there, imprisoned, as it were, in the clothes in which it has been wrapped through the solicitude of others. There is nothing elevating about the manger in which it lies, either, nothing even remotely corresponding to the heavenly glory of the singing angels. There is practically nothing even half worth seeing; the destination of the shepherds' nightly journey is the most ordinary scene. Indeed, in its poverty it is decidedly disappointing. It is something entirely human and ordinary, something quite profane, in no way distinguished—except for the fact that this is the promised sign, and it fits.

The shepherds believe the word. The word sends them *from* heaven and *to* earth, and as they proceed along this path, from light to darkness, from the extraordinary to the ordinary, from the solitary experience of God to the realm of ordinary human intercourse, from the splendor above to the poverty below, they are given the confirmation they need: the sign fits. Only now does their fearful joy under heaven's radiance turn into a completely uninhibited, human and Christian joy. Because it fits. And why does it fit? Because the Lord, the High God, has taken the same path as they have: he has left his glory behind him and gone into the dark world, into the child's apparent insignificance, into the unfreedom of human restrictions and bonds, into the poverty of the crib. This is the Word *in action*, and as yet the shepherds do not know, no one knows, how far down into the darkness this Word-in-action will lead. At all events it will descend much deeper than anyone else into what is worldly, apparently insignificant and profane; into what is bound, poor and powerless; so much so that we shall not be able to follow the last stage of his path. A heavy stone will block the way, preventing the others from approaching, while, in utter night, in ultimate loneliness and forsakenness, he descends to his dead human brothers.

It is true, therefore: in order that he shall find God, the Christian is placed on the streets of the world, sent to his manacled and poor brethren, to all who suffer, hunger and thirst; to all who are naked, sick and in prison. From henceforth this is his place; he must identify with them all. This is the great joy that is proclaimed to him today, for it is the same way that God sent a Savior to us. We ourselves may be poor and in bondage too, in need of liberation; yet at the same time all of us who have been given a share in the joy of deliverance are sent to be companions of those who are poor and in bondage.

But who will step out along this road that leads from God's glory to the figure of the poor Child lying in the manger? Not the person who is taking a walk for his own pleasure. He will walk along other paths that are more likely to run in the opposite direction, paths that lead from the misery of his own existence toward some imaginary or dreamed-up attempt at a heaven, whether of a brief pleasure or of a long oblivion. The only one to journey from heaven, through the world, to the hell of the lost, is he who is aware, deep in his heart, of a mission to do so; such a one obeys a call that is stronger than his own comfort and his resistance. This is a call that has complete power and authority over my life; I submit to it because it comes from a higher plane than my entire existence. It is an appeal to my heart, demanding the investment of my total self; its hidden, magisterial radiance obliges me, willy-nilly, to submit. I may not know who it is that so takes me into his service. But one thing I do know: if I stay locked within myself, if I seek myself, I shall not find the peace that is promised to the man on whom God's favor rests. I must go. I must enter the service of the poor and imprisoned. I must lose my soul if I am to regain it, for so long as I hold onto it, I shall lose it. This implacable, silent word (which yet is so unmistakable) burns in my heart and will not leave me in peace.

In other lands there are millions who are starving, who work themselves to death for a derisory day's wage, heartlessly exploited like cattle. There too are the slaughtered peoples whose wars cannot end because certain interests (which are not theirs) are tied up with the continuance of their misery. And I know that all my talk about progress and mankind's liberation will be dismissed with laughter and mockery by all the realistic forecasters of mankind's next few decades. Indeed, I only need to open my eyes and ears, and I shall hear the cry of those unjustly oppressed growing louder every day, along with the clamor of those who are resolved to gain power at any price, through hatred and annihilation. These are the superpowers of darkness; in the face of them all our courage drains away, and we lose all belief in the mission that resides in our hearts, that mission that was once so bright, joyous and peace bringing; we lose all hope of really finding the poor Child wrapped in swaddling clothes. What can my pitiful mission achieve, this drop of water in the white-hot furnace? What is the point of my efforts, my dedication, my sacrifice, my pleading to God for a world that is resolved to perish?

"Be not afraid; for behold, I bring you Good News of a great joy. . . . This day is born the Savior", that is, he who, as Son of God and Son of the Father, has traveled (in obedience to the Father) the path that leads away from the Father and into the darkness of the world. Behind him omnipotence and freedom; before, powerlessness, bonds and obedience. Behind him the comprehensive divine vision; before him the prospect of the meaninglessness of death on the Cross between two criminals. Behind him the bliss of life with the Father; before him, grievous solidarity with all who do not know the Father, do not want to know him and deny his existence. Rejoice then, for God himself has passed this way! The Son took with him the awareness of doing the Father's will. He took with him the unceasing prayer that the Father's will would be done on the dark earth as in the brightness of heaven. He took with him his rejoicing that the Father had hidden these things from the wise and revealed them to babes, to the simple and the poor. "I am the way", and this way is "the truth" for you; along this way you will find "the life". Along "the way" that I am you will learn to lose your life in order to find it; you will learn to grow beyond yourselves and your insincerity into a truth that is greater than you are. From a worldly point of view everything may seem very dark; your dedication may seem unproductive and a failure. But do not be afraid: you are on God's path. "Let not your hearts be troubled: believe in God; believe also in me." I am walking on ahead of you and blazing the trail of Christian love for you. It leads to your most inaccessible brother, the person most forsaken by God. But it is the path of divine love itself. You are on the right path. All who deny themselves in order to carry out love's commission are on the right path.

Miracles happen along this path. Apparently insignificant miracles, noticed by hardly anyone. The very finding of a Child wrapped in swaddling clothes, lying in a manger—is this not a miracle in itself? Then there is the miracle when a particular mission, hidden in a person's heart, really reaches its goal, bringing God's peace and joy where there were nothing but despair and resignation; when someone succeeds in striking a tiny light in the midst of an overpowering darkness. When joy irradiates a heart that no longer dared to believe in it. Now and again we ourselves are assured that the angel's word we are trying to obey will bring us to the place where God's Word and Son is already made man. We are assured that, in spite of all the noise and nonsense, today, December 25, is Christmas just as truly as two millennia ago. Once and for all God has started out on his journey toward us, and nothing, till the world's end, will stop him from coming to us and abiding in us.

Fullness Creates History

We often imagine the event of God's Incarnation, the birth and life of Jesus Christ, in this way: it is as if, right from the beginning, God had a purpose in mind for mankind, and that, in what the Apostle calls "the fullness of time", this purpose had been realized. With a view to this culmination God had first of all chosen one individual, Abraham, to become the progenitor of a chosen clan, and later Moses, to be the leader of a chosen people. Then, in the course of this so-called Old Covenant, God's intention became clearer and clearer: objectively, in that his word and promise showed an increasingly defined outline, and subjectively, in that the hearts of the chosen people were increasingly more inclined to take note of God's purpose, looking forward with ever greater yearning to the coming Messiah on the basis of increasing insight into their own guilt and the impossibility of atoning for it without God's redeeming help.

There are various ways of viewing this undeniable inner development, this dawn that grows brighter and brighter until the sun rises in radiant splendor. Like the ancient theologians and world historians who were imbued with faith, we can describe it as a succession of eons of the world that, unfolding, unveil the divine plan. Or, in a more rationalistic and Enlightenment manner, we can see it, like Lessing, in terms of an "education of the human race" or, like the Idealists, as the unfolding of man's religious consciousness. Common to both approaches is the idea that the Old Covenant was a slow ascent toward a culmination, and that, once this peak had been reached, something had taken place that was unsurpassable in every respect. This is the "fullness of time", something so final that, in a true sense, it signifies the end of history; it is something eschatological, anticipating the end; essentially, therefore, from this event on, nothing of significance is to be expected in world history.

It cannot be denied that something of this atmosphere can be found throughout the writings of the New Covenant. With Christ the end has come, so much so that the short pause between his Ascension and his return in glory does not count at all. It is only the end time, in which nothing decisive remains to be done, since, in Christ, the fulfillment of every one of God's promises has already come. The only possible and legitimate task left is to proclaim the event that has taken place to the whole world, to testify to what we have experienced to the ends of the earth. Of course, those who concluded from this that they could lay their hands in their laps and did not need to work anymore were sharply rebuked by Paul, who said that he who would not work should not eat either; but all the same the idea of "waiting" is predominant in the Gospel, particularly in the Lord's discourses concerning the time of the end—John speaks of "abiding" (*menein*)—and very emphatically in the Book of Revelation. By and large the time of the end is a terrifying prospect: hell is let loose, because evil, cast out of eternity, sees itself restricted to time's short compass, and, enraged at this limitation, wreaks its savage spite on the earth. It would be futile to offer any resistance, to attempt to outwit and outmaneuver the superhuman aggressor by human means; what counts is to stand fast, not to fall, to endure, to cling to the triumph that has already been won in the eternal realm. For, when time has run its course, this triumph will also be manifested in world history.

Yet this is not the whole of the Christian message. Christ did not come again; time continued to stretch forward and, to that extent, acquired a renewed significance. Centuries, millennia, passed by, weighed down with events of such importance for mankind that nowadays, even for Christians, it is not easy to see and hold fast to that birth two thousand years ago as something absolutely decisive for all historical future. For a while the history of the West was totally under the sway of this event. Not only the Church: the state too understood and fashioned itself as a representation, visible on earth, of the eternal Conqueror of the world, the Kyrios Christos. But then history hoisted its sails once again and journeyed to new shores. Many Christians lost their bearings; the events of Bethlehem and Golgotha seemed a mere symbol to them, an idea, perhaps even a myth, perhaps the purest and most fruitful myth of all, yet not the all-governing reality. It was a mere blueprint for the development of humanity, for the implementation of human rights, for reconciliation and forgiveness between men and between nations. In Christ, according to this view, the idea of the pure man entered history in a somehow supercharged way; subsequently the various cultures have endeavored progressively to develop this idea.

We must not forget that this view of things, too, is not foreign to the word of Holy Scripture. While it is true that God's Covenant with Israel works toward a culmination, toward the coming of the Promised One, toward the fullness of time, this "fullness" is never portrayed in either the Old or the New Covenant as a final destination rendering all genuine future history impossible. Jesus too, most of all, tells his parables of the kingdom of God that is approaching, that has come near. These parables use organic images, for example, the scattered seed and its "uneconomical" growth (most of it is lost, but the little that survives brings forth superabundant fruit), the good seed mixed with weeds and in general all the images drawn from cultivation, as seen by the farmer: "It is as if a man should scatter seed upon the ground, and should sleep and rise night and day, and the seed should sprout and grow, he knows not how. The earth produces of itself, first the blade, then the ear, then the full grain in the ear. But when the grain is ripe, at once he puts in the sickle, because the harvest has come" (Mk 4:26–29). Here we have an overwhelming picture of firm, ceaseless succession, of peaceful inner development, according to an internal law that is so strong and imperious that the one who stands watching it simply cannot intervene. He can rise and sleep, he can give a little help here and there by watering and weeding but even his weeding is restricted by another parable: he might be interfering with the continual growth process. Better to let the weed grow, for in any case it only grows due to the thriving of the good crop; it is its counterimage, its shadow, its byproduct. Undoubtedly, of course, the farmer *will* interrupt the laws of growth and, at some time that seems good to him, put in his sickle. And in the last sentence, when we see the glint of the sickle, Mark uses his favorite word, *euthus*: suddenly, at once, without delay: "But when the grain is ripe, at once he puts in the sickle, because the harvest has come." This harvest ripens through the course of world history. It is the harvest for which God himself has waited, so that he may celebrate his harvest festival together with mankind. "I shall not drink again of the fruit of the vine until that day when I drink it new with you in my Father's kingdom" (Mt 26:29).

Although on the Cross Jesus had accomplished all things, he himself felt that what he had done was a founding act, a core, a beginning. For him, the kingdom of heaven he had brought near was a mustard seed, destined to grow from the smallest seed to the largest shrub. That is also why he loved children and urged his hearers to leave the rigidities and culs-de-sac of adult life and return to the openness, docility and utter receptiveness that characterize childhood. Jesus' own life breaks off at an age the Romans regarded as that of a young man, and he promises his own disciples that they will do greater works than he, works that will be more visible in earthly terms, in the same discourse in which he tells them "apart from me you can do nothing". In old age and maturity, when he had gone beyond the initially one-sided eschatologism of the early days, Paul reached a more all-embracing view of salvation history and came to see the age of the Church as a period of growth of the social body of Christ, whose members are the individual believers. This body is actually only moving toward its real maturity, "to mature manhood, to the measure of the stature of the fullness of Christ" (Eph 4:13). This is the first mention of the word *vir* ("man").

But just as the child is father to the man, just as life and all it contains only develop the power and fullness of the personality that lie hidden and concentrated within the child, so, for the Apostle Paul, the Jesus Christ of history *is* the fullness. He will not be added to through the coming ages but will show, interpret, unfold himself as this fullness; by his own power he will produce, organize and control the growing "body", the Church, "the fullness of him who fulfills all in all", just as the jar of oil of the widow of Sarepta manifested its inexhaustible inner wealth in all the other full jars ranged around it. And it was not because this fullness had dried up that the oil stopped flowing but solely because there were no more vessels on hand to receive it.

No one but the Lord of history knows when this time of full maturity has come. So the warning stands: we must watch and pray and be ready at all times. And yet there are indications. These too are expressed in an organic picture, and thus they apply to us and concern us; we are challenged to understand them, situated within this ripening history as we are. "From the fig tree learn its lesson: as soon as its branch becomes tender and puts forth its leaves, you know that the summer is near. So also, when you see these things taking place, you know that he is near, at the very gates" (Mk 13:28–29).

There is one point, however, we may object, in which Christ's Incarnation *was* an end and not a beginning: namely, in the history of the Jewish people. Let us put aside, for the moment, the astonishing fact that a nation whose raison d'être consisted in its looking toward a future failed to see that its fulfillment had begun to take place, actually missed it and rejected it; surely we must maintain that the entire Old Covenant, with its limited (albeit supernatural) national religion, with its law and ritual tied to a particular cultural stage, with its many imperfections, was only intended to be "for a time" and could only claim temporary validity? But this is by no means certain. We only have to recall the degree of universality this religion had already attained in the Wisdom literature and the shape it took in Palestine and the Diaspora at the time of Jesus; such a religion might have been capable of bursting the constricting nationalistic form from within. What is even more astonishing is the initial proclamation made by Jesus' disciples in the wake of his Ascension and the descent of the Spirit at Pentecost.

They address themselves to the Jewish people almost as if the condemnation and crucifixion of Jesus were not something irreversible, as if these were simply a misunderstanding that could be made good by repentance; as if the true, real history of the chosen people were now about to begin. This is how Peter speaks to the people:

> And now, brethren, I know that you acted in ignorance. . . . But what God foretold by the mouth of the prophets, that his Christ should suffer, he thus fulfilled. Repent therefore, and turn again, that your sins may be blotted out, that times of refreshing may come from the presence of the Lord, and that he may send the Christ appointed for you, Jesus, whom heaven must receive until the time for establishing all that God spoke by the mouth of his holy prophets from of old. . . . You are the sons of the prophets and of the Covenant that God gave to your fathers. . . . God, having raised up his servant, sent him to you first, to bless you in turning every one of you from your wickedness" (Acts 3:17–26).

In this amazing passage we hear that, as far as the Jews are concerned, everything is still open. Nothing is irrevocably lost. They need only repent, and God will send them his Messiah from heaven; then will come the days of consolation, of fulfillment and reestablishment, the days for which Israel had hoped from time immemorial and for which it rightly continues to hope. The fact that the Messiah has already been there should not stop the Jews from continuing to expect him. No sin, not even that of his execution in Jerusalem, is so terrible that it cannot be expiated by this very same murder and eliminated in the sinner himself, providing the latter lays hold of the grace of repentance. Nothing has been lost; every day can still be Christmas if we really wish it. Nor did Paul think any differently when he emphatically asserted that God's choices are irreversible, though this was no doubt contrary to the general view of Christians at the time that the Jews had been rejected because of their heinous deed and hardness of heart. If God has chosen a people, he will not let them fall; if

God has determined to enter into his glory amid the jubilation of the chosen people, then "all Israel" will repent (Rom 11). And did not Jesus himself take merely temporary leave of his people: "For I tell you, you will not see me again, until you say, 'Blessed is he who comes in the name of the Lord' " (Mt 23:39). World history is everything that takes place between the first, parabolic entry into Jerusalem—unfaithful Jerusalem, Jerusalem the harlot—an entry that was full of treachery, and the second entry, when all will be fulfilled and, on the foundation of innermost truth, the chosen people will break into rejoicing.

In this twofold respect, therefore, Christianity is a religion of the future. For, rightly or wrongly, the Jews continue to wait and hope for the Messiah, and we Christians join them in this; and the gentiles unfold the fullness of the gospel's tiny mustard seed, and we Christians join them in that. The end of history, toward which all times are running, is transcendent, and so it corresponds to the best expectations of the Jews; but, as the kingdom of God, it is also immanent and springs forth from the world's field and thus answers the best expectations of the gentiles. We should wait for it with prayer and patience, with a positively superhuman endurance; and in doing so we Christians are continuing the work of faithful and believing Jews; with them we perform the task of waiting for salvation. We are to do this by active love, which knits the body of Christ together, limb to limb, and causes it to develop into a fully grown body; by so doing, we Christians share in the work of the gentiles who fashion the world into a unity through culture and technology and endeavor to lift it to a spiritual plane. Our cooperation should impart a more than secular significance to what they do in the secular sphere, yielding a harvest that will be gathered into the eternal store barns.

Now, having reached this vantage point in salvation history, let us look back at the event of God's Incarnation in Jesus Christ. The history of salvation slowly moved toward this event through the various stages of Old Testament revelation.

These stages and steps—from Adam, Abel and Enoch to Noah; from Noah to Abraham; from Abraham via Isaac and Jacob to Moses and Joshua and the judges and kings and prophets, up to the Maccabees and righteous ones of the last age—these same steps were, for God, a descending staircase, and for man an ascending stair. Not in a rationalistically obvious sense, of course. But in a mystery of which we have certain intimations: God in heaven and man on earth enter into a Covenant, and God descends to dwell and "tabernacle" among men in his Word, in his Covenant Ark and his Temple, in his *shekinah*, in his words in the law and prophets, in the spirit of the God-sent leaders and wise men. He is coming down; he is approaching. And the last person of the Old Covenant, the Handmaid of the Lord, already belongs to the fullness, to the New and eternal Covenant; she is already "full of grace". The Old Covenant was broken in a thousand different ways. But in the New Covenant, we do not know how, a stage of history has been reached in which God can take upon himself the destiny of man, his Covenant partner. God's Word no longer hovers above the flesh, no longer dwells in flesh merely for a time (as in the prophets), but *becomes flesh*. God's Word can take over the entire bodily being of a human life as its own, divine destiny; and God can acknowledge what a man, this *one* man, is and experiences, as a valid, real and ultimate expression of the divine, saving will with regard to the world. Moreover, he can recognize this man as a true expression of the divine nature that reveals and gives itself to the creature. Anyone who endeavors to reflect on this will find that it explodes all categories, so much so that in the future he will be much more cautious in speaking about human progress. What kind of progress could there be over and above this event? None. Except this: history, including secular, cultural and technological history, could come to an awareness of itself in the shadow, or rather, in the light of this event and could make the supreme effort to catch up with it, or (since catching up with it is impossible) at least get nearer to it. For it is not as if

God's dwelling among us had spoiled men's game—as an adult can spoil children's delight in play by foisting himself upon them, knowing and doing everything better, so that it is no surprise when they turn their back on the spoilsport and start their games somewhere else. No. Quite the reverse. In speaking words from heaven to us, words of love, mysteries from the heart of God, Christ has not told us anything that will solve the human, natural, historical problems. He has given us no instructions about the state and culture, and even less about technology, its possibilities and dangers, and no word about the harmony and tension between Christianity and culture, between man's being bound to the world and his heavenly destination. He has scattered his seeds; it is up to us to nurture them and enable them to thrive on all fronts. In giving us the freedom of the children of God, he has not relieved us of the human freedom to take risks, to make discoveries, to make a thousand faux pas and bring catastrophes upon ourselves before achieving one solid step forward. On the contrary: because God has personally intervened, so to speak, in world history, and because the history of mankind is not only a series of stages on the way to him but also a history that comes from him, a history with him and in him, a history he feels and experiences in his own body (for we, the Church, are the body of Christ)—because of all this he has given this ongoing history a meaning and a dignity that lift it, at its core and in its harvest, into the divine realm; he has made of it an event that resounds into the very depths of eternity. Of its essence, grace is always the enabling and ennobling of nature.

Perhaps we are not particularly interested in engaging in such far-ranging reflections at the Feast of Christmas. Surely the point is that, in the middle of the night, everything else—including questions of whence and whither—is plunged in darkness so that all our attention can be focused on the illuminated center: the Child in the crib, with the Mother who has given birth to him and worships him, with the husband who looks after both of them, and with the proletarian shepherds, who are by no means given to philosophizing, who hasten to the scene in joy and then return again to their sheep. Indeed, so it is. This scene would need no further commentary if we knew how to see and celebrate it as a *feast of the future*; if, instead of it gradually disappearing into a gray and increasingly inaccessible past, eliciting merely vague, sentimental memories, we saw it as an implosion of eternity into time; if we were to see it as something so fraught with significance that it simply cannot become past, because no time can digest it and thus lay it to rest; if we were to see it as an event that, as Peter said to the Jews, is coming today just as much as it was then. We suddenly understand why the Church puts the Gospel of the return of Christ at the beginning of Advent. For this Advent of the Lord is a *single event*, not two separate events: it is simply so great that, when it enters into time, it both towers above time and yet is the fullness of time. It is time's center and its end, its painful, crucified center and its victorious conclusion, its judgment and its redemption, the veiling and unveiling of its mystery as it is in eternity. Let us kneel in a childlike manner around this mystery like the shepherds, who did not understand much of it, but because they were childlike with the eternal Child, grasped more of it than the learned men at King Herod's court. Let us be childlike, that is, young and open to everything that is to come, full of excited expectation and ready to embrace any adventure. God's Incarnation is an adventure, an *aventiure* [in Middle High German—TRANS.], that is, something that comes to us, comes to meet us, *ad-ventura*, and thus essentially has a future. It is an adventure that profoundly concerns us in our celebrations, and our Christmas trees and presents must not lose contact with it; it must not be covered over by all the domestic side of Christmas and all the seasonal goodwill. For, in this event, Love has appeared on earth, absolute, unsurpassable Love, so great that it causes every lover to catch his breath, for it reaches to the uttermost end, to God-forsakenness and death on behalf of others; it goes far beyond the circle of friends and fellow-countrymen and familiar acquaintances to embrace the enemy, the stranger and the alien. More than all the others, Christmas, the feast of the future, is the feast of open doors, of the outstretched hand, of the built bridge. The bridge to the person who has no sense or receptivity for it, who is closed in on himself and determined to remain so. Is it not the case, in spite of every argument, appearance and evidence to the contrary, that our age is an age of opening doors, when it is impossible for man to live alone and for himself any longer? (And the same applies to countries, continents and superpowers.) Has not isolationism, the principle of egoism, been reduced *ad absurdum* by history itself? And as for the closed nationalism that until recently was regarded as so superior, is it not thoroughly and conclusively obsolete today, such that a relapse into it could bring about catastrophes of world proportions? Is it presumptuous for the Christian to have a hope that extends to the future as well, a hope that embraces the germs of coming history that are already there in the present? True it is that the kingdom of God will never coincide with world history. True, too, that the hostile forces will grow, concentrating their power bases and extending their domination. Nevertheless, in spite of all the political and economic realisms and pessimisms, or atheistic optimisms, it does not seem presumptuous today, on this children's feast—indeed, it seems imperative—to nurture a childlike, naïve hope with regard to the future, for it is God who is coming. *Adveniat regnum tuum.* Thy kingdom come.

Leveling Downward

It stands to reason that the shepherds were the first to be told and that they had only a short journey to the crib. Only then were the "kings" or "wise men" notified, and since they had a long journey, as Paul Claudel points out, they arrived considerably late. The Church Fathers had no difficulty in interpreting things allegorically: the shepherds are the Jews, who come first; the gentiles come from afar, and consequently they come second. We might say, and with more reason, that the shepherds were poor people, and all the same they lived next door to the Lord God; or as Claudel puts it: "They are so poor that the good God does not even notice; and his Son immediately feels at home with them."

According to the Gospel, rich people have a longer journey because first of all they have to climb over their sacks of money, or, if their wealth does not consist in gold and stocks and shares but in knowledge, for instance, they have to do a great deal of gymnastics to extricate themselves from their neat and tidy concepts, opinions, perspectives, experiences and world views, until they finally stand on the naked earth where the Child lies in the crib. We do not know precisely what the position of these three wise men or astrologers was or how the celebrated star fitted in with their calculations (or did not fit); we do not know whether the star made them set out on their path because it was the missing link in their calculations, or whether it was a completely unexpected phenomenon in the heavens, instructing them to set off on the road to Palestine. And perhaps it is not even terribly important whether the entire story of these three rests on precise historical truth: we have no way of checking it; and yet it is good and edifying to hear that even "scientists" undertook the journey to the crib, whether the star confirmed their wisdom or confounded it. In the former case they would have brought their intellectual riches to present to holy poverty; in the latter case they would have grasped the inner poverty of all human knowledge and so found their way to the divine poverty. It is lovely that they brought presents with them for the Christ Child—not inconsiderable presents either—but it is even nicer that they really did unburden themselves of them, as things of little value compared with the treasure found in a field, the pearl of great price. They are the first to sell all they have in order to be disciples.

This brings them down to the level of the shepherds, and so a first Christian community can be formed out of the two groups. We could speak of a leveling downward here, for the rich become poor, but the poor do not thereby become rich. All come down to *the* level adopted by God himself in his Incarnation: the level of poverty, crib, flight; of Nazareth, the wilderness, nomadic existence; of the Cross and the grave. "The Son of Man has nowhere to lay his head."

This is a most unusual leveling. Paul refers to it when he declares that the difference between rich and poor, master and servant is abolished, and yet he says that everyone should remain in the state of life in which he was when the call to be a Christian came to him. The shepherds remain shepherds, and the so-called kings return home as such, albeit by a different route. And the people in between, forming the spectrum from the proletariat to the large-scale capitalist, remain just that: the people in between. Be that as it may, one thing remains true: the grace of our Lord consists in this, "that though he was rich, yet for your sake he became poor, so that by his poverty you might become rich" (2 Cor 8:9). All of you, rich and poor, all together. But the riches you have received consist precisely in Christ's poverty; and he becomes poor by giving himself away. Our wealth is this: to receive this self-giving and to respond to it by handing it on. A process of love. It is possible that this exchange of love will really have an effect even at the level of social structures; indeed, we can say that only where this effect actually occurs are people really serious about Christianity. If people are not serious about it, communism must fill the gap with its version of leveling and pursue its own kind of seriousness. But in that case the nominal Christians would have lost their justification for existing, together with their fantastically organized congregations, parishes, parish councils, dioceses, parties and Catholic congresses. Then, at best, there might be a rerun of the original situation at the crib, with shepherds and kings, to see whether the lesson has been grasped better this time. Such a repeat course for backward Christians would be a great grace from the Lord and a sign of his great patience.

We must not forget, however, that the world in its totality remains a training ground and will never transform itself into the kingdom of God through mere evolution (whether slow or fast). We must remember that, right to the end, the Christian decision in favor of poverty in company with the Lord who became poor remains a free decision on the part of individuals; it is not something suggested by conditions, let alone a decision that operates automatically. In some ways, this decision may perhaps be harder in the future, because the machinery of economics and society has such overwhelming power now to use the individual as a mere cog, and will increasingly block the air holes through which he can breathe as a person. And yet, as long as men are still worthy of the name, they will retain one freedom: the freedom to be poor in heart in order to *make many rich*. For it is the naked heart that does not want to belong to itself that becomes bread and wine for all who are hungry. The shepherd can do this just as well as the king, and so can every ordinary man in between. It is something as unspectacular as our everyday meal, and yet it is so unusual that it takes God's breath away: "Truly I tell you, this poor widow has put in more than all of them; for they all contributed out of their abundance, but she out of her poverty put in all the living that she had" (Lk 21:3–4).

Holy Family

Uniting the Disparate

Since, this year, the Sunday between Christmas and New Year's Day falls on the last day of the year, the Church is celebrating the Feast of the Holy Family today. Let us keep the picture of the Holy Family before us as we bring the old year to a close and carry it to its grave forever. It is one year of our short lives, and also one year of mankind's and the world's long history; in both respects it is a year that is finished, never to return. Today, as we tear the last page from the calendar before hanging up a new one, we are impressed by the uncanny reality of passing time.

Let us look, then, at the picture given us by the Church's calendar. For the Christian believer it is a very strange picture of a community in which the members who make it up seem to belong to different worlds. In the middle there is the Child, the growing boy called "Yeshua", that is, "Yahweh saves"—a popular name in the history of Israel ever since Moses' successor, whom we call "Joshua". He will grow far beyond his namesakes and impart a totally unique meaning to his name: in him, God will save finally and utterly; he will unite and fulfill all God's words and promises in his own person; people will be able to say of him that he is the incarnate Word of God in person. Through him and in him, God's past, present and future plan for humanity as a whole and for each individual member of it will be revealed—so much so that none of us will be able to find the abiding meaning of his existence, his ultimate relationship with God, apart from this

Yeshua. He is God's personal address to all, and hence his personal address to me.

According to the Scripture, this Man who is yet but a Child was born of the Virgin, Mary, who conceived him when the divine Spirit overshadowed her. Whenever Jesus spoke of his Father, he did not mean a human being but the eternal God, the "Father in heaven", and he clearly distinguished his relationship with his Father from that of other men, who owe their existence to a human father. So, like himself, but in a different way, the woman he calls his physical Mother does not fit in with all the usual earthly categories. Certainly, the Old Covenant was acquainted with births that were miraculous insofar as God gave the power of begetting and conceiving to barren bodies. But now these miracles are heightened and uniquely surpassed: without the intervention of earthly seed, Mary conceives, carries and gives birth to him who will be the incarnate Word of God. Otherwise, as one of the ancient Church Fathers (Tertullian) says, he would have two fathers, which would be unnatural and absurd.

All the same, there is Joseph, who had already contracted to marry Mary and who, at the angel's injunction, instead of dismissing the pregnant Virgin, has to take her to himself. He will give the Child the shelter of a roof over his head, and much more: the right to call himself a son of David. He will take responsibility for the family's material and spiritual well-being, initiating the Son into his carpenter's trade, and in all things he will minister to the high and hidden designs God has for those he has entrusted to him. He embodies the Old Testament; in him it attains its highest flowering and maturity, fitted to accept the task of being completely open to God's New and definitive Covenant and, in renunciation, of being completely at its disposal.

A strange family: none of them is actually what he or she outwardly seems. The family is like a united outer skin covering an inner secret so that it can come to fruition undisturbed—so much so that later, when the skin splits and the secret begins to come out, those nearest are appalled and taken aback; they think this Son who has broken out of the family is mad: "Is not this the carpenter, the son of Mary?" (Mk 6:3); "Is this not the carpenter's son? Is not his mother called Mary?" (Mt 13:55); "Is not this Joseph's son?" (Lk 4:22). And then there are the references to Jesus' brothers and sisters who are well known in the village—that is, according to the Semitic usage, then as now, his cousins and other relatives. (Otherwise it would make no sense for Jesus on the Cross to commend his Mother to the care of a stranger, his Beloved Disciple, John, and not to his physical brothers, if there had been such.)

A strange family indeed, not fashioned and held together by the bonds of human sexuality but by the bonds of a divine mission and plan of salvation. But perhaps these are the stronger bonds, able to weld the most disparate individuals into a unity of a higher order and of greater promise.

At this point, in spite of and because of its uniqueness, the Holy Family constitutes an urgent challenge to all Christian communities and all human communities whatsoever, originating in and kept in being by family blood relationships, reinforced by additional bonds (freely adopted or forcibly imposed) and by human interests and ideals. As such these are legitimate and beyond question, but we can see the limitations of this socialization process everywhere. We see this in the worldwide crisis of the family, where young people no longer regard authority on the basis of blood ties as being self-evident. We see it in the crises experienced by other communities and societies, insofar as the human interests that hold them together are often limited and egoistical and can therefore hold the members together only loosely, conditionally and with reservations. At a higher plane there is the community made up of the various nations and races of mankind; again, this is a highly disparate family, and it is very hard to bring its members to reconciliation and collaboration on the basis of a common human nature.

It would be too easy to give up here and say that these are all just natural forms of community, formed according to the laws of nature and acting correspondingly. On this view, the Church would be a supernatural community above and beyond the natural one, governed by higher, divine norms: only in this way could a certain analogy to the Holy Family be asserted. No. No such clean distinction between the mundane and the supramundane is envisaged in God's plan for the world; and if the family and the free, national and supernational communities close themselves to God's plan, if they refuse to open themselves and submit to it as their highest norm, they are not on course for the ultimate meaning of all human life.

This may sound somewhat abstract, but in fact it is utterly practical. Take the natural family: at the natural level it is an essential structure if the relationship between man and woman is to flourish and if children are to thrive. But unless it takes its bearings from a religious norm that is higher than the (mostly egoistical) interests of individuals, the institution of the family—as is evident worldwide today—crumbles and constitutes a profound threat to individuals: instead of being safe on board ship, they are clinging to individual planks, adrift on the open sea.

Let us take the state institutions and the voluntary associations that are integrated into them. Unless they are oriented to man's eternal destiny and are concerned with promoting the dignity of every man, they become machines, functioning inhumanly, going round and round in a void; then, almost necessarily, they provoke the reaction we are experiencing today in the form of terrorism. The machine that rotates meaninglessly is equally meaninglessly destroyed.

Finally let us take the families of nations and races. Here the egoism of power that characterizes the natural plane is at its strongest and most ineradicable, and thus it is most apparent to the eye. Hence the endeavors of all right-thinking people are directed toward maintaining a balance between the egoisms of national politics by creating communities of nations within continents and ultimately within the whole world. The aim is, if possible, to subordinate these national interests to the common interests of mankind. This obliges individual nations, races, continents and power blocs to make real sacrifices with regard to their particular interests. This is infinitely difficult. Indeed, this is probably the one fundamental experience of the period of world history in which we live; but this experience also impresses on us the urgent necessity of mutual agreement: humanity can put it off no longer without condemning itself to extinction. More than ever before, mankind is faced with the problem of squaring the circle, that is, of bringing politics and ethics into harmony, cost what it may.

Our human race, with all its problems, will never become a Holy Family. Much would have been achieved, however, if it were to keep before it this unattainable ideal, which shows people as profoundly diverse as Jesus, his Mother and his adoptive father united in a community of life under God's loving will. Only if men learn to look beyond their narrow interests (often legitimate at the natural level but distorted by egoism) and embrace the good of the whole does mankind have a chance of survival.

As we look back at the year that has gone, we can and we ought to wonder how far we ourselves have progressed along this ascending path that brings salvation. We should ask ourselves to what extent we have seriously subordinated our own interests to those we share with others, to interests that are universal and that seek the good of all. Only when all men succeed in subordinating the all-pervasive egoism—of whatever hue: democratic, nationalistic or Communist-imperialistic—can that peace the angels sang of at Christmas come upon the earth. It is the highest gift heaven has in store for earth, and in principle it has actually been given in Jesus Christ.

Year's End

Examination of Conscience

Dear Listeners, Once again a year of the long history of the world, a year of our short lives, has passed. We cannot stop it; the most we can do, as the year flows away, is to reflect on how we have lived it. We can examine our consciences. It was more or less like all the others, most people will say, for great conversions or other changes of direction are rare in our lives. The year passed in an average, mediocre sort of way, as previously, and we are afraid that things will stay that way, more or less. Most of us are in a rut; we carry on in the same old track. We have family, work, leisure, our hobbies; we have many prefabricated amusements, like television, sports, week-end outings by car or bicycle. Then, of course, we have the usual worries that Swiss people have nowadays: political changes threatening in the constituent regions, affecting us to some degree or other; a stagnant economy; inflation.

Only a few people are aware that this Swiss "average performance", this mediocrity that has always been a chronic condition of ours, expresses a sinking level of vitality. Or rather, we do not notice it, or hardly, but others can clearly see it, and they talk about it. Our image in the world has changed a great deal in recent years, and not in our favor. Clearly it is connected with the high standard of living in our country and with what we expect of life, of our fellowmen, of our technology. We have high expectations, and so we are chronically dissatisfied. We have become a strangely joyless, carping, pettily critical and unfriendly people. I am not referring to a certain Swiss coarseness that can go hand in hand with wit and bonhomie. I mean that complacency that lacks spirit, that prefers to make demands rather than to fulfill them, that takes it for granted that everything one could wish for is readily and silently at hand. Such complacency does not realize that, in the midst of all this, we have lost a certain inner discipline and culture of the heart; it is vanishing like a fragrance.

Even up to a few years ago one could be served in small shops in a friendly and neighborly fashion. Nowadays such treatment is superfluous: one takes the plastic basket and wanders through the supermarket, picking everything from the shelves oneself. But this neighborliness that has vanished imperceptibly has not simply changed into nothing: in places it has actually changed into its opposite. I have often been profoundly shocked, in public places, to see foreigners and migrant workers treated by employees with a rudeness that would have been unthinkable as recently as ten years ago. Regrettably, the same applies to other state officials too. I am not accusing any individual; I am simply pointing to a symptom: the inner culture of the heart has dropped to a seriously low level in our country. Whether this is the same in other countries, near or far, does not concern us here. But I know from my own experience—as a student in a foreign country after the First World War—the sickening fears that can be left in one's heart as a result of encounters with a heartless bureaucracy that keeps people waiting for hours and days. Kafka in Seldwyla![1]

Someone might say: What can you expect in a country with such a high standard of living, where most people have access —without any effort, or with very little—to all the blessings of an overripe civilization? The poor countries would not even have any desire for these things if we did not continually dangle them before their eyes. And as for the decline of moral standards, it is simply a sociological law, overwhelming the

[1] Seldwyla is a small Alpine village in Switzerland. It is very beautiful and life there is very orderly—a utopia [Ed.].

individual's normal powers of resistance. A country whose overfed citizens are offered a new slimming recipe every day—which does not even require them to abandon their gluttony—can only be cured by a very different "lean regime". Such a regime would also heal the breach between the generations that makes youngsters from overrefined homes run away to create an underrefined counterexistence of their own. It is hard to blame them for rebelling against the style of life in which they have been brought up, though their rebellion bears the same fin de siècle characteristics as the kind of life they despise and leave behind and thus is of no help to them.

However, between these great sociological laws against which the individual can apparently do nothing and his personal decisions there are a great many intermediary stages. This is the sphere of initiative of individuals and groups, of associations, of businesses, of economic and political parties; this is the realm of decisions that can shape our country for good or ill, in its internal affairs and in its external relations, now and in the future. I have neither the competence nor the time to go in detail into the workings of these factors. But one thing is certain: every citizen has the power, by participating responsibly in public life, to contribute creatively to the common good. In times of genuine democracy people have felt this to be an absolutely fundamental truth; they knew it and lived it. It was the powerful insight that a community can be viable only as long as it is sustained by the sacrificial efforts of its citizens; that the individual is an indispensable member of an organism, and that he must not fail or refuse his service or the whole body will be damaged. It was the realization that the individual can only be really free if the community guarantees this freedom, and if, from the outset, he has voluntarily invested much of his freedom in the community. It is not enough for him simply to pay his taxes: a state is something more than an automatic cash dispenser. He himself, a man with his own particular name, is indebted to all his fellow citizens if he wishes to share in the goods of the community. The only difference (but it is a big one) between a free democracy and a totalitarian state, of the right or of the left, is simply that in the former the socialization of the person springs from the individual's voluntary initiative on the basis of his personal reasoning, whereas in the latter the *raison de'état* is pursued by compulsion and force on the basis of the logic of the "objective spirit" or of the party that coincides with it. The latter is necessarily the corruption of the former. Just as I must be interested in our democracy and play my part in it here and now, I must also apply myself to its *future*, as far as that is meaningfully possible. Here too there are questions to be put to our consciences: What kind of *teachers*—secular and spiritual—have I allowed to indoctrinate my children? What attitudes have I myself taught them; what lessons have they drawn from my own cozy and comfortable existence? No one who has a family is a private person.

We really ought to examine this word *private*. "Private" refers to that area of the individual's or the family's life with which the public authorities should not interfere. Well and good, provided the particular individual or family participates adequately in public life and does not close himself or itself to it. Furthermore, the community has a right not only to a few external contributions but also to the citizen himself, to his reason, his heart, his spontaneity and inventiveness. If he wants to be entirely private, he is robbing the community and will eventually forfeit the goods he shares with others. If he wants to be a "private" man, he will "deprive" others and will himself be "de-prived".

Here we must utter a Christian word to the churches. It would really be best to avoid linking the words *church* and *democracy*. All the same, the essence of the Church and our life in the Church transcends the realm of the private, and this transcending of the private is also the vital nerve of democracy. Every Christian has his personal relationship with God, his prayer of the heart, his unique sharing in God's love for the world, in Christ's suffering for the world. But this personal sphere does not exist in private seclusion; in its very intimacy it exists for the community. The Christian is fundamentally a man who has been dispossessed. He lives for God and his fellowmen because he knows that he is not the author of his own existence; thus, in gratitude for his life, he must lead a life of thanksgiving. He gladly does what he can and gives what he has. In practical terms there is probably a limit to this openness to God and our fellowmen: we need a personal area in which to recharge our batteries so that we can return to the field of action and expend ourselves once again. But spiritually and existentially this openness has no limits. The Christian must always be available, whether he is waking or sleeping, praying or working, speaking or being silent—because he has been made *in principle* available. Paul put this truth in its radical form: "For the love of Christ urges us, because we are convinced that one has died for all; therefore all have died. And he died for all, that those who live might live no longer for themselves but for him who for their sake died and was raised" (2 Cor 5:14–15). So: "None of us lives to himself, and none of us dies to himself. If we live, we live to the Lord, and if we die, we die to the Lord" (Rom 14:7–8). In the New Testament, however, in being dispossessed and given to God we are also dispossessed and given to our fellowmen. "As you did it to one of the least of these my brethren, you did it to me" (Mt 25:40). Ultimately, our obligations to God and our obligations to our neighbor are identical. Whenever we pray to God, it is also for the world and its good; whenever we serve those around us, we are also doing the will of God, ministering to the coming of his kingdom "on earth as in heaven".

At this point the religious dimension merges into the political, just as the political, if it is to be wholesome, needs the religious impulse and substance. Neither religion nor civic life is private, for each of them can only thrive if the intertwining of personal freedom and the sense of community is understood, protected and promoted. We have already spoken of the damage done in the civic area by an exclusively private emphasis: it has also had a strong influence in the religious area. The organism of the Church is being seen more and more in terms of the secular model of a torso wrenched in two, with a soulless, technically functioning machine on the one hand (pejoratively referred to as the "establishment") and a playground of "charismatic" individual initiatives on the other. This kind of dualism is utterly contrary to Jesus' and the Apostles' entire concept of a Christian Church. We shall not reinstate the meaning of the Church and of Christianity by emigrating out of the allegedly moribund establishment. Nor shall we raise the level of ecclesial awareness by feverishly changing the establishment's structures with which clerics, in particular, busy themselves. "The letter kills; it is the spirit that gives life." There is a vicious circle here, and whether in the Church or in the state, we must escape from it at all costs: the more print is produced, the more laws are enacted, the more paragraphs are written to support and enliven the spirit, the more assuredly it will die away; and yet, like everything that pertains to the genuine human spirit, it *needs* to be embodied, to be laid down in the community.

These reflections may seem very general and abstract in character, but if we return to our year's end examination of conscience, we shall find that we have exposed its central, concrete point with regard to both areas, the spiritual and the secular. For both areas interpenetrate and mutually influence each other; in fact, for a Christian people, they are only two sides of a single, living reality. The question we must ask ourselves is simply this: How far have I regarded myself as the center and referred everything around me, God and the world, things and people, to myself, thereby robbing them of their intrinsic value? Or, on the contrary, have I taken my bearings from God and my fellowmen and thus been a useful member of the whole? Everyone must ask and answer this question for himself alone. Those who live in glass houses should not throw stones. Let no one think he can deal quickly with this question: it bores into the very core of our existence. We can never get rid of it by regarding ourselves as completely righteous ("I did what I could") or completely sinful ("I failed in everything; my case is hopeless . . ."). In all probability there are points at which we genuinely tried to respond and others where we failed quite decisively.

There is a wholesome egoism, however. That is, an inner decision, at a fundamental level, to serve; a decision that is expressed and slowly confirmed in small, everyday acts of concern for our fellowmen and of dedication to God. We know that these little acts are the subject matter on which we will be tested in our last and final examination: "For I was hungry and you gave me food; I was thirsty and you gave me drink; I was a stranger and you welcomed me; I was naked and you clothed me; I was sick and you visited me; I was in prison and you came to me" (Mt 25:35–36). Furthermore, "When you give a dinner or a banquet, do not invite your friends or your brothers or your kinsmen or your rich neighbors, lest they also invite you in return, and you be repaid. But when you give a feast, invite the poor, the maimed, the lame, the blind, and you will be blessed." And what is meant here is not that I should merely fill out some green form for development aid or an Albert Schweitzer Hospital or read the *Gulag Archipelago*: what is meant is that I should do something here and now, very personally and yet very modestly, in the place where I have been brought up, in family, community, Church and state. Only on the basis of this kind of personal initiative can our country remain a unified nation of brothers—or become such once more. But we must realize that to do so we shall have to swim against the tide, the tide of our personal egoism and the tide of the general trend. Being full is different from being content. Let people realize this by the example we give. Let us be joyful of heart, let us spread joy around us, and then we shall still be content if things go less well with us than at present.

Appendix: Basic Questions of Christology

Four Talks for Vatican Radio

The philosopher Hegel once wrote that the events of Jesus' life were slipping more and more into the past; the result of this was that his teaching, to put it crudely, "would soon be no longer true". Hegel wanted to remedy this disappearance by distilling a general law from Jesus' historical life, death and Resurrection and by viewing the destiny of Jesus as its highest symbolical representation. But if we look at the general spiritual situation of our modern world, which appears on the surface to be so secular, Hegel's dictum itself seems to have vanished. No book is anywhere near so discussed, interrogated and the subject of such untiring commentary as the Bible, and the New Testament in particular. The debate about Jesus is more animated than ever, whether in internal Church circles, in the ecumenical arena, in the dialogue with Judaism or Islam or in the issue of liberation theology that is set to decide the spiritual fate of Latin America. The world may act as secular as it wishes: no one is more present to it than Jesus of Nazareth.

But is it not a fact that, ever since the Enlightenment, the internal Church debate as to how the Gospels should be interpreted has torn to shreds the earlier, homogeneous picture of Jesus, with the result that, for many unsettled Christians, this picture has become almost unrecognizable and Jesus' cause and party seem to be disintegrating, irresistibly, from within? They "seem" to be disintegrating, perhaps. But the strange thing is that somehow, bafflingly, the picture of the Nazarene, which seemed to have finally collapsed, is still whole and entire. Two inseparable factors have brought this miracle about: the Word, and the Spirit who indwells it. One after the other, the critical hypotheses all try their skill on the word of the Gospel; they pass on, one takes over where its predecessor left off but the Word remains where it is, and, with it, the Holy Spirit indwelling it. "Heaven and earth and all biblical criticism will pass away, but my words will never pass away." Here we have been focusing on destructive criticism; of course there is a kind of scholarly biblical work that is highly useful in helping us to understand the Word.

In these four short addresses we shall try to shed some light on the central questions of the modern debate, questions that concern the learned world in the first place but that also spill over into the semilearned sphere and even enter the area of popular literature in the form of slogans; such slogans, triumphantly produced and urged upon us, unsettle many believers in Christ. Accordingly we shall discuss (1) the preaching of Jesus prior to Easter; (2) the post-Easter interpretation of this preaching; (3) Jesus' self-consciousness, particularly with reference to his imminent suffering; and (4) whether or not Jesus founded a Church. All these topics are related. The first topic, to which we now turn, brings us right into the middle of the problem.

The Preaching of Jesus

There can be no doubt that, as he commenced his preaching, Jesus had a single, central theme: the kingdom of God was approaching; it was on the threshold, imminent. The first instance of Jesus' preaching in Mark, summing up all that would follow, puts it succinctly: "The time is fulfilled, and the kingdom of God is at hand; repent, and believe in the gospel" (Mk 1:15). However, this gospel, this Good News, is nothing other than the fact that the kingdom of God has come near. John the Baptist had also summoned people to repentance, but he pointed ahead to a coming final judgment. For Jesus, man's repentance means that he can look forward, not to judgment of sin but to the kingdom of God that has come near, which he has been invited to enter. But there is something else that distinguishes Jesus' message from that of the Baptist: the Baptist points ahead to something tremendous in favor of which he effaces himself entirely. By contrast, Jesus' word and deed, his whole being, is utterly inseparable from his message. It is not merely that he is entrusted with the task of heralding the imminent kingdom; rather, it is only in him that the kingdom's nearness is recognized; it is only in him that we *have* the kingdom. In that same first chapter of Mark they are all amazed and ask: "What is this? A new teaching! With authority . . . ?" (Mk 1:27). What is new, what amazes them, is precisely this authority that is visible and tangible in the words and actions of Jesus. The indissoluble connection between the proclamation of the kingdom and the Person of Jesus is affirmed by every pericope of the Gospels; there is not a single passage that contradicts it. We do not even need to cite such clear examples as the Sermon on the Mount, where Jesus, expounding the word of God, goes beyond the old interpretations of the law: "It was said . . . but I say to you." But if the kingdom of God and Jesus himself form such a unity, why does he speak only of the kingdom coming "near"? Why does he not simply say: I myself am the kingdom? Well, this nearness of the kingdom is mysterious. Somehow it is already there; thus he can say: "But if it is by the Spirit of God that I cast out demons, then the kingdom of God has come upon you" (Mt 12:28). But then why has it merely come "near"? Let us put it quite clearly: because Jesus himself is only in the process of coming. He is like a word that must be spoken in its entirety before it can be understood. In fact he is a word of three parts: life–death–Resurrection. Only after the final part—Resurrection—will the disciples be able to understand the whole word, and then the kingdom's "nearness" will have been transformed into its "presence": it will have fully come.

Now, suddenly, we understand the central teaching of St. John's Gospel, which speaks of Jesus as the *Word* of God. In the Old Testament God had spoken many words. But in Jesus the Word becomes flesh, that is, man. His words and deeds and suffering, his whole being as a man: this is the all-embracing, concluding Word that God has to say to us. Within it, all that was said before remains true, but the unity of the Word in the man Jesus makes everything new, gives everything an unexpectedly unified, surpassing, wondrous meaning. And on the basis of John's Gospel we now also understand why Jesus does not proclaim himself but rather the kingdom of the God whom he also calls his Father. He is not just any word, a prophetic word speaking about God. He is the Word in which God expresses himself. A human word never speaks about itself; it does not proclaim itself, but something else, a content. So Jesus can say: "If I bear witness to myself, my testimony is not true" (Jn 5:31). On the contrary, he proclaims something, Someone, his Father, at whose service, totally, he places himself and his whole being. "I have come down from heaven, not to do my own will but the will of him who sent me" (Jn 6:38). However, this Word that proclaims the Father's kingdom is inseparable from its content, as we have seen. It *would* be separable from its content if it were nothing more than God's "advocate" in the world (as Hans Küng says). No, in the Gospel—in all four Gospels!—the content, that is, the Father and the kingdom, has no other vessel than the Word, the Son. Thus, with razor-sharp logic, he says: "My teaching is not mine, but his who sent me" (Jn 7:16). But at the same time there is a unique, incomparable interpenetration of the one speaking and what is spoken—"He who sees me sees him who sent me" (Jn 12:45)—so unique that no other relationship between God and man can be compared to it. It is misleading to speak of Jesus promoting a "cause", because the Father who is in him and acts in him, while he is his absolute concern, is not some "cause" extrinsic to him.

John is only putting into words what is clearly present in the synoptic evangelists and the earliest preaching of Jesus available to us. From the very beginning, therefore, Jesus challenges people to believe in him. This being so, how could anyone who does not believe in him understand his absolute concern and his own person? But equally, how can even a believer reach the inner insight that an entirely new view of the living God is being opened up here, a sight never before seen? Here something so dazzling comes into view that Judaism and Islam both retreat in horror, as if confronted with something utterly scandalous: God is not only in heaven but also a man on earth! Moreover, God is not only the One who speaks and the One spoken, Father and Son; he is also the Spirit, the personal, freely given love of both, given to the world! God himself, and within himself, is triune love, and this is proved to the world through the sending of the Son and his being delivered up to death for us all. The dogma of God's Trinity and his redemption of the world is everywhere, latently or expressly, in the New Testament writings: it is built into the very being of Jesus. With full authority, and at the same time with reverence, Jesus points to the eternal Father; the eternal Spirit of God rests upon him; he follows the Spirit who will ultimately be in his gift.

The Church's Interpretation of Jesus

In what we said in the last broadcast we already *have* the fundamental answer to the objection, in various forms, that the post-Easter community produced an arbitrary interpretation of the words of Jesus. The objection can be summed up in this "headline": the preacher becomes the preached. That is, the one who only proclaimed the kingdom of God (and not himself) has been moved into the center of the proclamation: Jesus Christ, Son of God, Redeemer of the world, of one substance with the Father, true God and true man in a single Person. . . . But why not, if, as we have said, the kingdom of God that he proclaimed was inseparable from his Person? If, by accomplishing his destiny, through his death on the Cross and his Resurrection, he also perfected his message, with the result that the kingdom that had drawn near now actually arrived and became present in him?

At the same time we must remember that the Church's preaching is by no means restricted to the Person of Jesus; it always points to God in his totality. Jesus is now seen and understood as the visible epiphany of God's totality. Jesus himself proclaimed the kingdom of God, that is, more precisely, the kingdom of the God whom Israel knew as its Creator and Covenant Lord and whom Jesus called his Father, his "Daddy", "Abba", in a totally new and unique sense. He also referred to him as the Father who gives his Holy Spirit to all who ask him (Lk 11:13). This God exhibited the most beautiful, most vibrant features of the Covenant God of the Old Testament—his listeners knew perfectly well whom he was speaking about—and yet wondrously deepened features appeared in his face, deepened through the manner and the human behavior of Jesus himself. Without formulating a dogma about God, he lived out in an exemplary way God's Trinity and his infinite love for the world. The kingdom he proclaimed was no unintelligible abstraction but something colorful and concrete, as we see from the way he portrayed the Father's disposition and his Spirit's "blowing". His Father was the Merciful One whom we can and should imitate, the One who causes his sun to rise upon the good and the wicked. His Father was the Forgiving One, provided we accept his Spirit into us and forgive our debtors in turn. The man whose attitude is one of love, so says Jesus to one of the scribes, is "not far from the kingdom of God" (Mk 12:34).

Consequently the Church is only taking over the preaching of Jesus when, in the wake of the Cross and of Easter, she rounds out the word of God, which is now complete, and in doing so devotes explicit attention to Jesus, who previously was only implicit in the doctrine of God. In the preaching of the Apostles, the chief Agent is still God the Father, who, through the Incarnation, death and Resurrection of Jesus, convinces the world of the reconciliation achieved. And if we look ahead to so (apparently) late a document as the First Letter of John, we see the same thing: it is shown that God is love, and there is no other proof of this but that God gave his only Son for the world, for us, as his Spirit (given to us) bears witness. The Church does not proclaim an isolated Jesus but the God of love. And God's love is shown not by allowing some man or "advocate" of God to go to his death—what good would that be to the world?—but by surrendering his divine Son, who alone was capable of making atonement for the world's sin, as the Synoptics, Paul and John unanimously affirm.

Everything now depended on confirming and establishing the genuine divinity of the man Jesus. Right up to the fourth century the Church fought for this truth, on which all depends, in her theology and councils. With regard to this long process of formulation, people have spoken of a "hellenizing" of the Christian Faith because the councils used various Greek terms in order to secure the truth. In fact it was the very reverse: it was a case of getting away from the Greek philosophical concept of God, according to which there could be only one chief and true God, God the Father, in command, whereas the Son and the Spirit could only be subordinate powers. The councils, developing Christology and so guarding the triune mystery against Greek rationalism, were simply aiming to protect the integrity of the New Testament. In John, the Jews persecute Jesus "for blasphemy; because you, being a man, make yourself God" (Jn 10:33; cf. 5:18). This gives a clear formulation of the claim Jesus makes in his whole life.

It does not matter whether Jesus applied titles of rank to himself or not. He certainly did not want to be openly designated "Messiah": it would have led to too much worldly misunderstanding. It is highly probable that he called himself "Son of Man", but there is disagreement as to the precise meaning he attributed to this title; maybe we shall never know exactly. It is possible that he occasionally referred to himself as "the Son"; such a designation cannot be traced to late Greek influences, as was long maintained, but arose in connection with Old Testament ideas, as has now been clearly proved. And we must always remember that the sublime quality that radiated from Jesus' entire person needed no title: it was evident to everyone, friend and foe. The titles applied to him by the Church's preaching were nothing other than appropriate designations for what he actually was.

Of course, his nature remained infinitely mysterious, with the result that it was impossible to reduce it to a single formula. There were many christological attempts to approach the mystery from various angles and converge on it. These attempts did not contradict each other: it is foolish to use them to reconstruct a christological pluralism, which would render authoritative Church teaching impossible. It is clear that Christ's elevation from Suffering Servant to Lord of the World in no way contradicts the fact that, even in the state of humiliation, *kenosis*, he was always the Son of God. No one can *become* God if he is not God *already*.

As far as the Church's understanding of herself is concerned, she was and is still confronted with the profound mystery of her origin. Insofar as Jesus is the Messiah of Israel, the New and eternal Covenant is not a second Covenant beside that made with Israel but is its fulfillment, as the prophets themselves solemnly foretold. But insofar as Jesus was more than a mere human Messiah, and the New Covenant was founded in his sacrifice, his flesh and blood, the Church's reality goes beyond the prototype, Israel, just as the body is more than the shadow, as Paul says (Col 2:17; Heb 8:5).

All theology of God, of Christ, of the Church, of her sacraments, and ultimately all theology of man and the world too, is and remains only a means of approaching the Word that was in the beginning with God, was God and became flesh. In this Word God has interpreted himself, giving grace upon grace. And how good it is that this living Word is always greater than everything we can put into words and concepts! All the Church's pondering and speaking about God are never anything other than a spur to prayer, making us fall down and worship, acknowledging that God's majesty and merciful condescension are always greater than anything we can grasp.

The Self-Consciousness of Jesus

Certainly there can be no psychology of Jesus (as Guardini often rightly emphasized), and yet the theologian, and the believer too, cannot avoid the question of his self-consciousness. This much is plain when one reads the more recent works of exegesis, which claim to show that, initially, Jesus knew nothing of the death on the Cross that lay ahead of him—the predictions of the Cross were later interpolations—nor, when he realized that this death was inevitable, did he say anything about its saving power for Israel, let alone for the whole world: consequently he knew nothing of this either.

Of course this thesis contradicts the letter of the Gospels. There Jesus not only predicts his death and Resurrection in many, often quite central places: literally, as in the passage where he calls Peter "Satan" because he is trying to stand in the way of his suffering; and metaphorically, when he speaks of the "baptism" that he must receive and that fills him with anxiety, and the "cup" (of God's anger at sin) that he must drink. Moreover, Jesus speaks of his death as a *lutron*, a price of redemption (Mk 10:35), given for "many", that is, surely not for Israel alone but for an unlimited number. This mode of speech recurs in the words instituting the Eucharist: people try in vain to pare away at them too; but if criticism sweeps these words away, the Church's whole Faith regarding the Eucharist and the Lord's Supper will collapse, along with the presence of Christ that is bound up with it.

In the Synoptic Gospels, however, and even better in John, we see that Jesus lives with a view to a mysterious coming "hour" for which, according to Luke, he has "earnestly longed", an hour that began with the Last Supper (Lk 22:15). This is the hour that troubles his spirit and yet cannot be avoided: "Now is my soul troubled. And what shall I say? 'Father, save me from this hour'? No, for this purpose I have come to this hour. Father, glorify thy name" (Jn 12:27f.).

Since when has Jesus known about this hour that awaits him? From the beginning. This is not only the teaching of the Church Fathers, who vie with one another in insisting that Jesus was born ultimately in order to die, and to die this particular saving death; it emerges from the whole way he lives. His words show it clearly: he never risks saying anything unless he knows that it is backed up by the gold currency of his Passion. Furthermore, he proclaims the Father's forgiveness in advance and himself forgives sins in God's name: he can only do this because, by way of anticipation, he is already drawing on the reconciliation that his Cross will effect between God and the world. So too he performs miracles of healing on bodies and souls, which draw their power from his atoning Passion. He knows that he will have to pay for all these treasures he is distributing in advance. The Passion is by no means something that comes to him from outside, simply because he had the misfortune to antagonize the Jewish and Roman authorities—something that could have been avoided if, for instance, the scribes and Pharisees and Sadducees had had somewhat closer relations with him. It is far too little to say that Jesus "provoked" his own death. He never sought it either, as we see clearly from those occasions when he escaped, by flight or disguise, from the hands of those who wanted to kill him, precisely because his hour had not yet come.

But—so the objection runs—it was his mission as Messiah of Israel to lead the people back to God, and he had pinned all his hopes on carrying out this mission, as we see so movingly when he weeps over hardhearted Jerusalem: "How often would I have gathered your children together . . . and you would not!" (Mt 23:37; Lk 20:41). Would he have been able to take such trouble and show such zeal if he knew in advance that it would come to ruin? Yes. Most unreservedly, Yes. This is clear from the call of the great prophets, Isaiah, Jeremiah, Ezekiel: right at the beginning, when they were first called, they were told that all their toil would be in vain, and nonetheless they put themselves into their task with all their strength, all their prayer and all their hope. As far as I am aware, the exegetes have given far too little attention to this aspect.

But we must seek to penetrate even further into Jesus' self-consciousness. The Son of God came to teach us instead of the self-will and disobedience of Adam what is the true attitude to God, namely, obedience to absolute goodness and love, obedience out of love, obedience unto death on a Cross. And this, for him, means obedience unto the hour of darkness, the draining of the cup of God's wrath toward the world's sin. Through this obedience we are reconciled with God. Obedience is more than burnt offerings, we read in the Old Testament; obedience is also more than doing what one does, knowing what one knows. The Son's obedience is something far greater than what the Church Fathers and Scholastics—out of reverence, of course—were concerned to attribute to Jesus: a constant, blissful vision of the Father and an exhaustive knowledge of everything in the world, and in particular of his own path. If he knows everything better than other men, if he decides everything on the basis of total insight, how can he be open at every moment to the inspiration of the Holy Spirit, in order at all times to be doing not his own will but the Father's?

Jesus has precisely the knowledge necessary for him in his mission as Messiah of Israel and as Suffering Servant, that is, as Redeemer of the world.

First, therefore, he knows of his mission as Messiah of Israel: he is to lead the chosen people back to repentance and to the original understanding of God's Covenant and law. This requires total self-dedication at every step and the hope, constantly alive, that this step will succeed—"Zeal for thy house will consume me": we see this in all Jesus' preaching and miracles and in every instance of his forgiving sins.

Second, he knows that, despite all failure on earth, God's saving plan will ultimately triumph through him. It will triumph, that is, on the far side of that judgment that will take place in the "hour of darkness" on the "Day of Yahweh". The great atonement spoken of by all the prophets right up to Isaiah's "Suffering Servant", Jesus' gigantic mission of reconciling the world with God, will succeed in spite of everything: in some way that is beyond our imagining, the Lamb of God will take away the sin of the world. For after all, on the basis of his baptism, he is the beloved Servant and Son upon whom God's entire favor rests: to him, therefore, the Father's entire saving will is entrusted.

Third, however, he is strictly ignorant of the hour. "But of that day or that hour no one knows, not even the angels in heaven, not the Son, but only the Father" (Mk 13:32). This is crucially important; we must take it absolutely literally. Jesus knows that, whatever happens, the hour will come: "My hour has not yet come." But he leaves it entirely to the Father. He does not get in training for it, so that, when it comes, its pitiless attack will be in any way mitigated. He keeps to his own maxim: "Therefore do not be anxious about tomorrow, for tomorrow will be anxious for itself. Let the day's own trouble be sufficient for the day" (Mt 6:34). Though God's Son, he is also the first, the exemplary Christian.

He knows just as much and just as little as is necessary so that he can carry out his unique, all-embracing mission of world atonement. He has the unshakable faith that the Father will lead him, through all the darkness, to its consummation; he has unshakable hope in the God of Israel and of all peoples; he has the infinite love that worships all that the Father ordains—including his being ultimately forsaken by God, including the terrible thirst for the God he has lost.

But is not the Son of God also God? As such, is he not omniscient? Yes, but that does not mean that he wished to share all his divine attributes with his human nature. Here, doubtless, there are mysteries we shall never fully penetrate. But one thing we can say: just as the Son, as God, eternally receives full divinity (and hence full omniscience) from his Father, so he eternally gives himself, all that he has and is, back to the Father in gratitude: it is at his Father's sole disposal. Thus, in some way, we can understand that, when the Son's eternal "procession" from the Father takes the shape of a "mission" to the world, the Son deposits his divine attributes (without losing them) with the Father in heaven. For we read that he "emptied himself" of his divine form (Phil 2:7) precisely so that he could be humanly obedient unto death. God's eternal, threefold life is evidently so alive that it can encompass this possibility. Holy Scripture testifies literally to it, and it stands to reason that someone who is true God is also able to become true man. Only thus can Christian reflection faithfully trace the image presented to us by Jesus Christ.

Jesus Christ and the Foundation of the Church

It has become customary to cast doubt on the belief that Christ founded the Church, primarily because, to all appearances, he thought that the world was soon to come to an end. He seems to have regarded the prospect of the ruin of Jerusalem as contemporaneous with the final ruin of the world. And who would question that he foresaw the destruction of the city, especially as such premonitions constitute a frequently occurring and apparently natural phenomenon? Furthermore, and more importantly, the prophets had predicted the city's destruction in a very similar way, even describing it in detail. But at this very point we are reminded of Isaiah: Jerusalem will be annihilated, root and branch, but, astonishingly, the apparently dead stump that remains will put forth a new shoot, the royal scion, what the prophets called the "holy remnant".

According to Jesus, however, not only Jerusalem but also the world in its totality were approaching their end. Here even Catholic exegetes are at a loss. But let us see things from Jesus' point of view: his task is to reconcile not only the present and past world with God but also the whole of the world; thus he truly bears the sins of the coming generations. With his Cross he literally reaches the end of the world. And the Resurrection as such can only take place where our world ends, whether or not its chronological time continues to run as far as others are concerned. When he says to his disciples, "Be of good cheer; I have overcome the world" (Jn 16:33), this is true in an ultimate, eschatological sense. "But when Christ had offered for all time a single sacrifice for sins, he sat down at the right hand of God, then to wait until his enemies should be made a stool for his feet" (Heb 10:12), that is, until his eschatological deed has spread its influence through all remaining history. For him it was the end of the world, while, for others, historical time continued to run. Holding these two together was not a problem for him. This is shown by his saying: "Truly, I say to you, there are some standing here who will not taste death before they see the Son of man coming in his kingdom" (Mt 16:28), or "before they see the kingdom of God come with power" (Mk 9:1). For, according to what we said in our first talk, the Risen One, having accomplished his mission, *is himself* the kingdom.

Now we come to the disciples' much-debated visions of the Risen One. The whole of the Christian Faith depends on their being true. If they could be shown to be illusions or hallucinations, the Church would indeed be cut off from the umbilical cord of the Jesus of history. We cannot go into detail here with regard to the failure of the attempts to undermine Easter on the part of the Enlightenment and of liberalism; such attempts are doomed, because what the disciples experienced, in different ways, turned their whole picture of the world upside down, transforming their despair into certainty, their timidity into the courage of martyrs. But it is Paul's Damascus experience that provides the best evidence for the Easter event: How could a hallucination instantly change this rabid persecutor of Christians and turn his whole existence around 180 degrees? In the oldest New Testament text we possess (1 Cor 15:3–5), Paul puts the Lord's appearance to him on the same level as his appearance to Peter and the Twelve. No—only in the light of the Easter appearances could the disciples realize the meaning, now manifest, of the life, teaching and miracles of the earthly Jesus and, above all, of his Passion. Now that the Word had been spoken in its totality, it was possible, on the basis of the whole, to grasp the beginning.

Naturally it took a while before the gigantic whirl of events attained a certain logical order in the disciples' minds: while Jesus' work is complete in itself, it is continued in them; the Covenant with Abraham and Moses is simultaneously superseded *and* perfected; what is begun in the life of Jesus attains its definitive meaning with the future that is now commencing, be it short or long. As the months and years go by, the disciples realize more and more deeply the meaning of Jesus' words: "When the Spirit of truth comes, he will guide you into all the truth; for he will not speak on his own authority, but . . . will take what is mine and declare it to you" (Jn 16:31f.). Thus they understand that it is not only that the Holy Spirit creates continuity between Jesus and the Church: for they themselves were chosen by Jesus and sent out to preach and heal; they themselves left everything for his sake. And whatever, in terms of scriptural exegesis, we may make of the words "do this in memory of me", one thing is certain: on the basis of this scene at the Last Supper, and of the Risen One's breaking of bread among them, they realize that his gestures and actions are meant to continue; that they will be no less important and significant in the times to come than they are now. And after Easter, how they realize the whole range of the authority given to them to forgive sins on earth so that they are forgiven in heaven! In their preaching, not only can they point to the once-for-all atonement that took place on the Cross; they can also actualize it in entirely personal acts of forgiving sin—and, where it cannot be avoided, of retaining sin, so that, subsequently, such sin can be "loosed" all the more effectively. We find eloquent examples of this in the Letters of Paul and in the Acts of the Apostles.

How it all goes on as a matter of course! There are no discussions or debates as to whether the disciples of Jesus still possess these powers that once were given to them, or whether Peter still has a preeminence in the College of Apostles, or whether the Apostles may delegate their authority to others—as Paul, for instance, does quite naturally in the Letters to the Corinthians. So we need not be surprised to find that, later, the Apostles just as naturally hand on to their successors the powers necessary for governing the Church. They in turn will hand them on to others as a matter of course, as is shown, for instance, in the Letter to Titus: "This is why I left you in Crete, that you might amend what was defective, and appoint elders in every town as I directed you" (Titus 1:5). How unproblematically the whole mysterious Church structure unfolds, unlike any secular form of community. No one questions the authority of the leaders (stemming as it does from Jesus) or the fellowship that enfolds all: "One heart and one soul"; "You have one teacher, and you are all brethren" (Mt 23:8). The Church—again unlike any other society—penetrates and moves between the visible and invisible realms:

preaching, sacraments, ministry, witness: these are visible, but the greater part of the Church's life, as of the life of Christians, is invisible; "Your life is hid with Christ in God" (Col 3:3). Since the Church and her members draw their life from the whole of Christ's life, from his earthly existence, his death and his Resurrection, their existence too has one foot in this world and one foot in the world beyond, to which they have access because they have died with Christ. It is because they are rooted in eternal life that the Church and Christians acquire strength to carry out their mission in *this* world; they are otherworldly, but they are also this-worldly, addressing the world and its issues. These paradoxes of Christian existence were unquestioningly accepted; they were a given part of the picture from the very first, needing no fundamental change as the millennia unfolded. Viewed in this way the Church is a "spontaneous generation" comparable to the tremendous mutations of evolution; it is equally evident that her unitary being is entirely grounded in the life of the pre-Easter Jesus, like the butterfly in the caterpillar.

The Church's development did not need complicated founding documents and detailed instructions from Jesus. All that was necessary for the Church to develop from Jesus was his example, his choosing and teaching of the disciples, his eucharistic self-giving and the promise of the Spirit, who would lead the disciples into all the initially baffling truth and praxis. We can lay hold, tangibly, of both things: of how everything is grounded in Jesus and how the Spirit of God has built the Church on the foundation of Jesus. As Jesus said, "One sows and another reaps." "He who reaps gathers fruit for eternal life, so that sower and reaper may rejoice together" (Jn 4:37, 36).